Passing Judgements

Poetry in the Eighties

by

John Mole

for Mum,
with much love
from
John .

Bristol Classical Press

for Arthur Sale

This book first published in 1989 by Bristol Classical Press, 226 North Street, Bedminster, Bristol BS3 1JD.

Review-essays reproduced by kind permission of *Encounter.*

British Library Cataloguing in Publication Data

Mole, John
    Passing judgements: poetry in the eighties
    : essays from Encounter.
    1. Poetry in English, 1945 – – Critical
    studies
    I. Title   II. Encounter
    821'.914'09

    ISBN 1-85399-067-1

Printed in Great Britain by
Antony Rowe Ltd, Chippenham, Wiltshire

Contents

Foreword by Anthony Thwaite

The days of the majestically long review of poetry are long over: the copious dissection of the new Wordsworth, Keats, Browning or Tennyson has been replaced, these many years, by the 900-word round-up. This is not to denigrate one or two writers who usually manage to do an honourable and decent job within the restrictions of the later dispensation; but no one could argue that these occasional pieces are other than, at best, good journalism, or weeklydom.

Encounter, through its various literary co-editors, from Stephen Spender to Richard Mayne, has attempted to correct the imbalance. Certainly during my years on the magazine (1973-85) I tried to give as much space as possible to long, considered reviews of new poetry, as well as to the publication of new poems.

John Mole succeeded two other poets, Douglas Dunn and Alan Brownjohn, as the person to whom I sent almost all the poetry books and verse pamphlets that arrived at Encounter. What he took his brief to be, and how he tackled the job, he makes plain in his Introduction to this book. I very much welcome the putting-together of these sharp, generous, fair-minded, independent and entertaining review-essays. They form a chronicle of poetry in the 1980s, now given greater permanence than if they had been allowed to languish in their separate issues of the magazine; and they stand up well, as judgements and not just as journalism.

Introduction

I am not now, nor have I ever been, a professional critic. If that sounds evasive, let me put it another way. I write poems without ever quite knowing why, and with a similarly baffled but convinced trust in intuition I try to remain alert to the work of my contemporaries.

When asked to review a book of poems – or books *en masse* as in the case of these pieces for *Encounter* – I hope to find what is distinctive and individual, and to recommend it through a mixture of impressionistic description and careful quotation. I confess that wielding the billhook does not come naturally to me – though I keep a few knives in the drawer – and that I'm probably a bit of a softie. When I open a new book I want to make discoveries, and if I don't (though the failure might be due to my lack of adventurousness or just plain bad map-reading) then I prefer to say nothing about it at all.

As I sat waiting for the reviews of my own first collection to appear, I remember a literary acquaintance telling me never to mind what was said in them but always to measure the column inches – as if a sufficient number would add up to a reputation. I can only say that as a reviewer I consider it a matter of honour never to go over the page about a book which I don't think is worth it. From the many hundreds of individual collections, anthologies and pamphlets sent to me by *Encounter* I have selected the ones which interested me most (all having been, at the very least, glanced at), irrespective of the poet's standing or the cachet of an imprint. Certain eventful volumes could hardly be avoided. Not to have written about them would have been considered a wilful, even a petty, silence in the face of their noisy promotion, but it has given me much more satisfaction to find space for the quietists and the fugitive originals.

In a decade which has seen the fierce acceleration of the promotional tour, the packaging of poets as marketable products, the loud allure of national poetry competitions with their head-lined sponsors and large

1

cash prizes, and above all the uneasy confusion of reputation with public profile, I have come increasingly to admire the smaller publishers' stubborn faith and commitment, their tenacious enthusiasm for the authenticity of the individual poem as distinct from the attention-seeking Business of Poetry. If it appears that some well-known names are missing from the pieces gathered in this book it can be certain that they will have received their due elsewhere. I have often felt, and acted upon it, that if I don't put in a word for the less fêted no one else will. In this respect *Passing Judgements* is not so much representative of the Eighties as of one working poet's attempt to move around in them on his own terms.

So these judgements are passing in several senses of the phrase. At best they can only be provisional meditations on a cavalcade of review-copies – a personal record of taste and predilection. Obviously I should like to think that if I have written clearly and persuasively about poets whose work I admire, a few who come across this volume will search out some of the books, buy them, and help to establish the only valid reputation which resides in a lasting readership. 'Passing', too, I must admit in that, looking back over these pieces, I detect plenty of vacillation and even a little volte-face in my negotiations with the *zeitgeist*. There have been poets who began by delighting me but in the end, after a book or two, left me none the wiser. I have said so, but even that must be a passing judgement because in most cases there may be more, and possibly better, to come.

Since 1982, as a reviewer of contemporary poetry, I have never closed. As I walk out to post the latest envelope of copy to *Encounter* I trip over yet another monstrous jiffy-bag of 'product' dumped on my doorstep. Perhaps the final judgement must be mine upon myself for having connived in the extension of my term of office. Poetry? There are times when it is too much with me, when 'I too dislike it', when the sheer volume of others' lines makes me doubt whether I shall ever write another of my own. But then comes that unexpected discovery – the genuine new voice or the old prospector who has at last struck gold – and once more the serious game of making verses is afoot.

As for the effect of omnibus reviewing on my own poetry, it has made me aware of how there are more blind alleys than by-ways. Once, after going through a disappointingly dud pile of books, I came up with this as a post-script. I offer it now as a bridge to what follows:

Won't Do: A Memorandum

What won't: the occasional
Framed page from your journal.
What won't: the fashionable myth,

The heavy breathing of Death.
What won't: the slick
Mountebank, the sugar-pill Quack.
What won't: the hurt
Of a divided heart.
What won't: the contrived
Sentiment – *These You Have Loved* –.
What won't: the hired wit,
The mark others have hit.
What won't: the effusive
Ego, the self-abusive.
What won't: the Idiot's Tale,
The irresponsibly surreal.
What won't: the tipsy
Word games of a scholar gipsy.
What won't won't do. What might
Still insists that you write.

John Mole
July 1988

1
Modern Languages
January 1983

Poetry Review Volume 72, No.2
Thom Gunn: *The Occasions of Poetry* (Faber & Faber)
Edwin Morgan: *Poems of Thirty Years* (Carcanet)
James Fenton: *The Memory of War* (Salamander Press)
Thom Gunn: *The Passages of Joy* (Faber & Faber)
Christopher Reid: *Pea Soup* (Oxford University Press)
John Ash: *The Goodbyes* (Carcanet)
U.A. Fanthorpe: *Standing To* (Peterloo Poets)
Tom Rawling: *Ghosts at my Back* (Oxford University Press)
John Whitworth: *Poor Butterflies* (Secker & Warburg)

A FEW MONTHS ago, James Fenton gave an interview to *Poetry Review* in which he considered, among other things, some ways 'towards finding, in non-poetic language, what can be the poetic language of the future'. As I read this, I found myself recalling Yeats' celebrated, idiosyncratic radio broadcast on Modern Poetry – 'In my youth I heard much of the music of the future' – and his lofty bewilderment when confronted by what he saw as the non-poetic modernity of T.S. Eliot whose unromantic, impersonal initials one can still hear him spitting out in the BBC archives:

> No romantic word or sound, nothing reminiscent, nothing in the least like the paintings of Ricketts could be permitted henceforth. Poetry must resemble prose, and both must accept the vocabulary of their time; nor must there be any special subject matter. Tristram and Isoult were not a more suitable theme than Paddington Railway Station.

The Old Lion had had his day. Poetry was going to the dogs whose satirical intensity gave them a more feral bite. Long in the tooth he might be, but he could still manage the Grand Snarl – he'd bow out roaring on the wings of an old song while the next generation caught its prosaic trains to a future from which its grandchildren would be setting out on a space-craft to Mars...

How neat and historical this all seems now. Time has absorbed an urgent, living issue, pickled it and put it in the Museum. Yeats and Eliot, the one with his florid bow and the other with his neck-tie asserted by a simple pin, sit side by side in the same glass case while we busy ourselves with the new proscriptions, keep the old quarrel alive on a different footing, and are bent on appropriating the future according to our own temperaments. We choose our representatives, fight our style wars, seem all too often to argue about Poetry with a greater enthusiasm than we read poems, roll up the magazines, hit each other over the head with partisan editorials, talk about the *importance* of literature, the *politics* of literature, the *survival* of literature – and yet, if we're poets, we make our poems in spite of it all; we make them, as Yeats said, and however old-hat it sounds, 'out of the quarrel with ourselves'. We write 'as men have always written'.

Every battle of the factions is a campaign lost and won, the only survivors being the few good poems left standing. Of course the critical debate will go on (the fashions, the ins-and-outs of favour) because we'd be dead if it didn't, but as for this reviewer, now that he has finished piling on the rhetoric of his convictions, he hopes simply to be able to spot a few of these survivors whether they turn out to be in 'the poetic language of the future' or not.

What, though, are the chances for the omnibus reviewer as the books come flooding in? One of the current batch is Thom Gunn's *The Occasions of Poetry*, a collection of essays, some of them – and some of the best – autobiographical: 'In the late fifties and sixties' Gunn warns me 'I wrote a series of omnibus poetry reviews for the *Yale Review*. It is always good to make yourself read poetry with close attention, but I became more and more dissatisfied with the business of making comparatively fast judgements on contemporary poets. Specifically, there were books that I simply changed my mind about later on'.

I shall bear this in mind as I begin.

Edwin Morgan's *Poems of Thirty Years* is an omnibus in itself, a 442-page Bumper Book of wholly serious fun and games by a versatile poet who is probably best known for his shapes and sounds. He's *homo ludens*, par excellence, – an echo chamber of tongues and dialects, and a canny inventor of new languages:

> – Although a poem is
> undoubtedly a 'game'
> it is not a game.
> And although now it is even
> part of the game to say so,
> making it a " 'game' "
> is spooky, and we'll
> not play that.
>
> – Who are you kidding, said
> the next card. You just played.

Morgan is always playing the next card. Often his brilliant mind is a space-age Nautilus crammed with sonar equipment and instamatic cameras, and bristling with moral antennae. He's a humane Captain Nemo, alert to every signal from the darkest recesses of his ship. Many of the poems are cast in the form of Odysseys, extended sequential narratives which relish the strangeness of their own wordscapes, stretch the imagination and hint, wittily, at the responsibilities that begin in dreams: 'to me it seems/the virtue's in the questions, not the answers'. Certainly a profound sense of virtue is crucial to the impact of Morgan's vision. All the Sci-Fi paraphernalia is there to entice the ghost into the machine, and as one of the speakers comments in a set of Dialogue Poems, 'The Whittrick':

Machines can be persuaded to stumble on dreams...
The flash of imagination has been built in,
Its logic allows the leap of thought.

Logic, the leap of thought, and sudden flashes of illumination are what make these poems, at their best, both intriguing and memorable. Edwin Morgan is particularly good at transcribing audio-constructions into their component letters, so that some kind of alien intelligence can be heard on the verge of discovering a human voice – as in that artfully contrived arrangement of consonants, 'The Loch Ness Monster's Song', and in my own favourite, 'The Day the Sea Spoke', which doesn't appear in this volume, presumably because it was thought to be too purely a sound-device to make sense on the printed page. In reading a book of this size thoroughly and at length, it is impossible to avoid feeling that Morgan is sometimes in danger of becoming a victim of his brilliance, and that if one turns too many pages at one sitting his inventions return to plague the reader. As 'The Clone Poem' admits:

you can have too much of a good thing too much of a good thing too much
you can have too much you can you can too much of a good thing you can
have have too much too much of a good thing

But there are many good things. There are the celebratory/elegiac poems for Hemingway, Marilyn Monroe and Edith Piaf, deft little songs of innocence and experience like 'Song of the Child', poems of social observation – some of them instamatic snapshots and others, like the account of helping a blind man to the toilet in 'In the Snack Bar', more slowly and remorselessly developed with much painful detail and implicit judgement but – in keeping with Morgan's approach elsewhere – a minimum of explicit comment: 'Dear Christ, to be born for this!' Again and again, though, the poems return to a sense of human values defined and off-set by a deliberate futuristic chilliness: 'erase the exclamation mark. Surprise/comes from old microstructure thinking'.

In thirty years Edwin Morgan has come a long way from the 'strain and flash and fable' of his earliest work, an amalgam of Revelation, the New Apocalypse, Vachel Lindsay razmataz and Anglo-Saxon hammering. In one of these early poems he has Isaac Newton speak of 'Feeling, that chaos, /I sold for abstract tranquillity'. In his own case, the chaos of feeling was in time to order itself into patterns where the abstract and impersonal forms would convey a far less theatrical intensity.

There's certainly a theatrical intensity about much of James Fenton's poetry. It's full of mise-en-scène, cameos and verbal invention, but if early Edwin Morgan took the barn by storm, Fenton's tours de force are collegiate theatre – more sophisticated in their brilliance. Randall Jarrell once commented on the feeling a reader has when confronted by the writings of Robert Graves: 'Here is a man who can explain everything' – the kind of alert, omnivorous intelligence which never misses a coincidence or a connection. Reading Fenton's *The Memory of War*, my immediate reaction is 'here is a mind which can *contain* everything'. His poems are packed with information about the natural world and human behaviour. He travels as widely as he reads, writes with a bravura energy and has understandably been placed by his admirers in the tradition of Byron. Byron claimed that he wrote on horseback. Fenton, though, is a dazzling foot-soldier – he's had to be in order to reach some of the places he reports on – but he keeps his boots as supple as dancing shoes. Even his toes think.

It's easy, too, to see why he is often compared with Auden; – the moral landscapes, the bizarre machinery of his fictions, the sinister undertones, the idyllic calm of a precarious truce threatened by bulletins from the frontier:

> The square, the cafe seats, the doorways are empty
> And the long grey balconies stretch out on all sides.
> Time for an interlude, evening in the country,
> With distant cowbells providing the angelus.
> But we are interrupted by the latest post.

In poems as different as 'Nest of Vampires' and 'South Parks Road' it is as if the quick-fire intelligence of young Uncle Whiz were informing the erudite, gossipy syllabics of the later Auden, but beneath it all runs a disturbed, personal seriousness which reminds me of Robert Graves' *Pier Glass* period and of Auden's immense (unreciprocated) admiration for Graves which is too often ignored by those who see the apostolic succession of modernism as passing from Eliot to Auden. Fenton's nursery-worldish nonsense poems, 'The Empire of the Senseless', are peculiarly English – the Oxford of Lewis Carroll fallen into a state of lost innocence and taking a vacation in post-war Europe; a kind of Jabberwocky in jackboots. In his more sustained work, such as 'A German Requiem' and 'A Staffordshire Murderer', there is a haunting sense of the repressed and the unsaid: 'It is not what he wants to know./It is what he wants not to know./It is not what they say./It is what they do not say.' The horrors are oblique, hinting at the 'godawfulness' of a civilization at the end of its moral tether – values fragmented into a display of wit which is both coruscating and appalled. The best of Fenton's poems about the war in East Asia, 'Dead Soldiers', demonstrates this with great force, and in 'The Fruit-Grower in War-Time' he uses a collage technique to the same end, offering (along with the 'found poem *composé*' method of

'Chosun') his own contribution to the language of the future.

Fenton's greatest weakness is apparent when the poems, as some of them do, tip the balance towards mere cleverness and display. 'The Skip', written rather uncharacteristically in a self-conscious public-bar Larkinese, is an extended identity-fantasy in which the narrator throws his life on a skip and picks up another's found lying there. It's very clever, super-symmetrical and just too knowing by half; a poem full of laboured point whereas in the best work the moral concern is in the play of intelligence.

The play of intelligence has always been a distinguishing mark of Thom Gunn's poetry, and his critical essays show that it is what he values most in the poetry of others. Writing on the early work of Gary Snyder – a significant sign-post en route to his own Americanization – he singles out a poem which is 'about feeling the cleanness of the senses' and goes on to observe that 'cleanness, exactness, adequacy are the first impressions we have of the language and the rhythms...rhythms at one with the perceptions, neither their servants nor their masters'. It is this kind of firm grace, a lyrical pact between servant and master, the practice of an efficient sensibility, that Gunn has always seemed to go for. In his strongest poems he has achieved a balance of rule and energy where, with an increasing confidence in the handling of free verse and syllabics, the celebrated pose has gradually relaxed into a more mature poise.

The poems I like most in *The Passages of Joy* are, in the words of one of them, exercises 'in stance, and/in the muscle of feeling'. They are full of teasing questions of identity, and often turn on a moment of complex interplay experienced as a creative tension. In 'Night Taxi', Gunn assumes the personality of a taxi-driver and is soon caught up in considerations which reflect his own poetic preoccupations:

> Do I pass through the city
> or does it pass through me?
> I know I have to be loose,
> like my light embrace of the wheel,
> loose but in control...

This is dangerously close to Midnight Cowboy folksiness of the 'you can take the boy out of the city but you can't take the city out of the boy' variety, but Gunn's continual alertness to the need to be 'loose but in control' (or, as he reverses it in the sonnet 'Keats at Highgate', 'perhaps not well-dressed but oh no not loose') keeps the reader involved with his search for that fusion of passion and intellect which, for him, is the essence of a good poem. His scenarios have increasingly become the streets and bars of San Francisco or New York but they are not just those of a convert to the American way of life excited by local colour. They are occasions for the exploration of 'the cool source of all that hurry/and desperate activity', just as in the autobiographical sequence about living in London, 'Talbot Road', his memories weave their way between impressions of remoteness and pressing activity. 'A boy...in the house opposite' watching the street

> sat in his white shirt at the window...
> ...poised, detached in wonder
> and in no hurry
> before he got ready one day
> to climb down into its live current.

Gunn's imagination makes something talismanic out of that white shirt. It is luminous with an aura of precarious innocence, and the boy is his secret sharer. When, though, the poems become merely a part of that 'live current', when they are loose to the point of hanging out – as in some of the pieces which seem to do no more than celebrate *coming* out –, they seem very limp indeed. The free-booting innocent abroad, preoccupied with the 'warm teasing tickle' in the cave of a handshake which takes his mind off toothpaste, offers whimsical glimpses of the gay life but fails to make them more than a faintly embarrassing catalogue of local thrills. The gap between Gunn's best and worst poetry remains a vast one, and points to a paradox he has not yet resolved.

The kind of poetry Christopher Reid writes offers dozens of neat little hostages to those who don't warm to his particular brand of snappy wit. It is easy to take phrases from his new collection like 'in the play-ground of impromptu metaphors' or 'the tiny boudoir-church/that is my favourite' and stick them as labels on his poetic baggage. Nor is it hard to single out his 'grave rumpuses, flytings/of fanfare and frugal whoopee' and see him as a dinky Wallace Stevens. This would be to do him some injustice, though. His poems are pleasantly inventive, beatitudinous charms, or they are mischievously disconcerting like verbal/visual equiv-alents of Satie or Milhaud – 'a saxophone/oozing into/efflorescence'. What I find disappointing about them is – again to take one of his perfectly wrought phrases, of which there are just too many – that they don't amount to more than 'tokens of possible eloquence'. I've read somewhere that Reid is an admirer of the potter Lucie Rie, so he'll remember a comment she made about the moment when she opens her kiln being 'not a revelation – a surprise'. Reid's work is full of surprises – his pots are splendidly turned and immaculately glazed – but it never moves me to more than a feeling of wistful tenderness or a recognition that the world, viewed from a certain angle, does after a fashion look like that. The church painting where 'heaven itself/is graced by an off-centre patch of damp' is typical of the Reid frisson – that *graced* preparing for a delicious coup of witty bathos. Robert Frost observed that a good poem begins in delight and ends in wisdom. Reid's poetry, however serious its implications, begins and ends in delight.

Delight of a kind seems to be what John Ash is after in *The Goodbyes*. His surrealist eleven-finger exercises keep dissolving into themselves and, as he puts it in 'What Remains', all definitions are 'approximate and free'. I must confess to a preference for what Edward Thomas called the 'fixed and free' and to a degree of puzzlement when led, line by extended line, through a leisurely sequence of random associations. The trip is pleasing enough, although much of the scenery is made up out of the familiar stage props of Ash's French precursors, and I'm not sure that such all-out surrealism is anything but a dead-end however much the poet may slip in sharply-observed images of contemporary life. These poems – and not just because of their author's name – recall the widely-praised 'melodic trains' of John Ashbery: 'it is a kind of *movement* we want above all else', writes Ash, but movement as a raison d'être seems to me to be a poor substitute for poetic *action*. Poems in which little else happens but the poem itself last no longer than the experience of reading them:

> Similarly
> you will like the people here but if you choose
> to ignore them no offence will be taken...

> ...silences
> have to be orchestrated, portraits drawn with invisible ink
> if we are to know what is really taking place
> beyond this pale surface that is so satisfying in itself...

Of course, it is impossible to quote fairly from *The Goodbyes*. Whatever their limitation, the poems are at least whole or nothing, and indeed their surfaces *are* satisfying in themselves. Which is something.

So far the poets under review have been of particular interest because of their style and language. With the work of U.A. Fanthorpe and Tom Rawling we come down to English earth and a sensible, generous verse firmly rooted in social observation, daily routine and carefully tended memory. *Standing To* and *Ghosts at my Back* are both modestly excellent books and each, in its own way, is memorably human. U.A. Fanthorpe's gift is for looking on the worst side and reporting back with compassion. Her poems alternate between a gentle despair and a brisk stoicism nowhere more marked than in the fine 'Fanfare' which opens her book and in which she celebrates her thrifty, fatalistic mother; the woman for whom 'homes were only provisional,/Bivouacs on the stony mountain of living'. The poem sets up a beautiful contrast with 'my extrovert dog of a father,/ With his ragtime blazer and his swimming togs/Tucked like a swiss roll under his arm'. I finished 'Fanfare' feeling great affection for this redoubtable lady, her trench wit and her gloomy relish of every fresh disaster, and – I think – appreciating how a gift of temperament can be inherited. The daughter, now, is 'standing to' in her own way as a poet, 'making/Happiness keep its distance' but alert to occasions for compassion and love. In another good poem, 'The Guide', she writes of Virgil who, learning the secrets of his beemaster father, 'trudged further into suffering/And pity than other people,/Led to accept his vocation/By the annals of the hive'. The hive that has taught U.A. Fanthorpe so much is that 'lucent comb' – as Philip Larkin describes it – the hospital. She has worked for some time as a hospital clerk, and several of the best poems in *Standing To*, as in her previous collection, come out of this experience. Her range, though, is greater than this might seem to suggest. Among much else, there are four serio-comic monologues which explore how the masculine world of Shakespeare's tragedies looks from a woman's angle. They are outstandingly funny and wise.

Ghosts at my Back gets off to an inauspicious start. The first poem begins 'I am wandering through Dickinson's/Dictionary of Cumberland dialect' (oh yes?), and is closely followed by two equally flat openings – 'It's not nostalgia' and 'Enough to hear/The names of the fells'. *Isn't* it nostalgia? *Is* it enough? However, as soon as Tom Rawlings works his way back into the past (he's in his sixties and this is his first book of poems), he allows himself space to recreate it. Memory becomes imagination, and the poetry celebrates 'the bond with those who bred me' in sharp vignettes. There are also some fine poems about fishing, their skilled free verse rhythms attentive to the 'strategem of rod and line':

> Now in the dark pool
> Panic races, twangs the line
> Screeches the reel, runs
> Till the rod's spring compels
> Obedient circles,
> Flank-flash drowning in air,
> Drawn to the net
> Where my loaded club
> Kills.

Before starting to write poems, Rawling wrote numerous specialist articles on fishing, and this seems to have paid off in much the same way as did Edward Thomas's prose about country matters. In each case the material was obviously just waiting for its destined shape.

And getting even further down to earth, there's John Whitworth's second collection, *Poor Butterflies*. Its huggy-bear aggression and hectoring pyrotechnics force the reader into the ring as a contender. At Oxford, Whitworth tells us,

I stopped being a working-class culturemonger,
Inserting FUCK every fourth word,
Being by rote an offensive turd,
Confusing honesty with rudeness
And sexual success with lewdness.

I don't believe it. Or perhaps, on mature reflection, he decided to revert. His enjoyable, clever, scatological verse rejoices in offensive turdery, is honestly rude (or rudely honest?) and relishes the lewder anecdotes of sex. Added to which he can make rhyme do anything in any position. His poor butterflies are broken on the wheel and keep coming back for more. No language of the future here, only an eternal public-bar present.

2
Respectable Formalities
April 1983

Blake Morrison & Andrew Motion (eds): *The Penguin Book of
Contemporary British Poetry* (Penguin)
Derek Mahon: *The Hunt by Night* (Oxford University Press)
Anne Stevenson: *Minute by Glass Minute* (Oxford University Press)
Alistair Elliot: *Talking Back* (Secker & Warburg)
Paul Verlaine (trans. Alistair Elliot) *Femmes/Hombres* (Anvil Press)
Gavin Ewart: *More Little Ones* (Anvil Press)
Patric Dickinson: *A Rift in Time* (Chatto & Windus)
Gillian Clarke: *Letter from a Far Country* (Carcanet)
Michael Cullup: *Reading Geographies* (Carcanet)
John Loveday: *The Agricultural Engineer* (Priapus Press)
John Cotton: *Day Book* (Priapus Press)
Emma Rose: *Being Glass* (Priapus Press)
Emma Rose: *Flags for the Occasion* (Dodman Press)

GIVEN ITS PUBLISHERS, who hail it on the cover as a brilliant new landmark, *The Penguin Book of Contemporary British Poetry* must be considered as an event. Given the machinery of publishing, the commercial imperative and the demands of marketing, it must also be promoted as a *significant* event. In the publicity hand-out which accompanies my review copy, the word *major* is substituted for *brilliant:* – 'a major new landmark in anthologies of modern poetry'.

So the pressure is on. Another anthology destined to be tossed to-and-fro between the cachet of its imprint, the claims of its editors, the society of its chosen few, and the talents of its individual poets – if the trees can be singled out from the wood. The more brilliant/major a publishing event, the more it merely serves the moment it seeks either to define or transcend. It is a collusion of innocent and knowing opportunism; a book with serious intentions which flies in, bags its place on the conveyor-belt of contemporary culture and hopes to make a bit of fuss at the customs while getting through.

In this particular case, it was a good idea to have a pair of editors, two heads being safer (if not more imaginative) than one, and more likely to vanish conveniently into the eventful mirror. The idiosyncratic, passionate partisan is always a risk. He is likely to turn up too early for the event, or behave inappropriately at it. With luck, he'll be an immediate success, but by and large perhaps it's better to be careful. Certainly no single editor – least of all the already legendary Alvarez – could ever have written 'This is an anthology of what, over the last few years, a number of close observers have come to think of as the new British poetry'. With what subtle modesty Blake Morrison and Andrew Motion smuggle through their unexceptional taste as party members of an elite committee of propagation. The whole tone of their introduction guarantees an authentic, insidiously safe anthology *à la mode* – a neat package of what can comfortably and comfortingly be felt to be important. It's not all that bad, but it *is* dispiritingly faceless – or rather, where a vivid face would have been welcome, it wears the detached look of wisdom after the event. In places the modesty is tentative to the point of paralysis; '...it is now twenty years since the last serious anthology of British poetry was published...an unusually long gap, and to fill it with a representative anthology must in itself be some kind of service. We believe that we may be able to do rather more than that...'. *Some kind of, may be able to, rather more than*...Oh come on out and declare yourselves! (And, incidentally, what was so *un*serious about Edward Lucie-Smith's *British Poetry since 1945*, published by Penguin in 1970?). But maybe this is the limit of Morrison and Motion's capacity for declaration, once agreement has been reached. According to Morrison, quoted in the hand-out, things were not always so bland:

> Andrew Motion and I considered some fifty poets or so for inclusion but narrowed the choice to twenty: to do this we met, corresponded, exchanged phone calls, argued, compromised, agreed, changed our minds again, and finally reached our decisions – remaining, as we began, good friends. There were differences but our tastes coincided to a remarkable degree.

There is more vigour and sense of engagement in this short statement than in the whole of the judicious introduction (or rationale) as finally published. With the bald announcement 'this anthology is intended to be didactic as well as representative' the editors come back from vacation. There is a shift from what seems to have been a home kitchen to an institutional dining hall, and the excitement of planning a menu and concocting a meal gives way to the respectable formalities of eating in college under the shadow of the high table 'where tastes coincide to a remarkable degree'.

But what proof is in the eating? The poets are mostly under forty-five, with the exception of Anne Stevenson, Fleur Adcock, and of Peter Scupham who was born in 1933 but did not publish his first book until 1973. And no one who appeared in Alvarez's *The New Poetry* – however young he was at the time (e.g. John Fuller) – has been considered eligible for inclusion. Whereas, according to the editors, Alvarez 'presented language as a mere instrument in a therapeutic transaction between writer and reader', the twenty poets they have assembled (as against Alvarez's slightly more generous twenty-eight) are set out to demonstrate a new relish for language. They are led by Seamus Heaney – 'the most important new poet of the last fifteen years' – for whom language 'embodies politics, history and locality, as well as having its own delectability'. Forces of disintegration, particularly the Irish Troubles, are seen as being approached obliquely, rather than through naked confrontation, in poems which have been made 'to accommodate an uncommonly wide range of social responsiveness' through fictions, narratives, myth, emblematic landscapes, and analogues drawn from other troubled societies in which the artist finds himself an 'inner emigré'.

A sense of exile, where the poet – in Heaney's words – sits 'weighing and weighing/My responsible *tristia*' – predominates amongst several of the most serious and competent poets in the anthology, and (en masse) lies heavily despite the felicities of their surfaces. This is, perhaps, inevitable – although a poet such as James Simmons would have offered some variety without trivialising the theme – and the editors choose reliably from Heaney, Michael Longley, Derek Mahon and Tom Paulin, establishing in each case a strong, individual voice. Their selection from Paul Muldoon is distorted by their over-valuation of his clever extravaganza 'Immram'.

Tony Harrison and Douglas Dunn deserve their places – two poets whose uneasy relationship both with their provincial, working class up-bringing and with 'the cultural establishment' has been the source of much energetic and moving work. Harrison makes the stronger impact, while Dunn is given more space. Other good poets include James Fenton, Peter Scupham (made to look much more of a miniaturist than he is), Fleur Adcock and Anne Stevenson. These are various talents, presented even-handedly, and in most instances they endorse an apparent preference for intelligent, humane, well-crafted verse. There is nothing fugitive. Almost without exception they come from a well-established and narrow range of publishers who have nursed their reputations, but they do leave one wondering why the many excellent small presses must be seen as having contributed apparently so little of significance to 'contemporary poetry'.

Which brings me to what disappoints and worries me most about the anthology. Praising Heaney in his recent notebook, *The Private Art*, Geoffrey Grigson wrote:

> Sometimes a single image out of a poem goes up into the dark and hangs there by itself, and says 'Watch! Watch for more!' and we know of a new poet. For me that was so with the last stanza in Seamus Heaney's 'Sunlight'
>
> > And here is love
> > like a tinsmith's scoop
> > sunk past its gleam
> > in the meal bin.
>
> 'Watch' says the image, in its sudden possession of the dark, 'Watch', it says, 'but you may be disappointed.

This is certainly a fine image, arising as it does out of a depth of feeling, an exact, sensuous register of personal emotion; but in so much contemporary verse, as approved by Morrison and Motion, there are just too many smart images going up in the dark and hanging there, rootless. Introducing the so-called 'Martian school', brilliantly beamed up by Craig Raine and Christopher Reid, the editors note that these writers share a delight in outrageous simile and like to 'twist and mix' language – verbs suggestive of poker and cocktails respectively, and, in their innocence, witnessing to the superficiality which is rather anxiously denied in stressing that the Martians' ingenuity does not prevent them from expressing emotion. But, yes, they do play a game for quick returns, and they are intoxicating, and their influence and reputation continue to grow. They have taken the element of visual epiphany which is a vivid strength in Heaney, isolated it, mixed in the cunning of the riddler, and made it a device – monotonous in its little frissons of amazing freshness. They, and to a less spectacular extent other more anecdotal poets in this anthology, will sacrifice far too much to a verbal coup. That they should be given so much space in such a selective book is depressing. It's a selling short of the full resources of poetry, highlighting a fashion certainly, but giving far too much credence to a very partial story which should look infinitely more redundant in twenty years time than anything to be found in Alvarez. But, then, is that *should* mere wishful thinking? Maybe *The Penguin Book of Contemporary Poetry,* in its confident representation and didacticism, will contribute to an increasing detachment of the elements of poetry from poetry itself. I can only hope not.

Derek Mahon's new collection contains several poems good enough to place alongside his 'A Disused Shed in Co. Wexford', a justly celebrated piece, and one of the best in the Penguin Book. It is not only in his confident use of the familiar stanza form that Mahon can be seen as the Marvell amongst his contemporaries and compatriots. He is a truly witty writer, and his recent work reminds me of T.S. Eliot's observation that all too often one is confronted by 'serious poets who seem afraid of acquiring wit lest they lose intensity'. That this is a genuine risk is illustrated by numerous, honourable present-day poets, but in Mahon's case what Eliot calls 'wit's internal equilibrium' is immediately evident. Whereas there has always been a tough reasonableness behind his sometimes very slight lyric grace, there are all the signs that the lyric grace in itself is becoming tougher:

> I lived there as a boy and know the coal
> Glittering in its shed, late-afternoon
> Lambency informing the deal table.
> The ceiling cradled in a radiant spoon.

That *informing*, in the third line, is characteristic of Mahon's imagination and skill; it's a modest word but brilliantly exact, a perfect functional pairing with the more obviously 'poetic' *lambency*. In a poem which, like so many in the book, holds darkness and light in an intense equilibrium, it presents light as a virtue, as an element of the imagination possessing the material world and shaping it from within. Mahon's poems are full of radiant objects which shine all the brighter for their setting in a dark, chilly universe of exile and unrest, and a hard, crystalline energy informs the measured verse.

Mahon can, at times, appear a solemnly playful, self-aware doomsday dandy, and in 'Another Sunday Morning' he simultaneouly assumes and is amused by the stance. The echoes of Robert Lowell are unmistakable and, given the title, clearly deliberate, but the sardonic viewpoint is more reminiscent of Louis MacNeice in Regents Park than Lowell in Central. Mahon's temperament sets a limit to his sense of public responsibility:

> A chiliastic prig, I prowl
> Among the dog-lovers and growl;
> Among the kite-fliers and fly
> The private kite of poetry –

There are echoes of Dark Tower Yeats, too, particularly in the fifth stanza of 'To the Unborn', and assuming the persona of Knut Hamsun in 'Old Age', Mahon confronts one of Yeats's most celebrated lines:

> One fortunate in both would have us choose
> 'Perfection of the life or of the work'.
> Nonsense, you work best on a full stomach
> As everybody over thirty knows –
> For who, unbreakfasted, will love the lark?
> Prepare your protein-fed epiphanies,
> Your heavenly mansions blazing in the dark.

This is well-put and crucial, but Mahon's own epiphanies are protein-fed and he knows, with an exquisite guilt, that he's well-breakfasted. He's not going to deny his gift for the sake of an obligatory solemnity. The dark remains a backdrop to offset the vivid inventions of his verse, and when in the volume's title poem he posits for a moment that Uccello's marvellous rampant pageantry 'were not the great/Adventure we suppose but some elaborate/Spectacle put on for fun/And not for food' he catches exactly the tension set up throughout his work. His own hunt by night has a private beast in view – the anxious source of his vivid and generous imagination.

In some ways similar to Derek Mahon's, though lacking his kind of formal elegance – and, I suspect, mistrusting it – Anne Stevenson's recent poems are at the same time anxious and generous, brittle yet open to a wide range of experience which sometimes overwhelms them. *Minute by Glass Minute* is puritan and celebrant, and the glass that Anne Stevenson keeps looking through (the title of this new book is reminiscent of the earlier *Travelling Behind Glass*) both separates her from the world and irradiates it. 'When we belong to the world/we become what we are' she asserts at the end of 'Poem to my Daughter' but she knows that consciousness, the self-awareness of her art, is a holding back:

> Another day in March. Late
> rawness and wetness. I hear my mind say,
> if only I could paint essences...

She keeps hearing what her mind says, and she answers back with litanies of the actual. Several poems in the book weave their way philosophically in and out of exact, sensuous transcriptions such as:

> Beechbole, cheekbone of the interior,
> Sugaring maple, tap of sour soil,
> Woody sweetness, wine of the honeybark,
> Mountain trickle, bitter to the tongue.

But there is a strenuous, mannered air about the way Anne Stevenson registers her doubts and tentative certainties. 'Burnished' is an interesting poem in this respect. It begins:

> Walking out of Hay in the rain, imagining Blake
> imagining the real world into existence,
> I suddenly turned on him and said with energy –
> How dare you inflict imagination on us!
> What halo does the world deserve? And he –
> Let worlds die burnished, as along this bank.

'What halo does the world deserve?' The question is rhetorical and has a double edge; it is recriminating and, at the same time, hesitantly affirmative. At its centre is the quarrel out of which Anne Stevenson makes an authentic, if somewhat befuddled poetry. The tug between what, in the long poem 'Green Mountain, Black Mountain', she defines as 'ghost-pull' and 'animal-pull' leaves rather too much unresolved although it's fascinating as oblique autobiography and as an exploration of the contrasts between her New England upbringing and her more recent experience.

An incidental strength in Anne Stevenson's work is her acute feeling for moments of pain in human relationships – there's a world of horror and compassion in the portrait of her dying mother ('she was dying at us') – but in the same poem she can be modishly whimsical in her excessive use of simile. Stanzas 11-13 of section five of 'Green Mountain, Black Mountain' announce the Martian invasion of Vermont.

For Dr. Animus, in Anne Stevenson's 'Small Philosophical Poem', 'the world is the pleasure of thought'. It's a pleasure intensified by the 'small glass of doubt' which his wife Anima pours him. Alistair Elliot is a poet who belongs in such stringently meditative company where thoughts, as he says, are often 'like shop-windows standing between/us and our ease' but keep on coming and are shaped with relish into poems. In fact the poems themselves become a kind of ease, in that Elliot is an immensely *urbane* poet who has given back strength to that somewhat bland term. His work is full of scholarship, wit and observation, and it's appropriate that one of the poems should take as its epigraph Dr. Johnson's comment 'He that travels in the Highlands may easily saturate his soul with intelligence, if he will acquiesce in the first account'. Elliot's poems are certainly saturated with intelligence, but never enclosed. They are open to everyday experience, and some of the most moving of them in *Talking Back* result from a learned acquiescence to the commonplace. For example, the 'kitchen full of folk' to which he delivers a message in 'Ingredients of a Sleepless Night in Wales' is illuminated by the passing reference to Piers Plowman, fitted quite naturally into a conversational idiom. There's nothing precious about this – Elliot's poetic personality is far too gregarious ever to lay itself open to the charge of rarified erudition – but the approach it demonstrates is what makes poems which, on the surface, are about ancestors, families, travel and passing events, work effectively at a far deeper level.

Alistair Elliot's skill is equally evident in his dexterous, juicy versions of Verlaine's *Femmes/Hombres*. When asked what brush he painted his women with, Renoir is said to have replied 'avec mon chibre'. In this collaboration chibre has spoken to chibre across the years, and is obviously the only tool fit for the job:

> You are not the most fond of love
> Of women who have tried me on;
> You are not the most spicy of
> My women of the year just gone,
>
> But I adore you anyway!
> Besides, your sweet, mild body in
> Its final calm knows how to say
> All that is fatly feminine...

Fatly feminine and rampantly male, *Femmes/Hombres* is a catalogue of mutual delights without what Burns (and Elliot) call the 'consequential sorrows'.

And this seems a suitable point of intermission at which to mention Gavin Ewart's entertaining new collection of short poems, *More Little Ones*. There are limericks, clerihews, haiku, one-liners, all competing for the prize for the most memorable brevity. Some of the best are not that far distant from Verlaine ('Pantoum: Worship', for example) while others, such as the couplet on Seamus Heaney – 'He's very popular among his mates./ I think I'm Auden. He thinks he's Yeats' – are perhaps too complex in their multiple ironies to appeal widely outside the literary metropolis.

In a poetic climate which favours irony and cunning, and in which *content* is often the merely necessary means towards the desired end of stylistic novelty, Patric Dickinson's candid lyricism is as refreshing as it is rare. The poems in *A Rift in Time* are, to take Hardy's definition of poetry, 'emotion put into measure', and their authenticity transcends fashion. The language is unspectacular, the verse forms traditional, but they serve the purpose of a poet whose depth of feeling is best conveyed by the simplest means. I find Dickinson's work often very moving indeed; it is immediate, and subtle in its modesty – though the personality is too awkward, even irascible in its loves and hates, ever to be described as self-effacing. Dickinson's kind of straightforwardness is a balance of the commonplace and the idiosyncratic. Here is the second of two poems entitled 'Seathwaite Falls':

> Walking up the tortuous path
> Up through the rocks and bracken
> Towards the falls,
> I felt so heavenly shed
>
> Of being, yet nothing gone,
> An angel's nakedness,
> I stopped and you climbed nearer.
> I was so little dead
>
> So not alone with love,
> You had to be silent there
> By the never-silent waters
> And nothing heard, if spoken.
>
> – Your kind of coming back
> Our ever-flowing on.

This strikes me as an exemplary lyric. I have read it aloud several times, appreciating its pauses, repetitions and emphases: – the discreet impetus of that second 'up' at the beginning of the second line, the exact placing of 'heavenly' which anticipates 'an angel's nakedness' but might at first be mistaken for mere effusion, the 'nothing heard' in verse three which echoes and complements the 'nothing gone' in verse two, and the absolute clarity with which a complex perception is expressed in the last two lines. By no means all of *A Rift in Time* is as impressive as this, but even a handful of poems of such quality makes it a book for which to be grateful.

I admired Gillian Clarke's previous collection, *The Sundial*, but found rather too many of her vivid, sensuous nature poems marred by neat, moralistic codas. *Letter from a Far Country* trusts more in the power of metaphor to teach through revelation, and is a various, impressive book. The title poem, written for radio, explores the role of the home-centred wife and mother 'who ought to be/up to her wrists in marriage' in the context of place and history, those 'dead grandmothers' who

>...haul at the taut silk cords;
>set us fetching eggs, feeding hens,
>mixing rage with the family bread,
>lock us to the elbows in soap suds.
>Their sculleries and kitchens fill
>with steam, sweetness, goosefeathers.

From wrists to elbows, as the sense of history and restless disquiet intensifies throughout a poem which is – paradoxically – also a cele-bration. Gillian Clarke is best, though, as in her earlier work, at making her reader aware of what she calls 'the otherness of pain'. That is the farthest country of all. It crowds her poems with intimations, and she looks resolutely in its direction.

Michael Cullup, whose first book *Reading Geographies* brings together the work of sixteen years, is another poet who doesn't scorn subject matter and is attentive to the particular moment. He is quoted by his publisher as believing '...as Edward Thomas put it when writing of Robert Frost, in words being *bound together and made elements of beauty by a calm eagerness of emotion'*. Unfortunately, although the poems are well-crafted, there is a tendency for the calm to become blandness, and Cullup takes rather too many short cuts in his attempts to establish mood:

>There are leaves in my mind, dying leaves.
>It must be autumn, judging by the weather.
>Something is smouldering somewhere.
>The boughs creak.

There's a kind of precision about this, but it begins to seem like the after-effects of feeling – too measured a transcription – rather than a recreation. 'Something is smouldering somewhere' may be genuinely perceptive but it is also curiously null. The best poems in *Reading Geographies* are about people, and the best of all is 'The Ailing Gentlewoman' in which a clever use of banal parentheses catches the mood of twilight gentility:

>The world too being delicate as the snow was,
>So that the nature of one's disorder
>Fell so much without complaint to the ground
>One felt healed, in a manner of speaking,
>The ground being covered by snow
>As it were by a mantle, over all,
>So that one looked from one's world out onto it
>Lying there,
>With a sense of rightness at its being so
>Just as it was, fallen,

One was grateful, in a way, for its being like that:
Without hurt, white, and quite silent.

John Cotton's admirable Priapus Press has just celebrated its twentieth year in backroom business, and I'd urge anyone who feels that volumes like *The Penguin Book of Contemporary Poetry* are less than sufficient to send for its complete list. To do so at once, in fact, since today's decision so often becomes tomorrow's good intention. Among the press's recent publications three particularly successful items stand out: John Loveday's vivid rural vignettes from the 1930's and 40's, *The Agricultural Engineer*, John Cotton's own *Day Book*, which is a series of thirty-two 'fragments' moving adroitly in and around themes of personal and social concern, and Emma Rose's *Being Glass*. Emma Rose is a young poet of real promise. Although her imagery is often too tightly packed, and her intensity self-enclosed and brittle – 'Always inside I am looking out' – she has an excellent ear and a gift for touching in the minutest detail. Her imagination leans towards the surreal, and she needs to beware of whimsy, but her sense of a poem's necessary shape restrains her from excess. More of her work can be found in *Flags for the Occasion*, a beautifully produced pamphlet from the Dodman Press which also publishes the excellent poetry magazine *Grand Piano*, and this is a characteristic example: 'Ceremonial':

Glass and dust make a fine cutting edge,
but glass for all its brilliance is not
what they have come for, nor for dust, although
they hope to gain something from this.

The candle and the solemn dog.
A ring is poised between her thumb and finger,
around it promises and rituals
whose light strikes glass in patterns of frail gold.

3
Everyday Worlds
June 1983

R.S. Thomas: *Later Poems 1972-1982* (Macmillan)
John Fuller: *The Beautiful Inventions* (Secker & Warburg)
Patricia Beer: *The Lie of the Land* (Hutchinson)
Jenny Joseph: *Beyond Descartes* (Secker & Warburg)
Sean O'Brien: *The Indoor Park* (Bloodaxe Books)
John Latham: *Unpacking Mr. Jones* (Peterloo Poets)
Julian Ennis: *At the Frontier* (Peterloo Poets)
Hal Summers: *The Burning Book* (The Book Guild)

THE PUBLICATION OF a volume entitled *Later Poems* must necessarily raise interesting questions about its author, especially when he is still very much alive and, one hopes, a long way from writing his Last. The established ring of 'Later' is, of course, an endorsement of status, the measure of a distance covered. There's a conferred distinction implicit in its putting of a career in perspective, as if the poet could be seen to have moved into a rather splendid new house bought for him by his reputation. But has he taken the old furniture with him? Can his tracks be seen leading to the front door? As we look through the window, is he still at work in there? Are the new poems getting written? Do they promise to be more than a succession of mere appendices and a mere repetition of later, later, later until the ultimate repetition of last?

In the case of R.S. Thomas, the answers amount to a confident *Yes* to coincide with his seventieth birthday. *Later Poems 1972–1982* contains a careful but generous selection from his four most recent full-scale volumes, a mere five from his more marginal publications during this period, and forty three new poems, some of which are as fine, austere and commanding as any he has written. It is a book of sonorous and calculated rhetoric where condensed dramas of spiritual quest, fragments of the continuing search for an infinitely protean *deus absconditus* – 'the echoes/We follow, the footprints he has just/Left' –, combine the animation of a curious, interrogating mind with the cadences of a desolate patience. Since the appearance of *H'm* in 1972, Thomas's poems have become increasingly contemplative and at the same time more argumentative and intense. They are wilfully indifferent to the dangers of abstraction, taking on prosaic ballast as an earnest of the voyage's urgency, and usually getting away with it – though not always:

> Machines were invented
> To cope, but they also were limited
> By our expectations. Men stared
> With a sort of growing resentment
> At life that was ubiquitous and
> Unseizable.

This is prose by any reckoning, and dull prose at that, but Thomas has always been sceptical about the adequacy – for his purposes – of 'pure poetry'. As he wrote, twenty years ago now, 'A pure poet is one who, presumably, lives for his art, interested in the interior world of words and thought, rather than the everyday world of noise and pain and evil. I think, when I examine my own position, that I have never been a pure poet in that way. To make a poetic artefact out of words has never or rarely ever been my first aim or satisfaction. There is always lurking at the back of my poetry a kind of moralistic or propagandist intention'.

When his subect matter – back in what might be called the heyday of his Schools Anthology popularity – was the Welsh Hill Country, its landscape and peasantry, his moralistic eye perched bleakly and memorably on local detail; but even in those earlier poems, striking though many of their metaphors may be they are often laboured and over-extended, and it is really the accumulation and balancing of phrases – a kind of incantatory commitment to the vision – that distinguishes them from the ruck of rural verse. This seems to me to be what those critics resistant to Thomas's later work fail to recognise. They see him as having abandoned the rocky acres for a nebulous cosmos, and a firm poetic footing for an inconclusive and portentous space-walking, whereas in fact what has occurred is an enlargement of his concerns and a refinement of his technique. The fascinating paradox of his more recent poetry is that it confronts 'the everyday world of noise and pain and evil' even as it explores interior worlds of private doubt in the search for consolation:

> Seeking the poem
> In the pain, I have learned
> Silence is best, paying for it
> With my conscience.

The poem in the pain and the pain in the poem: this is what makes for the intensity of Thomas's work. And the silence is active, never the passivity of surrender. In poem after poem, he presents himself as watching and waiting 'somewhere between faith and doubt,/for the echoes of...arrival'. The silence 'belabours' him, and he contends, wrestling with its evasions through poems with titles such as 'Threshold', 'Groping', 'Probing', 'The Combat', 'The Interrogation' and 'The Truce'. These poems are often directly addressed to God in his various aspects which include the Hardy-esque 'disposer of the issues/of life', and their ransacking of the languages of physics, physiology, biology, even aeronautics ('The weather/is his mind's turbine') is explained in the argument of the poems themselves as a technique 'for registering the ubiquity/of your presence'. At times the titles cry out like an Old Testament Prophet 'Aie!', 'Selah!' or fall help-lessly silent – 'H'm'. The book's index alone reads like a spiritual temperature chart.

Despite the excesses and the moments when one almost suspects self-parody, *Later Poems*, along with *Selected Poems 1946-1968*, establishes R.S. Thomas as a poet of the first importance; by turns intolerant, compassionate, remote, intimate, but above all – while taking a full look at the worst – affirmative:

> A bird chimes
> from a green tree
> the hour that is no hour
> you know. The river dawdles
> to hold a mirror for you
> where you may see yourself
> as you are, a traveller
> with the moon's halo
> above him, who has arrived
> after long journeying where he
> began, catching this
> one truth by surprise
> that there is everything to look forward to.

W.H. Auden once commented that there's no such thing as a pretty good omelette, and I'd guess that John Fuller agrees. He's undoubtedly one of the best cooks since Auden – his ingredients are carefully chosen, his mixes often surprising, and the resultant dishes invariably rare. The meal is given a final stir for good luck, then served with decorum:

> Afterwards you may walk the block,
> Or collect your daughter from judo, noticing
> In the jut of lip and foot in the jostling
> For a fall, an equal determination.
> Then coffee, and music. And perhaps a cigar.

No perhaps about it. Definitely a cigar – and a toast to Auden. That flash of a world outside – collecting your daughter – partakes of the meal. The bonne bouche is a paradigm of the good life: the grub *is* the ethics. And reading 'Steamed Carp's Cheeks' – one of several poems in *The Beautiful Inventions* where cooking instructions emerge as a branch of moral philosophy, and where we're told to buy Chinese mushrooms if our grocer has them – I found myself remembering the ancient Chinese saying that you should govern a country as you would cook a small fish. Fuller is just such a fastidious emperor, issuing and acting upon instructions for the business of good government and craftsmanlike making. He has a delight in the workings of orderly little universes – beautiful inventions in themselves – which he sometimes recreates through the details of a protective rhetoric, as in 'Wasp Nest':

Be careful not to crush
This scalloped tenement:
Who knows what secrets
Winter has failed to find
Within its paper walls?

It is the universe
Looking entirely inwards,
A hanging lantern
Whose black light wriggles
Through innumerable chambers

Where hopes still sleep
In her furry pews,
The chewed dormitory
Of a forgotten tribe
That layered its wooden pearl...

The delicacy of this is admirable, and, in the main, I like *The Beautiful Inventions* best when it is at its most intricately riddling. There's nothing fussy or wilfully smart about Fuller's cleverness in such poems. Their small, exact occasions clear an ample space for tenderness and wisdom. What I'm less happy about are some of the brilliant, rhymed displays of metrical footwork – *copious* inventions, certainly, and in their way amazing, but they're a kind of Ira Gershwin gone nice:

I'd like to have your back to scour
And other parts to lubricate.
Sometimes I feel it is my fate
To chase you screaming up a tower
Or make you cower
By asking you to differentiate
Nietzsche from Schopenhauer.

There's a preciousness in this. It's like listening to the Kings Singers going through their repertoire of jazz items – bending the notes so self-consciously with such knowing accomplishment – but if you like that kind of thing, no one does it better than John Fuller and there's plenty of it towards the end of the book.

The last poem, though, is the most remarkable, and one of the best that Fuller has written. 'The College Ghost', in which the poet meets and listens without protest or interruption to a spectre which is not unlike his alter ego, manages to be both disquietingly modern in its edgy questioning of the value of University life and traditionally donnish in the manner of M.R. James. It's a poem in which the void whispers beyond the dreaming spires, and in a book that is in so many ways accomplished and complete it seems somehow right that a ghost in the works should have the last word:

> 'Now I appear to you because at last
> I have rejoined you for ever. Life has made
> Its choice. My affairs are finally quite complete
> And there is nothing left in the world to alter.
> Whatever you teach will make no difference at all.'

Patricia Beer's poems are full of ghosts. They move fleetingly across her miniature canvasses like figures in a pageant to the tolling of a passing bell. She is preoccupied with time, and her work has the monitory elegance of a collection of hour-glasses in which the light is continually catching the sifting sand. To take a phrase from 'The Spinsters and The Knitters in the Sun', one of the finest poems in her new collection, she works in a 'spotlit darkness', contemplating her own mortality as part of the shadow-play of history. She is attuned to intimation and rumour ('At the top of the lane/Wars went by', 'Somewhere a horse galloped') and this gives an edge to the precise, domestic observation which is one of her great strengths:

> I watch the shadows of the house climbing
> Slantwise and high up the back field.
> The east chimney puffs out a black ghost.

That 'slantwise' is tell-tale, an accurate perception both visually and as an indication of Patricia Beer's method. Like Emily Dickinson she knows how to tell it slant, so that nothing is ever quite what it seems although it is defined with great exactitude. The lie of the land is deceptive – and the pun in the book's title is surely intended. Patricia Beer's poems are full of images the cleverness of which is absorbed into the landscape they serve to depict, giving it an idiosyncratic character and perspective: she risks whimsy and turns the slightest effect to advantage – 'The trees are parsley magnified' or 'Today/Impromptu meres, whiskery/ In fields, raise half/A fence for an eyebrow'. A quizzical look, and Patricia Beer's eyebrow is raised back, a match for it.

My favourite poem in *The Lie of the Land* is 'Bereavement'. It has a pained beauty, an oddly hymn-like stately simplicity in which Blake meets with the Ancient and Modern Victorians. Its rhythms and rhymes (particularly the second couplets in stanzas 2 and 3) are haunting in their contrived blend of knowingness and naiveté: the Lamb of God is a lost child, fierce in its sense of betrayal:

> I was too young. I had to watch
> My heavy mother lie on her back to scratch.
> They never touched ground again, those brittle feet.
> I cannot eat what all the others eat.
>
> Foolish mother, rolling to death, how long
> Shall the deserted bare an aching tongue

To call for what is drying up inside you
As the afternoon trees begin to shade you?

Soon he will come, the farmer, and haul away
And hide that sheep, who treacherously
Lay down, where I can never find her
Nor go into the slaughter-house behind her.

The sharp May grass sings under my nose
And soon the farmer will hear a new voice
That lost the day wailing about hunger
But towards nightfall turns to anger.

Nightfall, again, as in so many of the poems, and time running out. 'The clock on the night storage heating/Ticks like a taxi waiting'.

Jenny Joseph is another poet of the quotidian but, unlike Patricia Beer, she's more obviously, remorselessly compassionate, and in her philosophical pieces she seems possessed of an intellectual fever. Nothing stays put for a moment, and she's bound upon the wheel of appearances in a turmoil of perception and thought: 'Only by doing again/Each done thing do we live a minute – you stop and you die'. In her poems, several of them of considerable length, rhetorical force and teasing complexity, unease becomes a moral imperative and she juggles her various perspectives accordingly. Her address to the reader is often direct, nervous and urgent – 'Are you there, Reader?' – a recurring demand for involvement, complicity, even reassurance: *agnoscis me, ergo sum*. Jenny Joseph's imagination is one in which the poet's existence is felt to be a collective responsibility, and response becomes a part of the process of her thinking:

And when I sit in your room, dear, and you reach across
To get a paper to show me something, have I
By looking forward lost you in the present,
Or having made you, understand you better
Than ever happens in raw life outside?
These mirrored mirrors lead us nowhere fast.
Solitary reader at night that I have conjured
Reaching across to pick up a picture that you
Imagined yourself into, turn round again.
Step out of the frame that I have trapped us in
Place your hand on my shoulder and take away the pen.

Beyond Descartes takes as its epigraph a quotation from Graham Dunstan Martin, '*Terra Firma* is rather a small islet' and its effect as a whole is to make one aware of how insecure even that small islet is. 'Here is shade/ And safety on the edge of danger'...'each must pull the fabric where he can/to shield him'. A number of the poems are cast in the form of journeys

– looking in on gardens or cosy interiors with a kind of sceptical longing before passing on:

> Traveller, you think you have gone far.
> You have learnt to pack, travel light, full of expertise
> To hold to the road, to be lucky, avoid plague towns;
> And one dusk you may, inadvertent, pass a place, a bit of air
>
> And from it will seize
> You in the gut the feral eye-beam of the animal,
> Old thoughts you thought swallowed and passed;
> And the spirits, for some time shrunk and tamed, once again
> Wild – all.

That feral eye-beam seldom lets up in Jenny Joseph's work – the shrunk and the tamed are constantly reminded of their timorousness and, by implication, of their irresponsibility. The poetry can be flabby and rather over-insistent ('But, human, need the human hope, and hope/Leaves us aghast at what the human is') or almost Whitmanesque in its strenuous romanticism ('Bird of my spirit, where are your lifting wings?/Song of my mind clear your lovely voice'). Length is perhaps a measure of her seriousness and impressive intellectual scope, but I do feel that she often doesn't know when to stop, and that a number of the poems lift off into stridency. *Beyond Descartes* is a book of intermittent brilliance which illuminates most when it is least exclamatory and self-conscious. A fine poem, 'Dipping for Diamonds', begins 'Dipping for diamonds, we were./I almost scooped one up when I wasn't looking'. Jenny Joseph's best work is done when she isn't looking. But, then, only the resolute prospector is blessed with such accidents.

Sean O'Brien's first collection, *The Indoor Park*, is an impressive debut. Fourteen of the poems appeared last year in the anthology *A Rumoured City: New Poets from Hull*, but there are fifty in this book, and the overall impression is one of considerable weight and seriousness. O'Brien owes much, by way of influence, to Douglas Dunn – applying the techniques of a benign and mellow surreal-cum-symbolist method to his city landscapes. Mallarmé's *adieu suprême des mouchoirs*, a sense of luxurious, resonant gloom embroidering details of decay, dissolution and loss, combine with a taste for more sprightly aestheticism reminiscent of Wallace Stevens; and this synthesis is in turn filtered through a modern urban sensibility. Echoes of 'Brise Marine' and the *Harmonium* poems merge into something interesting and strange:

> It will look like a posture
> Supportable only in summer,
> Like those embarrassed couples racked
> On postcards in primary colours

Of nuptial malfeasance and loathing,
Sent to prove a holiday was had.
Extended families of pain,
They float in batches to the shore
You reach beyond your book at night.
The sea, the blue comedian
Who rolls the drowned along the aisles
Of an interminable act,
Has autographed each card with love.

O'Brien, who announces directly in the collection's second poem 'I am in love with detail', is good at capturing those 'intensities of indolence' which can be as much felt in his solemn cadences as seen in his visual cameos. The poems are peopled by 'polite incapables', often young and caught between yearning and resignation. The most that can be hoped for is a modest, circumspect efficiency of routine in the face of 'the residue of time got wrong':

The best to be had is a biro that works
And some milk left for morning.
Let's go out now, to where we live,
The dead harbour, the pub and the station buffet,
North of the Word, where it rains in your face.

Sean O'Brien seems to me, again like Dunn, to distil a poetry from the symptoms of a culture he's lovingly addicted to but finds himself unable to approve. He's constantly drawing back from the sardonically critical into the helplessly romantic. His imagination thrives on ruin with an almost eighteenth-century relish for the picturesque, but his conscience qualifies every observation:

This is where the English live.
And we are foreigners. The bus to work
Braves Congos of complacent tat...

The evenings, though, are 'personal'.
I count the rooms. I count again.
I try to sit in one of them. I fail

And imagine pianos instead,
A Bechstein warehouse, grand and dumb,
With teeth as white as privilege.

That last line – oddly lyrical in itself but at odds with the vanished, symphonic splendours conjured up by the line which precedes it – is characteristic of what makes Sean O'Brien a poet to watch.

Another first collection is John Latham's *Unpacking Mr. Jones* in which many of the poems adopt a child's-eye view of things with varying degrees of success. A characteristic poem is 'Beneath the Walnut Table' where a small boy watches the lower parts of a family playing cards from knee (or crotch) level:

> A finger wearing Uncle Ivor's ring
> sneaks into view, sniffs the cobwebbed air.
>
> Carefully it wipes the gob of liquid on its tip
> along the grains. Aunt Lil's legs are thonged
>
> with purple snakes, which she follows, teases
> with her sea-shell nails, pinches meanly
>
> until they swell and blush. Susan's lace-fringed
> hand flutters vaguely onto Malcolm's knee,
>
> drifts north to a bulge like an ill-concealed
> revolver...

I find this, up to a point, clever and delightful, a cunning attempt to get the best of both worlds; to be, at the same time, innocent and knowing. Latham is good at catching the latent violence of infant sexuality – the half-cock, incipient thrill of it. He likes the verb *thonged*. It comes again in a rather nasty but convincing poem, 'Purple Cow', in which a small group of boys boil a girl's knickers with damsons so that when she puts them on 'purple trails' thong her thighs and creep down her knees. This is both visual and intensely visceral. There's more than a touch of prurience in the innocent eye, as Latham is intent on the effect he is achieving. What I mistrust is the element of showmanship in his method. He likes to end his poems with little frissons of horror, much as Roald Dahl concludes many of his stories, especially those in which children have a large part to play. When you come down to it, it's for Adults Only.

Nevertheless I enjoyed much of *Unpacking Mr. Jones*, not least the wholly and touchingly successful title poem. At the heart of John Latham's anecdotal recreations of childhood there's a nostalgia for fag cards, party girls with ribbons and lace frills, and a whole giggly, gossipy world of knickers and willies. Despite my reservations, it struck me as highly evocative.

If John Latham celebrates the lore of the playground and the back of the bicycle-sheds, Julian Ennis remains more soberly the school-master, decently concerned and with a quotation from English Literature for most occasions. The best poems in *At The Frontier* are the first few which come out of his recent retirement to Sidmouth. They are movingly honest in their acceptance of limitations:

> So we prefer to remain here
> Lying on the neat lines of grass
> And watch the wall we do not dare go over.
> Here, like birds, we find enough worms

> To make any gate welcome.
> For we seek the quiet life,
> Content to listen to whatever sound
> Is made by something somehow
> Between the silence and the roaring.

Julian Ennis *knows* that his imagination daren't go over the wall, and it's to his credit that he does. Not that he isn't uneasy in his acceptance of the circumspect: occasionally he attempts to bite, but it doesn't suit him. In 'Blackboard Jungle', after considering the seemingly callous reaction of his pupils to the death of one of their form-mates (rather inevitably called Smith), he ruminates: 'I tell the tale, am not sure of the moral to be learnt'. His limitation as a poet is that he finds himself, in general, over-anxious about the moral and only happy, it seems, if it comes readily to hand.

Finally, a collection which gives the pleasure of being in the company of a kind and modest man. There are no poems in Hal Summers' *The Burning Book* which made me sit *up*, but I sat down and read them all with appreciation. They are companionable, wise and unassuming. 'Sick Room' is a good example. It ends:

> Like one long absent coming home
> The sick man gazes round the room
> Brought back from nothingness, and sees
> How beautiful and sane it is.

Beauty and sanity are the hallmarks of *The Burning Book*. It cannot be memorable because it slips too invisibly into the genteel lyrical tradition which defines it, but at the same time such elegant niceness can be too easily overlooked altogether.

4
Expanding Elements
December 1983

Elizabeth Bishop: *The Complete Poems 1927-1979* (Chatto & Windus)
Christopher Middleton: *111 Poems* (Carcanet)
D.M. Thomas: *Selected Poems* (Secker & Warburg)
George Barker: *Anno Domini* (Faber & Faber)
Geoffrey Hill: *The Mystery of the Charity of Charles Péguy* (Agenda
Editions/Andre Deutsch)
Andrew Motion: *Secret Narratives* (Salamander Press)
Peter Reading: *Diplopic* (Secker & Warburg)
Carol Rumens: *Star Whisper* (Secker & Warburg)
John Levett: *Changing Sides* (Peterloo Poets)

'(NO IDEAS/BUT in things)' wrote William Carlos Williams, in parenthesis, and how that statement has kept returning to justify the minimal. The numinous object as an end in itself – palpable, crafted, the repository of an immaculate vocabulary – so often seems to be the Holy Grail of contemporary poets; an ambition to achieve much in little which remains resolutely little because the talent doesn't amount to much beyond a display of those qualities beloved of reviewers, 'a sharp eye and a feeling for language'. Words alone, alas, are not certain good. Obvious as it may seem to say so, there has to be a mind to arrange them. Poets must be possessed of the expanding element through which poems can grow larger than their occasion, otherwise it's like buying a dud Japanese flower and watching in vain for something to happen when you drop it in the tumbler. There are plenty of these duds to go round. Most packets contain several, some fewer than others, and on the rare occasion every pellet blossoms. In another of his wise little poems about poetry, Williams writes:

> Good Christ what is
> a poet if any
>   exists?
> a man
> whose words will
>   bite
>   their way
> home – being actual
>
> having the form
> of motion.

What's more, there must be a home for the words to bite *from* as well as *to*. Intelligence is the form of their motion, without which the actuality remains an inert precision, and poetry merely a game played with vivid counters.

Elizabeth Bishop seems to me a supreme example of bite and motion. The excellence of her work lies in the degree to which it is more than a total of the visual accuracies and startling metaphors for which it is celebrated. Not surprisingly it became the touchstone of perfection for a whole generation of highly intelligent, troubled American poets who envied her poise while recognising how very far from effortless it was. They were all ambitious and accomplished, but if their minds had mountains then somehow the air – and certainly the light – seemed clearer where she was. Randall Jarrell even went as far as to say that her poems were, quite simply, what poems ought to be, and I suspect that this may well have been because so many of his own, while seeking for a shape, kept becoming top-heavy with raw, plangent emotion. They seldom came out quite right, except the monologues. And one can see precisely why Robert Lowell, also, admired her; in one of her last poems, addressed to him *in memoriam*, she writes 'You can't derange, or rearrange, your poems again'. There's understanding in that, all right. She recognised the need to balance passion and perception, intelligence and grace. That was her ambition and, more consistently than for Jarrell or Lowell, her achievement. When Lowell himself wrote, in his 'Epilogue', 'Pray for the grace of accuracy/Vermeer gave to the sun's illumination/stealing like the tide across a map' he was voicing a prayer that had been answered for Elizabeth Bishop. And, incidentally, not only was the first poem in her first major collection entitled 'The Map' but Jarrell was amongst the first critics to liken her work to Vermeer's. Such telling coincidences reverberate, as do such marvellous lines as these:

> This iceberg cuts its facets from within.
> Like jewelry from a grave
> it saves itself perpetually and adorns
> only itself, perhaps the snows
> which so surprise us lying on the sea.
> Goodbye, we say, goodbye, the ship steers off
> where waves give in to one another's waves
> and clouds run in a warmer sky.
> Icebergs behoove the soul
> (both being self-made from elements least visible)
> to see them so: fleshed, fair, erected indivisible.

In another of her late poems, 'Santarém', collected for the first time in this *Complete Poems*, Elizabeth Bishop writes of a remembered landscape: 'I liked the place; I liked the idea of the place'. Her particular, enticing and profound talent can hardly be better characterised. Two apparently distinct observations are set up in juxtaposition within a single statement, the semi-colon telling the eye that perception and thought reflect each other in endless, incomplete ramification even as the ear registers a full-stop and is lulled into the false security of hearing a pair of straightforward remarks made with pleasing symmetry and assured, conversational ease. The delightful title, too, of a very early sequence

'Three Sonnets for the Eyes' indicates a similar tension between descriptive detail and the sustaining shape of the poem. For Elizabeth Bishop, a poet of remarkable *claritas*, nothing is merely incidental although every incident is welcomed as an amazing novelty. She is the most knowing and experienced of ingenues, at the same time deeply humane and dashingly witty, and it's her poetic method to be so. There's restraint in her brilliance, not least when she's most tempted to excess. She knows that 'just one luscious adjective/infuriates the whole damned band/and they're squabbling for it'. Hers is a most cunning diplomacy of the imagination.

In 'The Weed', one of her emblematic dream-fantasies, presented with an oddly haunting matter-of-factness which makes it so immediately a part of the reader's experience, there's a typical moment of ambush:

> Suddenly there was a motion,
> as startling, there, to every sense
> as an explosion. Then it dropped
> to insistent, cautious creeping
> in the region of the heart...

This seems to catch exactly the sensation of delight and disquiet felt when reading Elizabeth Bishop's poems. Whether her subject is a personality, an animal, an exotic landscape or a humdrum domestic interior, she first surprises – juggling our perceptions – and then, before we have realised it, she leaves us moved. At one level her poems are a 'theatre of the spirits:/objects putting the laws/of identity through hoops', but what this ingenuity serves is her keen, underlying awareness of how, in the end, we are all jumbled in a common box from cradle to grave:

> The passengers lie back.
> Snores. Some long sighs.
> A dreamy divagation
> begins in the night,
> a gentle, auditory,
> slow hallucination...
>
> In the creaking and noises,
> an old conversation
> – not concerning us,
> but recognisable, somewhere,
> back in the bus:
> Grandparents' voices
>
> uninterruptedly
> talking, in Eternity:
> names being mentioned,
> things cleared up finally...

Like those lines from 'The Moose', the poems weave their way
mysteriously in and out of the interstices between here and elsewhere,
always 'driving to the interior', aware that 'our knowledge is historical,
flowing and flown', and they certainly leave me grateful for a clear-
sightedness which is both the purest poetry and the most candid, gentle
and stoical celebration of the human condition.

Christopher Middleton is a very different writer from Elizabeth
Bishop, but equally one for whom poetic thought is a matter of arranging
objects. Many of the poems in a new selection of his work, dating back to
1949, are *about* the process, reading like experimental demonstrations
full of elipses, impacted phrasing and the kind of compression which
comes of taking notes while the bunsen is burning. They're far from being
mere activities of the laboratory, though, and their material is certainly
the stuff of human experience. Nevertheless there is a passionate, visceral
symmetry about them which seldom lets one forget that they are intent
upon results, and that these results are to do with definitions of poetry –
its possibilities and limits.

In a short prose piece, Middleton observes that 'the Historian, after
all, should move at a leisurely pace among the objects of his investigation, as a dog might, in a forest of lamp-posts, a lucid dog, that is, one who
knows the pleasure of dragging pleasure out'. I take it that, for him, the
historian and the poet are distinct, the one dragging it out, the other
packing it in. Intensity, 'the very nerve that sees' as he puts it, lights up
the lamp-posts for the poet, but it's a controlled and often rather *voulu*
intensity: 'The poem/Attacked by fleets of random objects/Had no purity
or perspective whatever'. Middleton allows little random behaviour
amongst his objects. Purity and perspective, his imperatives, require firm
discipline and a hermetic tightness. When he exclaims, in 'Ibeji', 'Lord/
What loops one lives in' it is possible to see each loop as both a continuum
and a noose, just as to read through *111 Poems* is to experience stretches
of clear, direct and moving poetry which suddenly clams up in bursts of
obscurity and scrambled intellectuality. This is fascinating if, in the end,
unsatisfactory, and it seems appropriate that Middleton's favourite shape
(to judge from its recurrence throughout the book) is the oval, that
tension between square and circle which is never really happy being
either.

For all his exact, artful spacings, placings and conspicuous
punctuation which, I suppose, have earned him his reputation (regretted
in the publisher's blurb) as a poet of remarkable oddity, Middleton can
write fine poems, several of which, here, come in the selection from his
1969 collection *Our Flowers and Nice Bones*. 'The Armadillos' is a beautiful piece, and an example of his vivid irony at its best. I think Elizabeth
Bishop, whose own 'The Armadillo' is one of her most memorable poems,

would have appreciated it. Three stanzas must suffice to give something
of its special quality:

> Don't fall, Harriet! Arthur, don't fall!
> We can't help it if the armadillos
> drop like bombs and catch only
> in the lower branches with their claws.
> Falling like that, they can't be lonely.
>
> Winters, they leave the trees and trundle
> to the end of the valley. In twos and fours
> they cluster there and comfort each other.
> The frost feels them under their bucklers;
> they taste it happening in their jaws.
>
> But in the trees where they build hides
> of cardboard boxes and paper bags,
> their main concern is believing summer.
> For my friends broken by special committees
> I hang out armadillo flags.

If Christopher Middleton sometimes seems too esoteric an arranger
of co-ordinates and polarities, D.M. Thomas is nothing if not pro-
grammed and prescriptive. For all his apparent experimentation, he
pre-empts the reader's imagination, barging in on it variously dressed (or
undressed) as lover, bard and analyst. He never gives short measure. By
turns torrentially libidinous and soberly in command of his historical,
family or futuristic fables, he is quite clear about the direction a poetic
career should take:

> The first book of a poet should be called *Stone*
> Or *Evening*, expressing in a single word
> The modesty of being part of the earth,
> The goodness of evening and stone, beyond the poet.
>
> The second book should have a name blushing
> With a great generality, such as *My Sister Life,*
> Shocking in its pride, even more in its modesty:
> Exasperated, warm, teasing, observant, tender.
>
> Later books should withdraw into a mysterious
> Privacy such as we all make for ourselves:
> *The White Stag* or *Plantain*. Or include the name
> Of the place at which his book falls open.

But this very clarity sounds the note of self-aware portentousness which
mars too many of his poems, giving them an air of solemn, claustrophobic
urgency. 'Exasperated, warm, teasing, observant, tender' they can certainly be, but at the same time they are too busy announcing that they are.

In his Preface to the *Selected Poems*, Thomas writes ' "Sex and the dead". said Yeats, were the only two subjects worthy of a serious man's conversation, and I'd go along with that. Sex, of course, includes all creativity, and death includes its own vanquishing'. I'd go along with that, too, including the *of course*, and I quite take the implied point that I am not a serious man if I don't take Thomas seriously. I do. I'm entirely solemn-faced when, for example, this instance of death and sex seizes him:

> A glint
> of family madness in her eyes, my love talks about
> dying. 'Fuck death,' I spit,
> and slide my hand along the pew, under her skirt.
> Invasive as a celtic saint,
> my finger opens her like the spine of a new testament.

The trouble is that on this occasion, as on so many, Thomas's fantastic earnestness makes me embarrassed to laugh, although he convinces me that laughter must surely be an important part of the truth. What, alas, is missing is a sense of humour and absurdity – a *perspective* on the experience which, far from trivialising his themes, might enrich them and make them seem less monolithic. As it is, the topics of conversation are Sex and Death and *how*! They flaunt 'the modesty of being part of the earth' with a rather immodest insistence, and when Thomas withdraws into that 'mysterious/privacy such as we all make for ourselves' they go with him, bag and baggage – to Vienna, Russia, everywhere.

The best poems in the book are directly elegiac and, refreshingly, eschew fantasy. On a smaller and larger/private and public scale, respectively, 'Rubble' – a portrait of his dying mother – and 'Requiem for Aberfan' are very moving indeed, showing – despite all reservations – what a good poet Thomas can be. Nevertheless, even when he is writing out of an immediate sense of shock, the cumulative insistence on significance can wreck the poem, as in 'Sun Valley' where an account of the mass killing of poultry is presented as a Dantesque vision. The experience of reading this is unnerving in the wrong sense. To begin with, a poem of keen personal observation is strengthened by the allusion to Dante implicit in the terza rima form and in the subtle inversions of syntax which lend a slight but not obtrusive air of antique courtliness to the poem's development. This highlights the horror, but then, at the end, a direct reference to the Inferno suddenly makes the whole poem take on the retrospective air of having been a literary occasion. It becomes another example of original perception worked up and over into so much less than it could have been by a self-conscious artistry.

The title poem of George Barker's *Anno Domini* is very nearly the complete volume, and a work of quite remarkable bravura. Its vivid, self-generating rhetoric goes over the top while the reader – engrossed – stays with it on a rare circuit of celebration, despair, satire and incantation. In the name of all that is alive and uncertain, Barker castigates the fixed, the arid and the complacent: 'at a time of categorical imperatives /to guess about clouds:/at a time of politicians/to trust only to children and demi-gods' – and so on, through instance after instance, and sequence after sequence of parallelism. 'Anno Domini' is psalmic, bizarre, profound, banal, a canticle of wisdom and bathos in equal, invigorating measure. If you stop to think – which the poem, at least for its duration, ensures that you don't – it would be sentimental lunacy to trust only to children and demi-gods, but the whole enterprise reads like the work of a childlike demi-god blessed with more than a little mature insight and sophisticated humour. Even as, for example, God is addressed as a Frankensteinian professor whose monstrous creation 'could have come from nowhere save a mind/capable of inventing the idea of evil' one responds to a driving passion which transcends the rather absurd machinery and the cluttered rant of the vocabulary. There is a deep and terrified level at which a passage like this calls out for assent:

> What does this shambling machine whisper
>   as it crawls and stumbles among rocks and ruins,
> its clockwork eyes clouded with selfhate, its
>   terminals cancerous, wetware and wordwrite
> alphanumeric, phonemed,
>   automatic forks pick-
> ing up isotopes, robotics utterly grouched,
>   the reproductive generator hanging
> down like an obsolete decoration, the
>   anthropic spirit skinnered, the
> enigma cybernized,
>   the circuit of the nervous system worn
> to a nexus of Freudian wires,
>   what does this shambling machine whisper
> when it encounters, down the dark path,
>   halfway through a Black Forest, of
> a midwinter midnight,
>   the huge god riding on a dead white horse?
> What, what does it whisper?
> "I am a man"?

The other poems in *Anno Domini* are an elegy for several of Barker's contemporaries, including Louis MacNeice who 'knew that poetry begins/where the philosophical propositions stop' but confronted that knowledge in very different ways from Barker, and an apocalyptic ballad, 'The Ship of Fools', where the elite passengers swill, guzzle and screw while:

> The priest stood priestifying at
> his little wooden ark.
> 'Beloved' he said, 'God is not dead.
> He's whistling in the dark'.

Barker, pagan and priestifyer, continues to get the best of both worlds. The historical occasion of Geoffrey Hill's new poem is the life, death and apotheosis of Charles Péguy. Péguy was a national socialist, poet, bookseller, a 'radical soul' whose 'dream of France, militant pastoral' was implicated in the murder (July 1914) of Jean Jaurès, the socialist leader. He had admired Jaurès up to the point where he came out against France's entry into the First World War, but subsequently rounded on him, calling for his blood and receiving his answer from an assassin's bullet. Péguy, a complex patriot, was fired by a vision of the 'national revolution', of a leaping into cleanness, which transcended conventional socialist allegiances. His conception of patriotism was 'regenerative and sacrificial' and, of its essence, inflammatory: to adapt Yeats' not entirely dissimilar question, asked in another country a few years later, did certain words of his send out the man who shot the leader? As Hill puts it in a prose postscript to *The Mystery of the Charity of Charles Péguy*, Péguy was at the same time moved by violent emotions and violently afflicted by mischance. The violence and the mischance coincided in his death on the first day of the first battle of the Marne in September 1914.

So much for the notes of the poem's theme, but as with most of Geoffrey Hill's work its impact is the total of its variations. These are many. They are densely layered and impacted. The historical occasion is only a part of the poetic event. *The Mystery of the Charity of Charles Péguy* is in ten sections, and is as intricate and allusive a pavan of violence and ambiguous redemption as Hill has yet written, an accumulation of beautiful and demanding lines, each in itself a facet for contemplation. It is also, though, remote in its sonority and its making of ex-cathedra statements, as if it were being delivered to a particularly erudite congregation from the other end of the cathedral. When Hill meditates on suffering and action, doubt and faith, reputation and redemption, he often comes dangerously close to sounding like a parody of Eliot's priests addressing the Women of Canterbury:

> Drawn on the past
> these presences endure; they have not ceased
> to act, suffer, crouching into the hail
> like labourers of their own memorial...

He's a brilliant phrase-maker, though, and each phrase is witness to a complex passion – an intense marriage of doubt and faith – which seems a match for Péguy's. The simplest combination of words, for Hill, is a feast of associations: 'the guilt belongs to time', 'Death does you proud' etc. Like the blood that, emblematically, dribbles from Péguy's skull on the battlefield it is 'a simple lesion of the complex brain'. In fact, the whole poem could be viewed as a succession of moments at which Hill's theme and method coincide in a celebration of his art and of Péguy's example. It is as self-conscious as it is selflessly admiring, and some of the stanzas are extraordinarily beautiful in their finish:

> Landscape is like revelation; it is both
> singular crystal and the remotest things.
> Cloud-shadows of seasons revisit the earth,
> odourless myrrh borne by the wandering kings.

> Happy are they who, under the gaze of God,
> die for the 'terre charnelle', marry her blood
> to theirs, and, in strange Christian hope, go down
> into the darkness of resurrection...

Above all it is that 'strange Christian hope' which reverberates throughout the poem, from the opening lines where Jaurès dies in the 'wine puddle' of his own blood to the final stanza where Péguy offers up his 'body's prayer'. The power is that of a poem which hopes where it cannot prove, and which very elegantly founders, as did Hill's 'Lachrimae' sequence, 'in desire for things unfound'. As he writes of Péguy in the postscript, 'he had...rediscovered the solitary ardours of faith but not the consolations of religious practice. He remained self-excommunicate but adoring'. Who, really, is this describing? *Solitary ardours, self-excommunicate, adoring*? The more one reads this poem, the more one feels that it may well be the closest Hill has come to giving us an oblique autobiography of the spirit. And grandiose as that may sound, it is appropriate to the whole tone of the poem.

Andrew Motion's *Secret Narratives* is a book of fluent, pleasantly readable if rather gratuitously baffling poems. They have a quiet levelness of tone despite the multiplicity of voices at play within their modest confines. Full of ambiguous, fugitive pronouns which hide inside each other, seeming by turns to evade their author and to establish a complicity with him, they keep raising the question of who exactly is writing whom or what. The idea behind many of them seems to be that snatches of conversation and anecdote, held in place by a loose narrative structure, should resonate and expand into something resembling a completeness of story. Motion is good at establishing mood if you stop worrying about what it all adds up to. In fact, what it all adds up to does appear to be mood. He's an old-fashioned impressionist *à la mode*, experimenting with the latest techniques of fiction, and he achieves some poignant atmospheres of loneliness, desolation and betrayal. The best poems in *Secret Narratives* speak with a single voice, as in 'The House Through' – a poem of sweetness and delicacy with a frisson of the supernatural. It's reminiscent of A.E. Coppard's wonderful short story 'Adam and Eve and Pinch Me' and points up the essential Englishness of Motion's work:

> Here at the door I am
> identical with its thin paint.
> Then one step and darkness
> falls in a furious storm
>
> of grains, splinters, rings
> until daylight appears again,
> and the hall, and his voice
> outside in the garden singing.

Motion also has a touching sympathy with the Englishman in exile. His portrait, in 'From the Imperial', of Edward Lear 'lonely/and bigongulous, wishing/he were an egg' is appropriately eccentric without being in the least sentimental. He could trust to his sense of oddity much more than he does. Often he seems far too intent on making safe, acceptable poems.

There's nothing safe about Peter Reading's work. He slaps on the detail with relish – great splashes of angry, viscous colour – and his poems are often as hilarious as they are painful. At one point, in his new book, he quotes Graham Greene's remark 'There is a splinter of ice in the heart of a writer' and adds 'I savour/the respective merits of one/kind of mayhem over another'. He is obviously attracted to the desperate and awful but there's nothing gratuitous about the way he dramatises the droll horrors. I'd complement that observation of Greene's with another of Aldous Huxley's – from *Ape and Essence* – that 'tragedy is the farce that involves our sympathies; farce, the tragedy that happens to outsiders'. The more one laughs at Reading's brilliant scenarios, the more one recognises the real private and social horrors they represent, and in several cases one is pushed beyond laughter to sheer amazement and despair. 'At Home', an account of a brutal attack on an old lady, is an extraordinary poem: its last section is spoken, in persona, by one of the teenage thugs who invade her house, and his gross, semi-articulate itemising of the gang's various acts of cruelty is chillingly done:

> It was
> dead great, how she screamed and screamed and
> how her hair come out in handfuls.
> Gibbo gets this bleeding budgie
> what she had in this big cage thing
> and he got its wings and lit them
> with his old fag-lighter. It was
> dead great how this parrot-thing went
> up in smoke. Gib bit its beak off.

That was dead great, how he done it.
Then we found her purse and all it
had was bleedin one pound fifty
so we give her fingers the old
snap-snap like and Gibbo tells her
'If you don't say where you've got it
hid, I'll give ya boilin water.'
An he did. That was dead great like.
There was dates – I don't like them much.

My only reservations concern the inevitable element of performance in this, as in much of Reading's work, and the sense given that things are often so desperate that merely to reveal them becomes the full extent of possibility. Perhaps they are, and perhaps it does. Certainly Reading has no time for humanitarian cant, and lines like 'Accentuate the dignified resilience/that humans, or some, are capable of still' are immediately undercut and deflated by irony. *Diplopic* is an entertaining, worrying book by a talented, idiosyncratic writer. If the double-vision is sometimes the reader's, after the battering administered, at least that reader is compelled to think about why he got hurt.

Carol Rumens' poetry is becoming more distinctive, when she lets it, but she's yet to break away from the fashion parade. Nineteen pages of her second collection, *Star Whisper*, are taken up by a smart, metropolitan sequence of little poems entitled 'Regent's Park Crossings'. This is dedicated to the 'Onlie Begetter' who will presumably be readily identified by all those with a nice dress sense as Beau Raine. It's a stylish performance all right, and a convenient display of current reflexes. There's high-class copywriting – 'et in Arcadia ice-cream' – shocking sensationalisms lurking amongst the clusters of similes – tulips at night 'sleep like the guns/of good fascists' – and at least one act of direct homage in the line 'the world is pure television'. The whole whimsical enterprise may delight some readers, and certainly it will flatter those in the know, but I found it all rather synthetic. It might have made a pleasant enough pamphlet, but the book never really recovers from the fact that the sequence occupies over a quarter of the space. The intermission is over-long. Ad infinitum ice-cream.

This is a pity, and I'm dwelling on it only because several of the other poems in *Star Whisper* are very good indeed, showing independence and originality. Carol Rumens' real talent is for poems of some substance and length where she is able to develop her perceptions into a considerable weightiness of meditation or argument. 'Heart Sufferer', 'The Most Difficult Door', 'The Emigrée', 'An Easter Garland' and 'Double Exposure' are particularly impressive, although she should beware of filling out lines with ready-mades like 'the home's true heart' or 'the whole of time'. *Star Whisper* also contains a successful villanelle which is really about something, a rare achievement and further evidence of Carol Rumens' increasing confidence and skill:

> Then on our hearts the whole world beat
> And of our hopes the whole world said
> But these are not what children eat.
>
> Two shadows shiver on our street.
> They have a roof, a fire, a bed,
> A shelf of books, a little meat
> – But these are not what children eat.

Finally, an excellent first collection. John Levett's *Changing Sides* opens with 'The Insect House' which won him the 1982 New Statesman Prudence Farmer Award. Its minute attention to an intricate, curious collection of glass tanks full of clicks and flutterings amounts to an impressive vehicle for conveying those 'introverted privacies of fear' which occasion the poem. There are several more complete successes, too, mostly in the vein of a wrily tender personal observation which Levett manages more effectively than satirical comment. I particularly liked 'A Letter from my Aunts' which ends:

> Exposed to guilt, I read it through once more,
> Surprised again how innocent and shy
> Old fashioned words of tenderness still are,
> Like echoes of the schoolroom where they claim
> That eloquence beyond vocabulary,
> The tiny kiss, the star beside each name.

There is, though, a tendency to rely too heavily on regular iambics to push the poems along, while the fine detail by no means always breaks free of the monotony. This is less of an impediment than it might have been, because that detail certainly abounds – vivid, humane and continuously surprising.

5

The Reflecting Glass

March 1984

Ted Hughes: *River* (Faber & Faber)
Alan Brownjohn: *Collected Poems* 1952-1983 (Secker & Warburg)
Fleur Adcock: *Selected Poems* (Oxford University Press)
Peter Scupham: *Winter Quarters* (Oxford University Press)
Tom Paulin: *Liberty Tree* (Faber & Faber)
Paul Muldoon: *Quoof* (Faber & Faber)
Kevin Crossley-Holland: *Time's Oriel* (Hutchinson)
David Constantine: *Watching for Dolphins* (Bloodaxe Books)
James Michie: *New and Selected Poems* (Chatto & Windus)
Elma Mitchell: *Furnished Rooms* (Peterloo Poets)
Norman MacCaig: *A World of Difference* (Chatto & Windus)
Kit Wright: *Bump-Starting the Hearse* (Hutchinson)
Ian McMillan: *Now it Can Be Told* (Carcanet)

Join water, wade in underbeing
Let brain mist into moist earth
Ghost loosen away downstream
Gulp river and gravity

TED HUGHES HAS never really been away from the river. It's his blood-stream. Dark brown god, soft sweet runner, muscle and fluency, primeval depths and surface dazzle, it has served him as a living metaphor – a tributary for patient contemplation, and a headlong rush inviting total immersion. When, as he often does, he speaks of fishing, his observations are those of a poet defining his art: 'The sort of fishing where the angler sits beside the water and waits is just as curious as the sort where he wades up or down the river sometimes up to his chest in the water. I've enjoyed both'. Readers who know Hughes' work well will smile at that word *curious* on which the observation turns. It couldn't be less innocent, just as it is impossible to imagine Hughes sitting anywhere without already being up to his chest (at least) in an ether of primal energies. He has always been the most possessed of observers. Even his patience is impetuous, tense and populated with the poetry it is about to become. So fierce, in fact, is the sense of *presence* in his often overwhelming poems that any attempt to disengage their author from these energies – and to sort out the genuine from the manufactured – feels like an intrusion for which a price will have to be paid. Where criticism is concerned, it sometimes seems as if Hughes has become invulnerably indentified with the sensational drama of his method, and one is not a little reminded of that Punch cartoon in which a timid visitor stands at the doorway to William Blake's workroom and calls out, through a teeming cloud of phenomena, 'Mr. Blake, may I speak with you *alone?*'

For the time being, though, it must be enough to say that his latest collection, *River*, – a bursting package of all that is best and most suspect in Hughes – is a lavish production. Its forty-three poems, accompanied by Peter Keen's cold-crystal photographs, celebrate a year in the life of the river, watched at all times of the day and night, and the life and death of everything that surrounds and is contained in it. '*Only birth matters*/Say the river's whorls' and the tone is sustained at a high pitch of amazed and grateful witness where death takes equal shares in the glamour, where for 'An October Salmon' 'this was inscribed in his egg./This chamber of horrors is also home'. For Hughes, life and death are always seeking a communion, or synthesis. They chase each others' tails while the river, in certain moods, 'Acts fishless.../Fully occupied with its callisthenics/Its twistings and self-wrestlings' or, in others, is the 'primitive, radical/Engine of earth's renewal' or renewing *itself* with a sort of charmed viscosity:

> It keeps
> Making the effort to burst its glistenings
> With sinewy bulgings, gluey splittings
> All down its living length.
> The river is trying
> To rise out of the river.

The poems ingest images plundered from every level of experience. In 'A Rival', for example, a cormorant's 'fossil eye-chip' unites prehistory with advanced technology, and then, having briefly undergone a Hammer Horror transformation into 'An abortion-doctor/Black bag packed with vital organs/Dripping unspeakably', the bird is off 'over the sea's iron curtain' with a cleverly timed frisson of contemporary politics left troubling the waters. This is brilliant, but there seems an element of opportunist contrivance in Hughes' exhaustive pursuit of analogies. The bird itself is swallowed up by the invention it has given rise to, and no amount of beautiful sound – 'Sanctus Sanctus/Swathes the blessed issue' – or vigorous stretches of language can give it the simple life it also deserves.

To suggest that Hughes often goes too far is, no doubt, an ungrateful, short-sighted response to his work. Every page of *River* is as full of sustained and challenging complexities as it is of random phrase-making. Nevertheless too unquestioning an involvement in a process where he seems to be appropriating the universe is in danger of repressing real doubts as to whether he is sometimes not also floundering in a vacuum of brilliance. A considerable degree of uncertainty cannot detract from his stature, though, and as a witness to poetry's sheer power of affirmation he has few equals:

> This is the sun's oiled snake, dangling, fallen,
> The medicinal mercury creature
>
> Sheathed with the garb, in all its inscribed scales,
> That it sheds
> And refreshes, spasming and whispering.

Spinal cord of the prone adoring land,
Rapt
To the roots of the sea, to the blossoming

Of the sea.

For Alan Brownjohn, a river more representative of our time is the
A202. It makes diversions but is essentially directionless:

It leaves its despondent, foul
And intractable deposit on its own
Banks all the way like virtually all

Large rivers, particularly the holy ones, which it
Is not. It sees little that deserves to be undespised.
It only means well in the worst of ways.
How much of love is much less compromised?

Brownjohn is not unaware of the long perspectives, even though for much
of the time he seems to doubt whether we're suited to them. Over the
thirty years from which his *Collected Poems* are gathered he has
developed a method of wry, meditative investigation, worrying away at
the point where civic and personal values intersect. Clearing a space there
for exact but tentative insight, he makes a virtue of hesitancy and
qualification in poems which conjure an almost stately lyricism out of the
most random – even tawdry – occasions. He gives loss such full scope,
such generous measure, that it becomes in the process a kind of gain, and
although the aspirations of the numerous characters that populate his
poems – lovers, employees, executives – amount to an implicit criticism
of contemporary British society, Brownjohn gives them various voices
which are seldom interrupted by his own unless it serves to reinforce the
values by which they live and by which we must be judged. He is too
nostalgic for the present, too aware that he is addicted to window displays,
brand names, the melancholy attractions of obsolescence, to be a mere
satirist. Instead, he is a witness to malaise – private and public – whose
gift is for the accumulation and manipulation of nuance, whose eye never
misses a gesture and whose ear transforms intriguing commonplaces into
poetry. In this he is remarkably similar to Harold Pinter. Indeed there are
times when Brownjohn's poems read exactly like Pinter's stage directions,
charged with a sense of something evasively significant contained within
a set of movements so immediately recognisable:

She rises with the cigarettes pointing.
She goes to the second woman first, who refuses.
The lights flicker as if his eye had blinked.

She goes to the second man second:
He accepts. She goes back poising her own cigarette.

The draught teems at the stopped-up door.
From her chair she offers now the first man
A cigarette. He takes it quickly, and nods.
A spray of rain patters the reflecting glass.

Like Pinter, too, Brownjohn is drawn continually to interiors which exist
in a nomansland between fantasy and reality, the disturbing and the
precariously secure: 'We dispose to think mostly indoors, for/Outdoors
only stay the limited/Tactics of inanimate things'. Although he is very
good at describing these limited tactics, much of his best work is preoccupied with what takes place 'in the near space/Between the unfolded
pale screen and the bed' and with all those sudden interruptions 'coming,
unignorable and restless, to fret your neat room'. A sense of disquiet and
threat lurk not so much in the dark corners as in the very composure of
a well-lighted place full of civilised objects:

> – Or, posing a record, leaving it
> To settle itself, to play;
> Or, an immovability about certain white cards
> In a shelf-row...
> Such things, therefore. And I dare
> You, I dare you, disorder.

It is just such disorder – a mixture of fear and desire – that opens out the
long perspectives, and it is here that the central theme of Brownjohn's
work lies. The society he depicts in so many poems is one of systems, grids,
organisations, 'virulent proprieties' – traffic 're-organised/Into an irre-
versible One Way' – where the apparant height of ambition is to have
'paid off the Datsun in just under five months' time' and where poetry is
'striving to root in a tub of dying plants/Put down on a vinyl landing'. Yet
the higher the gloss of materialism, the darker the chasm of loss and
confusion that lies beneath it, and for all his strategies of detachment,
Brownjohn is no stranger there. He dares it, watching and sharing what
in one poem he simply and memorably calls 'human play at the deep end'.
An often playful sense of depth and of familiar human activity as endlessly, sadly fascinating are what make Alan Brownjohn's poetry feel so
close to home and give it its particularly immediate appeal.

Towards the end of 'Mornings After' – an early poem but entirely
characteristic in its edgy, candid elegance – Fleur Adcock asks:

> And are the comic or harmless fantasies
> I wake with merely a deceiving guard,
> as one might put a Hans Andersen cover
> on a volume of the writings of De Sade?

This question, in various guises, remains as the source of much of her best writing to date. She knows only too well that nothing, or nobody, she wakes with (least of all herself) is as harmless as may appear, and anyone who has read Hans Andersen at all carefully will certainly not be deceived into thinking that to use him as a cover for De Sade is to hide much in the way of pain and cruelty. Like Robert Graves, whose combination of fastidious classicism and violent phantasmagoric effect has served her as a model, Fleur Adcock is caught in her own cool webs and has seen the spider. Part Alice, part Cat-goddess, the personality which emerges from her immaculately crafted poems is sensible and dangerous, inquisitive but seldom less than puzzled to distraction. Her imagination works most effectively on a shifting ground between sleeping and waking where the landscape partakes of both and it is never clear which is illusion:

> I am not at all sure that this is the real world
> but I am looking at it very closely.
> Is landscape serious? Are birds?

It is typical of Fleur Adcock to ask this question in a poem which has already looked at the 'real world' with an exact attentiveness. She just can't quite trust the evidence, just as in her many poems of travel she cannot feel at home in any of the places she so vividly describes. Coming back to England after a visit to her native New Zealand, she asks (always these *questions* in a poetry which is, on the surface, so secure in its accomplishment) 'By going back to look, after thirteen years,/have I made myself for the first time an exile?' No she hasn't. Exile is the condition of her art. 'I merely opened a usual door/And found this' she writes in 'Unexpected Visit'. What she finds is 'Not my kind of country' (what is?) –

> there is no
> Horizon behind the trees, no sun as clock
> Or compass. I shall go
>
> And find, somewhere among the formal hedges
> Or hidden behind a trellis, a toolshed. There
> I can sit on a box and wait.

The last sentence is a fine example of Fleur Adcock's tense composure under the stress of disorientation. She will sit there making a poem out of the experience to carry her back through the door until the next dislocation returns her to the same (or nearly) spot. The pleasures of her poetry are various: vivid observation of nature – particularly small animals which evoke a protective, unsentimental tenderness –, the details of love-making recorded in its erotic particulars (her often anthologised 'Against Coupling' is outflanked by the many poems which ignore its advice), and her humorous observation of the literary and social scene. But it is her awareness of how at any moment she may be seized by a terrible strangeness that admits the most compelling note into her work:

> ...something has caught me; around my shoulders
> I feel barbed wire; I am entangled.
>
> It pulls my hair, dragging me downwards;
> I am suddenly older than seventeen,
> Tired, powerless, pessimistic.
> I struggle weakly; and wake, of course.

Of course. But...

Peter Scupham is another poet for whom formal elegance is a means of defining and controlling an often amazed sense of displacement. Certainly, at first sight, he appears stubbornly unfashionable – a horder of beautiful antique phraseologies, an allusive antiquarian addicted to the pursuit of apt quotations – but to see him merely as a kind of rococo plasterer who hides the brickwork of immediate response behind the distractions of ornament is to miss the peculiar, haunted life of his building. In a poem from an earlier collection he wrote that 'ghosts are a poet's working capital', and he has gone on investing them in the present with increasing confidence. A bookish sense of history, a feeling for the continuities of place and human activity, and an urge to retrieve the clarities of primal sensation combine to produce poems which often group themselves like talismans around a cluster of images designed to spell away the very darkness they admit:

> Nights turning in, fold upon awkward fold,
> Leaves of a burnt book whose dull pages crumble
> Their brittle edges and discolorations.
> The stitching weakens; flesh and spirit split.
> Black epiphanies: a spring of night-sweats,
> A text of dreams, a dance of matchstick bones
> And soundless windows opening on no-place.
> The hour-glass nips my sand against its fall.

When in the central sequence of his new collection, 'Conscriptions, National Service '52 – '54', Scupham gives attention to an episode from his own personal history, he does so with the ghosts at his back working overtime. Far from crowding out his response to experiences of poignant absurdity and ritual humiliation, of which as a temporary corporal he was forced to become a participating witness, they populate his imagination, providing a companionship which puts things in perspective. His capacity for seeing through trivial events to a larger community of put-upon fellowship sees *him* through: 'Don Quixote leans there at our shoulder:/ Gestures and angles underneath his whiskers,/A furious windmill of small arms and cane'. Or with a delicious, vivid wit on the assault course:

> We sink with Carver Doone to the abyss,
> Tipple with Moriarty to the Falls,...
> Shake hands with Alan Quatermain, Tom Sawyer.
> Through, over, under, off – a stocking stitch:
> There's no doubt left that we must pull our socks up.

This finely-worked college of idiom, myth, and Boys Own bravado, from which emerges sudden flashes of plain compassionate desolation as in the portrait of the inevitable 'Scapegoat' – 'You are our crying need,/The dregs and lees of our incompetence,/A dark offence, a blur on the sharp air' – is in many ways like a small-scale, fragmentary version of David Jones' *In Parenthesis*. *Winter Quarters* contains several more successes. Another, shorter sequence, 'Fachwen: The Falls', is spectacularly gracious in its playful animation ('the brilliance, versatility,/With which the waterfall adjusts its dress'), three delightful tributes to M.R. James, Walter de la Mare and Rudyard Kipling claim the title 'Possessions' – yet again demonstrating Scupham's courteous appropriation of his ghosts – and the book closes with 'The Candles', a densely written poem which superimposes affectionate memories of a Polish airman encountered in wartime childhood on stark images drawn from more recent events in Poland.

The ghosts that haunt Tom Paulin's poetry are ancestral – at various removes – and his response to them holds a middle ground between recognition and detachment. On a recent tape-recorded reading from his work he speaks of his admiration for the novels of Joseph Conrad – particularly *Under Western Eyes* – and his own preoccupation with a map of Ulster in which history and fiction dissolve into each other would seem to owe not a little to Conrad's method of narration at a distance; a technique of creating perspective and clearing spaces within which character, event and ideologies can jostle and cohere into analysis. One can almost hear the knowingly bewildered tones of the Professor of Languages speaking in 'Martello': 'Can you *describe* history I'd like to know?/Isn't it a fiction that pretends to be fact...?', and the reply is fact that presents itself with all the selective, atmospheric detail of fiction:

> And the answer that snaps back at me
> is a winter's afternoon in Dungannon,
> the gothic barracks where the policemen
> were signing out their weapons in a stained register,
> a thick turbid light and that brisk smell of fear
> as I described the accident and felt guilty –
> guilty for no reason, or cause, I could think of.

The guilt, perhaps, is occasioned by the artistry at work on the material, the very effectiveness of the perception becoming (like a prize-winning newsreel shot) reprehensibly vivid, 'snapping' back in two senses of the word. But, then, the observer is also Paulin's creation, and what may at first seem like confession becomes – in the context of the various voices of the book as a whole – part of his analysis of guilt. The juxtaposition of dialects, slogans, locations at the same time exact in their topography and symbolic in their resonance ('the dead centre of a faith', 'The territory of the Law' etc.) set up a scenario in which the poet is manipulator, investigator, and just one more character picking his way across an echoing minefield of private and public concerns. This is much more the case in *Liberty Tree* than in Paulin's previous collections where the poems often stood more confidently on their own, and the result involves a degree of confused obscurity, but taken overall as a montage of cross-cutting full of brilliant flashes and linking commentary done in different voices it demands thoughtful reading.

The obscurity in Paul Muldoon's work is much more evasive, and often downright teasing. He's a sophisticated high-gloss technician, managing rhyme and stanza forms with dazzling accomplishment but the greater the verbal clarity in his poems the more puzzling they seem to become. His third collection, *Quoof*, (the family name for a hot-water bottle) is prefaced by an account of an eskimo shaman and begins and ends with poems which make reference to psilocybin. This sets the tone and the scene. Throughout the book Muldoon seems intent on taking anecdote and recollection as the starting points for exercises in pushing the actual through a series of transformations, breaking them up into hallucinatory fragments. Whereas for Paulin 'action is solid', for Muldoon it is anything but, though his shapely poems give an illusion of firmness. He'll often begin with a plain statement, something vivid and recognisable (even cunningly reassuring) and go on to develop it in a manner which confidently insists on its bearings even while readers may be losing theirs. Everything stays marvellously in focus, but what is happening? As one of the many voices in the volume's last, long poem (a tour de force of secular shamanism) declares:

> The other world to which mescalin
> admitted me was not the world of visions;
> it existed out there, in what I could see
> with my eyes open.

This seems to give some clue as to Muldoon's method. His fantastic imagination is not so much wool-gathering as mushroom (or cactus) gathering – 'Mushroom Gathering' being, in fact, the title of the volume's first poem. It acts upon what he can see 'out there' with his eyes open, and puts the pieces together in bizarre new formations. His reader is admitted to the sometimes whimsical, sometimes scary world of an artfully controlled trip. Along the way there are moments of tender lyricism and accessible humour but they keep loosening into a kaleidoscopic spin that lets nothing settle. This tiny poem 'Mink' is, in small measure, typical:

> A mink escaped from a mink farm
> in South Armagh
> is led to the grave of Robert Nairac
> by the fur-lined hood of his anorak.

Authoritative, neat as an epigram, provoking as a riddle, but with just a slight suspicion that the reader is being led by the sensitive tip of his nose.

Time as a window through which one looks from either side is the central metaphor of Kevin Crossley-Holland's new collection, *Time's Oriel*. His poems are full of first and last things affectionately described. Daylight is tinged with sadness, but the dark is always light enough. So much of what he notices seems, as he puts it in 'Postcards from Kodai', 'trapped in place or time, hazy or shiny' – and it's far from being just an Indian light, though several of the poems result from travels in the East. It's the particular temperamental glow of his intelligence which likes things mellow and burnished. Attracted to Anglo-Saxon literature – of which he is well-known as a translator – he certainly doesn't ignore its hinterland of desolation and darkness, but it's all those crafted artefacts and resonant wordhoards that really engage his imagination. 'Dazed brass gleams like a fallen moon' in another of the Indian poems, but it could just as well be doing so somewhere in the distance along The Wanderer's journey. Indeed a translation of 'The Wanderer' is placed among Crossley-Holland's own journeys in *Time's Oriel*: – 'Here possessions are fleeting, here friends are fleeting,/here man is fleeting, here kinsman is fleeting,/the whole world becomes a wilderness.' Yes, *in extremis*, but what is set against that has the last word in Crossley-Holland's much more comfortable travels. A safer outing, a more civilised itinerary with its minor but precious occasions, is enough for him:

> Time's wind bristles. But what
> is left in its wake is stubborn
> and persistent: emblems
> of an undying enchantment.
> Only keep your head well down
> alert for the telltale signs.

It's as 'emblems/of an undying enchantment' and of an undying relevance to immediate concerns that David Constantine experiences the Greek myths which provide him with numerous analogies, narratives and sources for some vigorous translations in his second collection *Watching for Dolphins*. The title poem is concerned with translation of a visionary nature – where the passengers on summer crossings to Piraeus gaze with various degrees of curiosity and longing for a sight of the dolphins which is never granted them:

>...Every face

>After its character implored the sea.
>All, unaccustomed, wanted epiphany,
>Praying the sky would clang and the abused Aegean
>Reverberate with cymbal, gong and drum.
>We could not imagine more prayer, and had they then
>On the waves, on the climax of our longing come

>Smiling, snub-nosed, domed like satyrs, oh
>We should have laughed and lifted the children up
>Stranger to stranger, pointing how with a leap
>They left their element, three or four times, centred
>On grace, and heavily and warm re-entered,
>Looping the keel. We should have felt them go

>Further and further into the deep parts. But soon
>We were among the great tankers, under their chains
>In black water. We had not seen the dolphins
>But woke, blinking. Eyes cast down
>With no admission of disappointment the company
>Dispersed and prepared to land in the city.

The point, of course, is that the poem itself is the sighting. It is about the transforming power of imagination (echoes of Yeats, a bit too insistently in the 'cymbal, gong and drum') and embodies a concept of poetic truth which is 'centred on grace' – a kind of certainty as palpable yet elusive as Rilke's angels. Or Constantine's dolphins. What is impressive about Constantine's poetry is the manner in which he can invest domestic occasions with this sense of the numinous while showing no sense of strain (as in 'Islands') and, at other times, rework a familiar myth with the freshness of original perception. His best poems combine firmness of diction with a sensuous fluency. Classical measures are danced out in a contemporary landscape, and contemporary concerns put on an antique clothing with only the occasional whiff of mothballs.

James Michie's *New and Selected Poems* is a welcome collection. It contains several well-known pieces from his 1959 volume *Possible Laughter*, including the delightful 'Park Concert' which many readers may have first come across in Auden's commonplace book *A Certain World*, and a number of more recent poems. Michie is known as a translator from Catullus, Martial and Horace, and his own work is, not surprisingly, a nice blend of the epigrammatic and the discursive. His quiet, witty but always rather anxious poems belong, in their edgy urbanity, with those of Norman Cameron and James Reeves. He's a paid-up member of that rather gentlemanly awkward squad whose polish only thinly disguises a stubborn, even stoical, devotion to the occasions of disappointment. For all its sprightly elegance ('the long-faced grasshoppers' is a marvellous touch) 'Nine Times' is a haunting analysis of failure, and its final sentence – out on the end of an oh so neat but hammering triplet – is the terrible plain truth:

> Nine times, too, cooler than Nora
> Walking out of her Doll's House of sham
> With a flourish of doors is the quite soundless slam
> With which inspiration leaves. Back jumps the Sahara,
> Bringing the long-faced grasshoppers which are a
> Burden, rubbing their legs and making grimaces,
> Till paper becomes the parody of an oasis,
> A patch of drought in a world of jeering garden.
> God knows how those divine girls can harden
> Their hearts against the old devoted beaux
> Who fucked so boisterously once. God knows
> How poetry greys insensibly to prose.

'To work (within one's capacity)/At a neatly demented desk' is the ambition of the speaker in 'Room Seven is Leaving Today' from Elma Mitchell's third collection *Furnished Rooms*, and a kind of hard-bitten, distrait fastidiousness – short lines, clipped sentences, tight stanzas – is characteristic of the poems as a whole and in danger of becoming a mannerism. Several of them end with punchy, deliberately trite last sentences – 'That's right. That's life', 'I like it here', 'I wouldn't, if he'd asked me' – and the overall effect is of a somewhat suburban Dorothy Parker. No illusions, but not too many hard feelings either. Although she's accomplished and bracingly sharp-tongued, it is hard not to feel that Elma Mitchell's earlier poems, though equally domestic, were written less within her capacity and were much more resonant. The best poem in the collection, 'Expatriate', can also be found in the beautifully-produced first issue of Harry Chambers' Peterloo House Journal *Poetry Matters*, and Elma Mitchell reads from her work (in company with U.A. Fanthorpe) on the first of what promises to be a series of Peterloo poetry cassettes.

For Norman MacCaig, in his latest collection *A World of Difference*, 'experience teaches/that it doesn't'. It always has. MacCaig delights in the variousness of things and rings every possible change on them. A number of his recent poems have been preoccupied with themes of death, but they are as inventive as ever and the vigour of their conceits gives the Old Boy a run for his money:

> I hate death, the skull-maker, because he proves
> that destroying and making happen together.

He'll be no friend of mine, as long as I'm still
a feathery pigeon or a scrapeskin dogfish.

– I mean a man, whose skull contains
ideas death never thought of.

They'll cheat him, for they'll lodge in another skull
– or become nothing, that comfortable absolute.

MacCaig is for the ascendency of quick-witted invention in the face of mortality, and his brilliance with metaphor is a kind of escapology. If at times he seems just too prodigal for words, so that his language crumbles into those whimsical 'flibbertigibbet fripperies' he claims to cherish in 'How to Cover the Ground', it is impossible to dislike these excesses. They come with the man, and, besides, they don't come too often.

'Laughter-smithing' is how Kit Wright describes his craft in 'Birthday Poem for Gavin Ewart' from *Bump-Starting the Hearse*, and at first glance another poem, 'The Divine Comedy', seems to offer an introduction to the art of side-splitting:

Laugh? They were sick.
They rolled on the floor, they

Didn't seem to see it,
The funny side.

Doubled up, curled up,
Fell about, they

Pissed themselves, all
Utterly helpless,

Roared and screamed
And rocked and cried: they

Just couldn't see it.
Laugh? They died.

Looked at more closely, though, this clearly never leaves the Inferno. It's about anything but laughter. The pain is real, and although the terms ('doubled up', 'pissed themselves' etc.) are all those usually used to describe helpless jocularity they are not serving that purpose here. These are the damned whose fate is never to see the funny side. Kit Wright's often hilarious, vastly entertaining, and above all *desperate* poems are mostly out on the end of a tether. They just manage to reach for laughter and go wild with relief. They celebrate the funny side of desperation and invite one to join in with their frequent refrains and rollicking metre. They lighten the darkness with a brilliant levity – interspersed with quieter, more reflectively observant pieces like 'The Day Room' (a moving 'notebook' sequence from mental hospital), and others such as 'The Losing of Liverpool' and 'The Yoke' where although the lightness remains in the metre all else is 'energy torn from exhaustion like despair'. *Bump-Starting the Hearse* is Wright's Survival Kit.

Ian McMillan's poems are more innocently entertaining, although there's plenty of roughage in their playfulness. Apparently McMillan's ambition is to be a stand-up comic, so he'll probably know the situation gag where a policeman approaches a man who is behaving suspiciously, says 'Come on, lad, you'd better watch it!' and receives the reply 'Yes, Officer but where *is* it?' The title of his second collection, *Now It Can Be Told*, raises something of the same question as to what *it* is. McMillan rejects the label 'surrealist' but his poems are nevertheless an engagingly odd behaviour cobbled together with a random, free-flow jokiness in the face of routine, dull authority and anaemic good intentions. Some of them, like the splendid 'From the Section dealing with The Loss of Grace' (a copy of which should be sent to every trendy vicar in the country) have real targets:

> And the priest shall answer:
> *Walk past the white caravans*
>
> The communicant shall walk past the white caravans.
> At the fifth caravan, the greyhound
> shall burst from the darkness
> and shall bite both legs of the communicant.
> The faces shall appear at the caravan windows.
>
> And the gypsy women shall shout:
> *Kick it, mister. Kick it, mister.*
>
> Alternative Forms:
>
> A: The communicant shall kick the dog.
> B: The communicant shall not kick the dog,
> and shall continue to walk past the white caravans.
>
> If alternative B is followed
> the priest shall say the following:
> *Enough. Shout back the greyhound.*
> *Switch off the bedroom light which is always on...*

However, most are simply happy to improvise on whatever spot they happen to be – which is usually close enough to a recognisable place to give pleasure.

6
Selves and Sequences
June 1984

John Hollander: *Powers of Thirteen* (Secker & Warburg)
F.T. Prince: *Later On* (Anvil Press)
George Szirtes: *Short Wave* (Secker & Warburg)
Michael Hofmann: *Nights in the Iron Hotel* (Faber & Faber)
Elizabeth Bartlett: *Strange Territory* (Peterloo Poets)
George MacBeth: *The Long Darkness* (Secker & Warburg)
Laurence Lerner: *Selected Poems* (Secker & Warburg)
Laurence Lerner: *Bible Poems* (Secker & Warburg)
John Cotton: *The Storyville Portraits* (Headland Publications)

SOMETIMES I CAN'T help feeling that too many poets find the idea of writing a sequence irresistible, and for dubious reasons. Perhaps it's a bid by old-timers to stay in the ring after they've lost confidence in their footwork, a mid-career anxiety to increase the odds in the posterity stakes, or a beginner's urge to be a cuckoo among the fledgelings. The nature of the market, such as it is, doesn't help. Faced with the prospect of a lifetime filling little spaces between book reviews, waiting to be 'fitted in' by editors, ambition becomes impatient, and experience develops ploys for attention. Small, real talents begin dreaming of the full page. Their fragments are sent out all over the place, marked with the tell-tale signs of spurious intent: *from Notes of a One-Eyed Jack* or *Sonnet XII*. Here, they imply, is a serious poet with purpose, an incipient book. And when the book, if it does, appears, it's full of all those bits cobbled together, threaded with numbers, asterisks and sub-headings. The blurb writer heralds a 'new sequence', the reviewer marks the occasion with a brief, tepid assessment, and at the bottom of his infrequent column a new contender – having waited for months to appear – is biding its time while further fragments pile up behind it. So much for poetry. And who pays for the damage?

Well, something like that. Of course there are some fine, inevitable sequences being written at the moment – such as Tony Harrison's *Continuous* – which create genuine excitement and anticipation, and whose source is, at the deepest poetic level, imaginative, but there are many others which could – and often do – just start and stop anywhere when the controlling, opportunist impulse reckons the time to be right. A few good poems, as good poems must, leap to attention from the rickety framework, but even then they can have a hard time of it and tend to look like accidents. Somehow one is grateful to them, as to smuggled contraband, simply for having got through. They are memorable, not least, for being memorable. Poet X, we say, is lucky at the customs. What a pity, though, that he needed to hide his gifts at the bottom of so many suitcases and beneath so much luggage.

Perhaps most alarming of all, though, is the book-length sequence of fearsome intellectual ingenuity by an established poet assured of his readership. His purpose can be in little doubt. He has set himself a task and slogged away at it, desk-bound, an exemplar of endeavour, deceiving no one but himself. 'A darned clever bunch!' we exclaim, echoing Ezra Pound's pilgrim, to which he'll no doubt reply 'But I meant them for poems'. This kind of poet, who is usually much honoured by Universities, belongs in his own Creative Writing Class for one. He knows all the pegs and how to hang his lines on them. His book is exhaustive and in its way (which has little to do with poetry) admirable. It's an instruction manual, demonstrating how to do it and how to keep it going. *What* it is, and *where* it's going, and *why*, are questions at the same time raised, and shamed, by the earnest immensity of the effort.

John Hollander avoids falling into this last category by the skin of his poems, though the skeleton of his latest enterprise could fairly be said to rattle with remorseless ingenuity. *Powers of Thirteen* – 'this/mess of amazing amusements I've been working through' which also aspires to be a 'grammar of storage' – is a sequence of 169 thirteen-liners, working out at 2197 lines, each of thirteen syllables. A quick turn on the calculator comes up with the figure of 28,560 or, in the words of line 7 of poem 27 (ironically titled 'At the End of the Line' since it's very far from being that), 'twenty-eight thousand, five hundred sixty syllables'. And just in case we haven't twigged, or would like it put yet another way, one of the notes at the back explains that $28,561 = 13^4$. So much for that. Once alerted to the rules of this power-game, one starts seeing the number everywhere. Often it announces itself directly (in poem 21, for example, as the stars of the thirteen original colonies of the USA) or comes thinly disguised as in poem 83, each line of which begins with the letter M – obvious enough not to need a note. Poem 134 announces: 'M's verses (wrote the boring lady bard now dead) smelled/Of the lamp' and continues with a meditation on lamps which, in turn, leads to the nostalgic recall of 'the metallic smell of my small flashlight sweeping out/Pale demonstrations in the sky of the summer night/That awakened my wide, thirteen-year-old longing eye'. A convenient age to have been at the time. After a while, the hunt can become obsessive. Zechariah and Ezekiel are glossed in a note from which we learn that the Ezekiel reference is to 3:1. Since the Zechariah reference is to 5:1, I can only suppose either that Zechariah was disobliging or that Ezekiel was in on the game but had cross-vision. There is also a perfectly rhymed sonnet buried in poem 51, offering a do-it-yourself exercise in the placing of the caesura (14 into 13 *will* go!), but enough. I mustn't spoil all the fun, or give the impression that the game isn't worth *any* of the candle.

There is, in fact, some fine writing in *Powers of Thirteen,* and it is only fair, at this stage, to quote a poem in full:

The pine with but one thought regards the water against
Which it rises, the wide bay with so much on its mind –
Clumps of nearby island and smudges of distant rock,
Other firs at the end of the long meadow which cut
Into the water's extent of consciousness, and at
The faraway edge of the day, an elaborate
Serial narrative of sundown. Now a long yawl
Crawls wearily into sight: the pine of one idea
Points to it as if it should remind the water of
Something; but the bay, as if in some old joke about
Absorption, is reminded of the sky – everything
Reminding water of the sky – despite its bazaar
Of reflections. This puzzles the single-minded pine.

The title 'Opacities of the Pine' points up Hollander's debt to Wallace Stevens, as does the whole poem with its vivid metaphorical exploration of abstract thought – of idea in action –, but it is more tribute than pastiche, and it sounds beautiful. The ghost of pale Ramon Fernandez must be nodding his assent in that world of supreme fiction to which, at his most inventive (as distinct from ingenious), Hollander also aspires. And there's Whitman, too: 'Now I am at the work of confection even when/Loafing, not irrelevantly, near the oven door/Where what goes on is no longer in my hands'. Just such a mixture of 'confection' and 'loafing' is what *Powers of Thirteen* really has to offer. Bauble and nourishment in equal measure, although the pun on 'loafing' is typical and belongs neither to Stevens – who would have owned to the confection – nor to Whitman, despite the borrowed word, but to Hollander the possessed verbal trickster. When 'what goes on is no longer in my hands', *Powers of Thirteen* relaxes into poetry, but for too much of the time, Hollander gets his hands on everything and whips it through the hoops of a brilliant, self-indulgent, performance. In the end, despite my admiration for such dazzling artistry and – yes – showmanship, I found the book tedious, and its length only numerically necessary. A handful of excellent poems stand out from the various groupings on themes of love, identity, place, making, and the phenomena of recurrence and déja vu, but they are eventually swallowed up by the voracious context. I'm afraid that the lady bard, now dead, might have passed the same judgement on H's project as she did on M's poems.

Where Hollander gives the impression of being a poet who yokes his poems too systematically together with a loud, demonstrative cleverness, F.T. Prince displays a modest, unstrained gift for quiet and original arrangement. He has a musician's instinct for varying his themes into coherent movements, and for him a sequence is a complementary patterning of shapes and cadences. His verse is, in the very best sense, civilised. It's the exercise of a subtle poetic intelligence rather than of an intellect commandeering the resources of poetry. Each of the three long poems which make up his new collection, *Later On*, seems written in one breath and with an intimate attention to measure, although each is very different from the others. 'The Yüan Chên Variations', based on Arthur Waley's translation of poems by the T'ang Dynasty poet Po Chü-i, groups a series of five-line stanzas into four sections. They celebrate Po Chü-i's friendship for Yüan Chên, and achieve a ghostly, impressionistic narrative of companionship, ageing, loss and memory. The movement of the verse is limpid, a translucent wash inscribed with delicate observation which never blurs or sentimentalises. At the risk of confusing musical and visual analogies, I'd say that the experience of reading these variations is like looking at a series of Hokusai landscapes and imagining them as backgrounds to a conversation piece. Prince's careful syllabic count and scrupulous rhyming hold in focus sentiments which could so easily become mannered, and they keep the balance between the elderly poet-narrator's discreet frenzy – sharply conveyed – and a pervasive mood of literary contrivance. At times it is almost as if the later Yeats had taken to water-colours:

> Yet sound above, beneath
> I have 'green' old age:
> still have eyes and teeth –
> still strength and will to see,
> and play the sage
> through strange wild scenery...
>
> Waves glint and tap.
> Thinking 'Here you
> could never have been'.
> I pause: but have been seen
> by a dipper with blue
> wings, who gives us his nap.

This is precise, elegant and accomplished. So, too, are the rather more compacted, argumentative stanzas of 'A Byron-Shelley Conversation' in which the two posthumous romantics relish the opportunity of exploring the differences between each other's life and work, and the ways in which they have been appropriated or misunderstood: 'Come, why should we repress/now, talking each to each//such things as we might stick/to say out once, as not/polite or politic? –' No reason at all, though some might consider that neither of them stuck to say out much when alive. Good, scholarly knock-about, drawing on several literary sources, and turning on fascinating issues of politics and the 'sweet degradation' of love.

Most remarkable of the three poems, though, is 'His Dog and Pilgrim', a canine autobiography in five sections. Its narrator is the companion of the legendary St. Rock and, through his fragmentary observations – made with a kind of gnomic, subservient courtliness in which a doggy pigeon-English imitates His Master's Voice –, the saint's story is obliquely told. This attendant hound seems almost, at times, The Dog, as he arranges crumbs of perception into cryptic offerings of wisdom. It's impossible to quote briefly from such an original oddity without making it sound like teasing nonsense. The poem's delight is in the sustained, solemn playfulness of its language, its quaintly lyrical jokiness on a serious theme – something of Joyce's 'moo-cow' or of Russell Hoban's Riddley Walker, but much more of *itself*. Canis Ludens is no mere bow-wow, *Later On* is a hugely enjoyable book, and F.T. Prince – too often referred to as the quondam author of 'Soldiers Bathing' – should be reckoned one of the best poets of his generation.

One of the poems in George Szirtes' new collection, *Short Wave*, is entitled 'Against Dullness' – a stricture which seems blithely irrelevant to his concerns. He couldn't be dull if he tried, because if he did the clouds would come gift-wrapped. His imagination is edged, even at its darkest, with a silver lining, and colour is the very life of his designs. In 'A Pheasant' he quotes Shakespeare's Feste: 'He that is dead need fear no colours' – and in his own work, as if to insist on the vivid uncertainties of living, the animated play of tints and shades carry many of the poems' intimations. Their frequencies, given Szirtes' equal delight in formal verse patterns, are a kind of sound made visible, a kaleidoscope of resonant glimpses. He delights in precise ambiguities and the endless possibilities of variousness clearly defined, but his quick intelligence usually saves his most dandified performances if not from a certain mock-sententiousness then at least from becoming mere show. As he writes in 'Redcurrants', it is 'the fate of jewelry, to go/forth into the world as concentration/without a thing to wear except one colour'. One is simply not enough. Its price would be fixed, and for Szirtes everything is always on offer. His world, too, is one of objects, numinous trouvailles, the discovery of which – as his poetic horizons have broadened – has brought him into closer touch with his middle-European background:

> My people, by whom I mean those curious sets
> Of non-relations in provincial towns,
> Sit ripening brightly in the *Weltanschauung*
> Of other poets. Here is one who follows
> A second-hand pair of shoes into the Courts
> Of Social History. Another ransacks
> His late unlettered father's bedside drawer
> And finds dead ukuleles littered there.
> What heraldic yet surreal landscapes!
> To lie in the bed of your ancestors
> And feel the fit...

That enticing, yet ominously haunted, link between a second-hand pair of shoes and the Courts of Social History indicates a direction Szirtes' recent work appears to have been taking. The light entering his studio, though no less brilliant, is now becoming not so much refracted from a consortium of neatly-placed aesthetic items as absorbed by rather more weathered properties whose familiar shapes have been cut or woven by history. Whereas his earlier domestic interiors tended to suggest a poet getting used to each room and learning how to write in it, a poem like 'Bedroom Verse 1' from his new collection reveals home to be the starting-point for more foreign concerns:

> It's true we have our scandals – no one knows
> what happened when the lights went out or didn't
> or what was said at certain hours of night
> beyond the passport office of our clothes,
> the secret codeword to the waiting sentry,
> the brief descriptions and the formal entry.

The entry is still formal, neo-Audenesque, – if anything, more so than in the previous volumes – but the 'passport office' admits Szirtes into more darkly populated areas of the imagination despite the often debonair insouciance of his sunnyside manner:

> You grab your coat and hat and go outside,
> leave doorsteps filthy with anxieties
> while treading a fine undulation, cracks
> for hopscotch and the promised gold of trees
> in autumn, the dull streets of human pride.

It will be interesting to see where he goes on to direct his feet.

George Szirtes does not appear in Michael Schmidt's new anthology, *Some Contemporary Poets of Britain and Ireland*, despite the editor's wish to encourage 'an aptitude for discriminating and pleasurable reading' based on those aural skills that he finds 'most wanting among younger readers'. On the other hand 'the truncated stories and vignettes' of Michael Hofmann – the youngest *poet* in the anthology – are offered as part of that encouragement. Presumably Schmidt agrees with Hofmann's publishers that he has 'a unique tone of voice', and I suppose in his flat rainy-pavement sort of way he has. In the words of a poem published since *Nights in the Iron Hotel*, there's a 'chemical sadness' about Hofmann's bitter-sweet contemporary scenarios, an acetate gloom. If George Szirtes is a studio painter, Hofmann is a cinéaste. He *runs* his poems, rather than utters them, and his voice – such as it is – seems as non-committal as the mechanism of a projection booth. This has the effect of concentrating attention, as it were, on the screen where his images flicker. They are certainly minutely observant, full of the play of a hyper-tense,

X-ray irony, but it's all chillingly impersonal, and even love is watched coldly from a distance:

> Our feelings are shorter and faster now.
> You confess a new infidelity. This time,
> a trombone player. His tender mercies...
>
> All night, we talk about separating.
> The radio wakes us with its musak.
> In a sinister way, you call it lulling.
>
> We are fascinated by our own anaesthesia,
> our inability to function. Sex is a luxury,
> an export of healthy physical economies.

This is confident, skilful writing of its kind, but the first sentence of that last stanza could all too easily be Hofmann's poems defining themselves.

A glance at any section of the contents page in Elizabeth Bartlett's *Strange Territory* gives ready warning of what one is in for. 'Opting Out', 'Senile Dementia', 'Psycho-Geriatric', 'Rain', '999 Call', 'Night Duty', 'The Intruder' (a limited number of guesses as to what *that* is!). For the last thirteen years, Elizabeth Bartlett has worked as a secretary and receptionist for a GP and the Home Care Service, and her poetry is witness to the suffering in which she has been implicated. Vulnerably human, there is no distinction between the professional and the personal where her response to others' pain is concerned, although she is often all too helplessly aware of being the enemy:

> ...he was an arrogant man the neighbours said,
> who once sent hats to Buck House and Ascot, in his time,
> (those festive hats, those aristocratic faces). .
> I felt I'd done him dirt, poor chap, and look up
> at his louvred windows late at night hoping to see a banner
>
> ELIZABETH, I FORGIVE YOU. NOT YOUR FAULT.
>
> I look, but it is never there.

This is the work of a remorseless truth-teller, and *Strange Territory* is a collection of desperate situations survived, it would seem, through an equal measure of hurt love for the individual and driving anger against inadequate systems. Poem after poem promises to be numbingly depressing – after those titles, just look at some of the first lines – but Elizabeth Bartlett's courage is, in the end, triumphant. Hers is the day-book of a night-nurse of the soul: forceful, pessimistic, it deals in the kind of reality far too easily categorised as 'documentary reportage'. There's very little to enjoy, and some readers may certainly feel like edging away from such a grim presence, but, make no mistake, these are poems.

Compared with such uncomfortable, authentic work as Elizabeth

Bartlett's, George MacBeth's celebration of last and first things in *The Long Darkness* seems, for all its eloquent sonority, a disconcertingly easy read. These new poems, many of them occasioned by the death of his wife's mother and the expectation of a new child, are at the same time a guided tour of his Norfolk demesne – or a proprietorial survey of it from his study window – and a sustained exercise in neo-Victorian pastiche. The Tennyson of 'In Memoriam' is everywhere in MacBeth's autumnal vistas and night thoughts, and domestic occasions are all the time lifting off into lofty utterance through 'the heart's high door'. Paralleling his meditations on human mortality, the death of small creatures is recorded in elegant, mournful stanzas, and the 'claw-strike' of his ubiquitous cat is knowingly Darwinian. The recurrence of such emotive captions as 'the marauding claws', 'the inevitable mouths', 'the crumbling dark', 'the last red admirals' all too soon becomes predictable, and although the book's more playful pieces insist that 'what's begun/In quirky humour, ends as reverence' the humour invariably seems strained – as if it just can't wait to become reverence. And when the reverence comes the trouble begins. Despite the intimate, personal concerns of *The Long Darkness* its overriding tone is one of self-conscious debt to the nineteenth century, and although throughout MacBeth reminds us of his own presence – 'Now that I think of it...', 'Yes, I know/How many of us feel...', 'Nobody, though – be honest – really feels...' etc. – he is far too readily overwhelmed by his tutelary ghosts. The echoes are distracting: 'the tormented, buzzing fly/ Glazed by the weeping window-pane', coming at the climax of an otherwise powerfully independent poem would claim, I suspect, to be itself but is, in fact, more than an allusion to Tennyson's famous blue fly line from 'Mariana'. Or, again, the redwings in 'Feeding the Birds' which 'gather twittering' belong so exclusively to another poet's autumn where they appeared as swallows that they really have no business here.

MacBeth has a reputation as a games-player who can get away with anything, but as yet his new-found elegiac cloak, spangled with a benign, whimsically paternal glitter, seems an uncomfortable fit. *The Long Darkness* is the work of a prodigiously accomplished poet in transition. Interesting things are happening all right. It's just that as he moves around his emblematic estate he still appears too much like a gifted actor strutting his hour upon the stage.

Laurence Lerner's act is a versatile one, and often very entertaining. His *Selected Poems* is a thought-provoking volume full of well-designed poems which make points and offer themselves for discussion. Lerner is a natural for school anthologies, and I don't mean that disparagingly. He favours the small-scale dramatic monologue, and although his different voices have a tendency to sound the same, that sameness is always approachable and attractive – a clever, decent levelness of heart and head

with a sardonic edge which adds a certain bite. Even his popular com-
puter couple A.R.T.H.U.R. and M.A.R.T.H.A. are a curiously sensible pair,
and their supposedly innocent and accidental witticisms are nicely controlled by what I suspect to be Lerner's discreet moral censor. Their
random self-analysis becomes the reader's illumination, as does their
baffled attempt to size up human behaviour – on which, needless to say
they always have insufficient data. In fact, human behaviour looked at
from the standpoint of speakers with insufficient data is a recurrent theme
in Lerner's work. In 'The Merman' for example:

> When humans talk they split their say in bits
> And bit by bit they step on what they feel.
> They talk in bits, they never talk in all.
> So live in wetness swimming they call 'sea';
> And stand on dry and watch the wet waves call
> They still call 'sea'.
> Only their waves don't call.

The best poems, though, are those in which Lerner dispenses with contrived perspectives and writes with a memorable directness. Nearly all of
them come from his 1980 volume *The Man I Killed* and are included here.
The finest of all is 'Raspberries', a meditation on love and death which,
for me, leaves George MacBeth standing. There are a few good poems,
too, in Lerner's new collection, *Bible Poems* – a reworking of biblical
narratives, mainly from the Old Testament – but rather more merely
clever ones. For much of the time I find myself too close to A.R.T.H.U.R.
and M.A.R.T.H.A. territory for comfort. 'I shall decide the moment' says a
remotely smiling God, 'for I control the game'. So does Lerner. There's
a lot of modish, in-jokey academic reference on the one hand – 'If you
deconstruct Job's discourse...', 'Joseph chose the future/And set to work,
decoding their deep structure' – and glib demythologising on the other.
The poems are embarrassingly full of nudges – 'We all know the story...'
– and those laughter-seeking parentheses for which 'plain speakers'
always have a weakness: 'He had a lot of children/(As Kings of Israel do)',
' "The Philistines will triumph. Blood will flow./Your sons and you will be
with me tomorrow" – The usual stuff'. *Bible Poems* contains too much of
that 'usual stuff' we tend to get when witty poets go to work on familiar
stories. At times, Lerner seems to promise more, as in the excellent
'Wrestling with the Angel' and 'The Three', but only fitfully.

For John Cotton it has always been 'a function of art to snatch
order/From life's disorderly house', and coming up with such confident
nuggets of definition which just avoid the platitudinous has remained a
characteristic of his attractively dogged poetry. *The Storyville Portraits* is
of a piece with his earlier collections in that it celebrates the uniqueness

of small, humdrum occasions and modest histories. When these histories are personal – notably in 'Somme Man: July 1916', an elegiac tribute to his father – Cotton's recording of them is immediate in its impact, and deeply affecting. He is the self-deprecating laureate of life's under-studies, attracted to those often anonymous figures which have accidentally found themselves on the fringe of significant events. Much of his work is a sort of wistful rescue operation, a naming of the bit-parts, 'a fine feeling for the ephemeral'. He is particularly attentive to old photographs:

> And Adele,
> Which one was Adele?...
> Was it you pinned by the camera to the door,
> In your best street clothes,
> While your companion sleeps in the crib?
> You look vulnerable enough.
> The weak need the weak,
> Only the strong should risk consolation.

Despite occasional bursts of lyricism, Cotton is a prosaic poet; nevertheless although he seldom lets a flutter of metaphor go unchecked by some sensible, rhythmically inert comment, this very awkwardness is in the end so consistent as to become the poems' guarantee. If he keeps putting his foot in them it is because *both* feet are already so firmly on the ground that neither of them can miss. He is unpretentious and undeceived, and one can only hope it is with affection that the Delphic Oracle parodies the rather bluff and breezy manner which sometimes threatens to reduce his serious themes to banality:

> 'Push-off Cotton' it said,
> 'You've had your future.'

I'm sure it knows his first name, really, and is expecting him back.

7

From Wave to Cave

December 1984

John Ashbery: *A Wave* (Carcanet)
Amy Clampitt: *The Kingfisher* (Faber & Faber)
Medbh McGuckian: *Venus and the Rain* (Oxford University Press)
Selima Hill: *Saying Hello at the Station* (Chatto & Windus)
Paul Hyland: *The Stubborn Forest* (Bloodaxe Books)
Herbert Lomas: *Fire in the Garden* (Oxford University Press)
Connie Bensley: *Moving In* (Peterloo Poets)
Philip Gross: *Familiars* (Peterloo Poets)
Philip Gross: *The Ice Factory* (Faber & Faber)
Patrick Hare: *Aeroplanes in Childhood* (Peterloo Poets)
B.C. Leale: *Leviathan* (Allison & Busby)
Frank Kuppner: *A Bad Day for the Sung Dynasty* (Carcanet)

IT SEEMS APPROPRIATE to open this review by considering the work of a highly-regarded American poet whose entire opus to date has been a sort of never-ending overture. To take a phrase from the long title poem of his latest collection, *A Wave*, John Ashbery's is a poetry of 'consistent eventfulness'. Everything happens where he is, and almost anything goes. *Where* it goes, though, is not so much a destination as the happening itself:

> And the serial continues:
> Pain, expiation, delight, more pain,
> A frieze that lengthens continually, in the happy way
> Friezes do, and no plot is produced,
> Nothing you could hang an identifying question on.

Besides, there's no time to stop for questions. You don't get off the serial loop of an Ashbery poem at any stage. Some of the noises may bewilder you but there's no danger of the tape getting snarled up in the machine. It runs with a hypnotic smoothness and the confidence of total efficiency. 'We get lost in life, but life knows where we are'. Ashbery is very fond of making statements like this. He can be as portentous en route through a poem as he can be gamesome in his titles – 'Ditto, Kiddo', 'Just Someone you say Hi to' etc. – but whether or not you give your assent there can be no doubt that to substitue *the poem* for *life* in that particular statement is to come up with a fair definition of what it often feels like somewhere in the middle. The poem knows where we are, all right. It put us all there in the first place, Ashbery included. He's the delighted victim of his own ingenuity. Not for him 'the tedium/Of self-expression'. Anything but. All is subordinate to the process of defining the process. As he says in a witty prose piece 'Description of a Masque'

> Then we all realised what should have been obvious from the start: that the setting would go on evolving eternally, rolling its waves across our vision like an ocean, each one new yet recognizably a part of the same series, which was creation itself... And the corollary of all this was that we would go on witnessing these tableaux, not that anything prevented us from leaving the theater, but there was no alternative to our interest in finding out what would happen next.

I feel this exactly as I read the poems. I'm certainly interested, intrigued even, but there's no alternative to my curiosity as to how Ashbery is going to get out of it this time. He *will* of course – he's outstandingly accomplished – and yet, for the duration, I'm totally absorbed by the display. Poem after poem reminds me of the jazz pianist Earl Hines' remark: 'Every night I like to find a different harmonic route to a certain point, and when you see me smiling you know I'm lost'. Ashbery is smiling all the time, and it's the confidence that does it. He's the supreme improvisateur, an aesthetic adventurer who gets lost without ever losing his cool. The more elaborately he can tease his material, himself and his reader so that 'we...all become part of a collective movement' the happier he is. 'I know that I braid too much my own/Snapped-off perceptions of things as they come to me' he has written in a poem from an earlier volume, and in another –

> What is writing?
> Well, in my case, it's getting down on paper
> Not thoughts, exactly, but ideas, maybe:
> Ideas about thoughts. Thoughts is too grand a word.
> Ideas is better, though not precisely what I mean.
> Someday I'll explain. Not today though.

Not in A *Wave* either. Ashbery has gone on evading those 'identifying questions' like the Protean master he is. Always he's somewhere else already, relishing a new dimension – 'the segments of the trip swing open like an orange'– and sporting in it, juggling those snapped-off perceptions:

> I think all games and disciplines are contained here,
> Painting, as they go, dots and asterisks that
> We force into meanings that don't concern us
> And so leave us behind...

But what does concern us? Occasionally these poems disturb with a truly memorable or chilling line – 'Being alone at the center of a moan that did not issue from me' – but I can never quite believe it. It's too close to 'the tedium of self-expression'. No, the game's the thing. When 'suddenly the lonesomeness becomes a pleasant city/Fanning out around a lake' – that's the quintessential Ashbery event. Yet another opportunity for intelligent discourse in a cool, well-lighted place.

Amy Clampitt's well-lighted place is the guest room where

> we get a fire going, listen
> to Mozart, read Marianne Moore, or
> sit looking out at the eiders, trig
> in their white-over-black as they tip
> and tuck themselves into the swell, almost

as though diving under the eiderdown
in a *gemütlich* hotel room at Innsbruck.

Her first full-length collection, *The Kingfisher*, is a most impressive debut. The English edition has been slimmed down from the American volume which contained an additional eighteen poems and some explanatory notes, but it is still a substantial book. Amy Clampitt owes much to what Elizabeth Bishop, describing Marianne Moore, called her *chinoiserie* of manners, and reading *The Kingfisher* puts me in mind, too, of Bishop's delightful account of how her friend, when not at her desk, used a clipboard with the poem under construction on it, carrying it about the apartment 'even when I'm dusting or washing the dishes, Elizabeth'.

I imagine Amy Clampitt with a similar clipboard in the several guest rooms she has occupied throughout what seems a provisional but mellow cosiness of exile – even on the Dorset farm recalled in her excellent poem 'On the Disadvantages of Central Heating' with 'big eager sheepdogs/ muscling in on bookish profundities.' Her's is an exquisite vocabulary of objects, deployed with a precision which seldom becomes precious throughout poems remarkable for their sustained passages of meditation. She seems aware of that predilection for 'bookish profundities' and is often nicely ironic at her own expense:

> Hemmed in by the prim
> deodorizing stare
> of the rare-book room,
> I stumbled over,
> lodged under glass, a
> revenant *Essay on Color*
> by Mary Gartside, a woman
> I'd never heard of, open
> to a hand-rendered
> watercolor illustration
> wet-bright as the day
> its unadulterated red-
> and-yellow was laid on
> (publication date 1818).

Moore and Bishop would have approved of both the exactitude and the humour of that parenthesis, but Amy Clampitt's particular, demure, self-aware way of stumbling is all her own. She seems to me least successful when her carefully-worked images are too obviously merely themselves and not fully absorbed by her meditations on botany, art, music and friendship. This is particularly noticeable when she looks at what Ashbery calls 'the topiary trash of the present': 'Daily the cortege of crumpled/ defunct cars/goes by by the lasagna-/layered flatbed/truckload...' Another martian bites the dustbowl. But not too often.

The cover illustration for Medbh McGuckian's second collection, *Venus and the Rain*, is a detail from a painting by the 19th century Secessionist Jan Toorop. It has been well-chosen – a fluid, densely-textured canvas reproduced in shadowy monochrome. The perspective recedes into a forest of prominently-rooted, sinuous trees which gather round a dark, standing pool, and the whole scene is ambivalently enchanting and sinister. In the foreground, a child sits in a high-chair – as if *indoors*, and as if the backdrop of the forest were only a painter's illusion. Immediately behind the child, a young woman is standing in what appears to be a half-opened doorway. Is she coming out or in? Is she choosing the natural world or an elaborate fantasy? Or is she already the victim of a choice made for her in which the child is a crucial element? To look closely at this picture is to be drawn into a close, teasing world of vital, unanswerable questions which are at the same time about the illusions of art and of domestic experience. To go on, then, to read Medbh McGuckian's poems is to continue the experience in colour. She's a fantasist of the everyday, and her's is a thoroughly up-to-date verse – 'retelling the story/Of its own provocative fractures' – which applies many of the symbols of aesthetic romanticism to a thoroughly contemporary exploration of love and motherhood. Often she seems a rather more robust and domesticated Dame aux Camelias:

> Each lighted
> Window shows me cardiganed, more desolate
> Than the garden, and more hallowed
> Than the hinge of the brass-studded
> Door that we close, and no one opens,
> That we open and no one closes.

That juxtaposition of the desolate and the hallowed is characteristic, just as McGuckian's tone keeps shifting from the bewildered to the benign. However, it would be quite wrong to suggest that these poems are at all straightforwardly expressive. Self and others are a cluster of images to be arranged and rearranged kaleidoscopically:

> No matter
> How hysterically the clouds swing out,
> They may not alter by one drop of rain
> The safari of the garden beds, or make
> Louisa's dress with its oyster-coloured overlay
> Of moss, kidnap me kindly for a day,
> As though a second wife were sleeping
> Already in your clothes, the sewn
> Lilies near the ground growing downwards.

Sun, rain, house, garden, forest etc. become both the constituents of personality and a means of defining relationships. At one moment the elemental is impinging on the domestic – 'a waterfall/Unstitching itself down the front stairs' – and at the next a household prop transforms itself into an emotional strategy – 'Except for the staircase that delivers you/ Like a jetty into the middle of a lake,/There is no measure of arrival, no/Negotiation...' This goes on all the time, a considerable poetic confidence at work on an obsessive ground of private enquiry. Medbh McGuckian's poetry, impressive though it is, does raise the question of how far it's possible to take a coded practice before it becomes a restrictive one. She is in some ways an obscure writer despite the attractiveness of her imagery. Rather too often I feel that I have to take it on trust that, for example, 'the change in your voice when speaking/Is like an orange in a snowdrift', and it's easy to get lost on one of her extended, metamorphic trails although she seems aware of this and even goes so far as to make it (by implication) one of her credentials when she suggests that 'my longer and longer sentences/Prove me wholly female'. Yes, but it could also prove her simply rather indulgent.

What impinges on Selima Hill's world of family life appears to be not so much the elemental as the tamely transcendental. She is intrigued by ancient history, particularly by the Egyptian deities, is continually surprised by double-take, though never to the extent of having her composure shaken:

> When I meet her at the station, I say
> *Hello, Mum!* and think *Hello, Thoth,*
> *This is the Weighing of the Heart.*

This is also the beginning of pretentiousness. Despite a pleasing humour, Selima Hill cannot avoid the curse of tedium which seems to be casting its spell at the moment over several poets much published in what the blurb for *Saying Hello at the Station* rather smugly calls 'leading literary journals'. Like them, she chooses to mess about on the inlets of narrative, creating little eddies of counterflow – all those lower-cased, casually interjected voices, many of which turn out to be a digest of the poet's current reading list: 'In "Above Tooey Mountain", I am indebted to the letters of Sir James Melville, James Joyce's mother, and Gerard Manley Hopkins (written on the day that he died).' All well and good, but the result is an absorption of those writers' personalities into a flat monotone of utterance. What Hill lacks overall is any sense of rhythm or daring beyond what is licenced by the vogue. In anecdotal poems such as 'The Flowers', 'The Bicycle Ride' and 'Chicken Feathers' she shows what she could do if she were to trust more to her gift for candid, direct observation:

> He went to his room with an orange
> in his hand and died there
> sometime during the afternoon.
> My mother spent her day in the kitchen.
> When I came in from the garden
> I was sent upstairs
> to call him down to tea:
> he was sitting by the window
> with his back to me.
> On the table beside him
> were four boats made of orange peel,
> with the pith piled neatly inside them.
> My mother couldn't stand up.
> She kept saying she was sorry,
> but she couldn't stand up.
> *It must be the shock* she said.
> It wasn't grief.
> *Come and sit down* she said,
> *And have your tea.*

Good, and deceptively modest. Selima Hill has the makings of an individual voice which will stand more chance of being heard if she can resist going for the flatness of a fashionably contemporary one.

If Medbh McGuckian and, to a lesser extent, Selima Hill are sibylline keepers of the mysteries, there's something in Paul Hyland of the gamekeeper at home. He's a plain speaker, and his is a rugged, hewn, earthbound poetry which works hard to make clearings in the natural world where past and present can be seen as contiguous. However, although bones are very much alive for him in his thoroughly informed, historical imagination, he can rarely make them live for long in his verse. A typical poem is observant – 'You mind things; you'm observant I can see' says one of the several countrymen he celebrates in *The Stubborn Forest* – but, as he admits himself, 'I am all eyes, pointing things out'. Too much of his work is just too closely packed for my taste, and his predilection for a matching density of language in the Anglo-Saxon vein reinforces the sense of verbal clutter which is strangely at odds with his desire to share an 'open ground'. In 'Fin de Siecle'

> Patrons no longer jostle naked flanks
> nor do pigs sag on hooks, strain senseless snouts
> to scents raised from the sawdust by their blood.

As Tennyson once said, 'Get the geese out of those lines'. There'd still be plenty of room for the pigs.

Despite these reservations, and my suspicion that his portentous radiophonic workshop sequence 'Domingus' which rounds off the book is the kind of thing better left to second-rate imitators of Ted Hughes, I admire Hyland's work and his example. He's an excellent topographer. His Purbeck poems are a gritty clutch, and his portraits – particularly those which describe the endurance of old-age – are often very moving indeed:

> her knuckles whiten as she lifts the cup's
> thick rim, so gently, to her parched blue lips,
> steam clouds her eyes, and gently, as she sips,
> age beats the living daylights out of her.

So nearly an embarrassing contrivance, that striking last line is one of a number of similar tropes that Paul Hyland earns by the seriousness of his endeavour and gets away with by the skin of his teeth.

I'm not so sure that Herbert Lomas gets away with this (from his poem 'Sad Cows'):

> Horses have a sense of humour, but these cows
> Do not. Their slow gait has the float of hopelessness.
> One hoists from the field like an old-age pensioner
> Who's just remembered the loo and plods slow-motion,
> Humping, as if into a gas chamber, leaning
> On her shoulder-bones towards a place that's lost a meaning.

The kind of shock-tactic deployment of similes, here, whereby thoughts of the loo become the imminence of a gas chamber amounts to a mixture of whimsicality and horror which I find disconcerting. Lomas is something of a satirist, and presumably I'm supposed to, but there seems to me a case for suggesting that if sentimentality is – as Eliot defined it – emotion in excess of the fact, then lapses of taste can often be recognised by allusiveness inappropriate to the emotion. Certainly Lomas makes you *think* about last things. His enumeration of them is uncompromising and vivid. In 'Nunhead Cemetery' 'Some find the blackberries stewing here delicious:/Heat from the gravestones and corpsemeat nitrogen/Fatten up great black clots from the juice of citizens'. We're all citizens, yes, and in it together, but as verse these lines are as congested as the graveyard – heads of the characters hammering up blackberries – and Lomas rams his dark poems into the light with remorseless irony. 'Even in the sun it's an air of funeral'. His theme, a striving to achieve the redemption of that pervasive irony, is the unexpected suddenness of grace. In church – still as distracted by the godawfulness of things as in the graveyard – he seems about to give up when 'here bums in a blue-chinned Greek-looking worshipper,/Pockets stuffed with evening newspapers, coat/Flapping, and grabs God by the throat//...And suddenly I'm in it: his grace has snatched/Me out...'. What Lomas witnesses to, here, is moving, and *Fire in the Garden* does contain some memorable poems – particularly 'The

Bridges that Matter', 'Elegy for Robin Lee' and 'With the Pike Behind Her' – but a feeling of overkill remains. Grace is snatched like a quick bite at lunchtime in the public gardens of a city full of the mighty roar of mortal traffic, and the result is too often indigestion.

Beginning her poem 'Self Selection', Connie Bensley exclaims: 'At last Safeways/Has made a notable contribution/To everyday philosophical thought' – as if she had been waiting all her life for it to do so, without for a moment believing that it ever would. This catches exactly the tone of much of her work, an ironic relish for life's little surprises (by no means all of them pleasant) within the more pervasive context of a compassionate, if somewhat chilly, acceptance of domestic routine. The poems in *Moving In*, her second collection, are sharp, intelligent, vulnerably immaculate, and they make much of their impact by pulling the shreds of whatever carpet remains from under your feet. Working against these strengths, though, is a minimalist tendency which reduces the scale of painful experience to what can be accommodated in a few snappy lines of desolate irony. Here is the whole of 'Short Story':

> As I knocked the cup from the shelf
> my mind flashed up reprises:
>
> that glass you dropped, the dark hotel room,
> my letter in the rack, your car driving away;
>
> a masterpiece of précis.
> The cup hits the floor. I turn to pick up the pieces.

This is certainly accomplished – a skilful précis, if not a masterpiece of the art – but I find it just a bit too coolly fixed in its selectivity. The details are like stills outside a cinema, motion (and emotion) frozen into familiar attitudes and thereby isolated into cliché. *Moving In* is an apt title in several ways. It is, of course, the photographer's means of getting a close-up, and stresses Connie Bensley's talent for startling the reader by suddenly focussing on an intimate moment of pain or shock. Also, as well as suggesting her awareness of how fragile and temporary any kind of residence is – and the most sympathetic side of her work derives from this – it points up her ironist's compulsion to move in for the kill. She can be devastatingly accurate, and poems such as 'Scandal' and 'The Innocent' are penny peepshows – miniature, authentic horrors of the commonplace. I'm less happy, though, about her over-readiness to go for the closure of a bite-on-the-bullet, laconic ending – 'I hurry on. It looks like rain', 'All it takes is time, rehearsal/and one's own gullibility' etc. A wry, terminal smile will only stretch so far. At most it provokes the shrug of assent, a *c'est la vie* complicity which is not far removed from the knowing wink. Although seldom comfortable, and with no illusions which have not been paid for, this can nevertheless appear to be a kind of *Safeways* poetry – brave hearts in the supermarket, a too carefully-processed, bittersweet stoicism. It would be good to see Connie Bensley knocking tins off the shelf more often.

Due to the perspicacity of Harry Chambers, who recognised a talent before it came to wider attention by winning the National Poetry Competition in 1982, fifteen out of the forty poems in Philip Gross's first Faber collection have already appeared (plus three others) as a Peterloo volume, *Familiars*. Or rather, in several cases, as the acknowledgements in *The Ice Factory* point out, versions of them have. Gross is a conscientious poet who beavers away to get it right. In some cases, with these reworkings, he has cut the poems by (and almost in) half as with his impressive 'The Displaced Persons Camp' – a title originally carrying the modish prefix 'From' which he has wisely dropped. In others, the changes are minimal but significant. 'First Encounter', about the birth of a child, and rather an over-written piece before and after treatment, seems to have been subject merely to a bit of tinkering to make it seem more immediate. 'You would not be denied:/a moth-tap at the glass, a blip of fear//on a dark screen, homing' becomes 'You were not to be denied./A flicker of static, of morse: yes, yes./ A blip on a dark screen, homing'. It's interesting to see a good new poet learning like this. 'Yes, yes' is an improvement, certainly, and yet...it does seem a trifle conscientiously worked-in after the impulse in order to give an otherwise inert poem the air of urgency.

Gross is the real thing, though – a poet already finding out how to go his own way. The compacted detail and ceremonial, elegiac stateliness of the title poem, 'The Bone Ship', 'Ignis Fatuus' and others owe plenty to the early Geoffrey Hill, and recollections of childhood – transposed into the third person – like the excellent 'The Musical Cottage' – recall the later MacNeice. The sooner he grows out of such Martian whimsicalities as 'Crab' and 'Snail Paces: ('They left small frills/to glide and teeter, balancing their shells/like the family china') the better, but a poem like 'Beside the Reservoir' is impressive entirely in its own right:

A surface still as marble. Drystone masonry
runs straight in, under. There is no other shore
but a thin brilliance of mist. One tree
stoops, waist-deep. At the small thud of a door

the gulls flush upwards briefly. By the car
two figures stand as if breath-taken. Once
they would have talked, talked, talked, troubling to share
this luminous distance. Now, he points

to bird-flecks drifting far out: a precarious

> species, winter visitors. She takes his arm,
> keeps company, through certain silences
> accepted like the need for water, for the drowned farm.

At first glance, Patrick Hare appears to be merely one more purveyor of amiable, medium-length, comfortable fits of reminiscence. Conversational, unhurried, he dwells on his early years in a Derbyshire village. I must admit to having been resistant, and hardly encouraged by a frequent self-conscious properness of syntax which keeps stiffening an already rather pedestrian verse into what seems an almost pedantic concentration on grammatical accuracy. There are sentences which read like parts of a translation exercise in an old Latin Primer – 'Had not the wall anchored him he would have/Hammered my bones...' – but I finished *Aeroplanes in Childhood* with more than a little admiration. There's a touch of the genuine visionary in Patrick Hare. His poems are a variety of burnished, heraldic nostalgia. Milk churns shine 'like armour dented/From championship', the face of a shadowy poacher is 'a moonlit mask', and the sky behind those childhood aeroplanes is an 'unaltered blue faithful as in a story'. This sense of being part of a myth not entirely of one's own making is something Hare has in common with Edwin Muir whose Orkney recollections kept coming to mind as I read. Like Muir, Hare still has one foot in Eden, and firmly enough to prevent him from becoming sentimental. When he recalls a field full of cows in 'Convoy Accident, 1943' he has not forgotten how 'The grass creaked in their guileless mouths'. That's a marvellous line, and his book is full of such luminous details. They're intensified, too, by a continual fear of exile or even excommunication; 'Sister Perpetua on the landline...her rebuke, her sure arrival'. In one poem, 'The Misses Duke', he describes an occasion when

> in the parlour
> With Papa in a haloed snap
> Eternally teasing them,
> They ate the cake that failed.

What has certainly not failed for Patrick Hare is the *light*. A 'haloed snap' is just what several of his best poems become, much as Samuel Palmer's 'Valley of vision' could be called a series of haloed paintings. The village of Two Dales is his Shoreham. Uneven, often clumsy, *Aeroplanes in Childhood* is nevertheless a distinctive achievement.

Several of B.C. Leale's poems are *about* paintings or, in this case ('Sketch by Constable'), concerned with the early stages of a very well-known one:

> The dog knows it's an early draft. He's
> full of destinations and joy as he
> rounds the first bend from the house –

his shadow sharp, vibrant. Even the
path's edge is of frisky earth.

About five years later he's finished.
His short run by the water's edge completed and
he's famous. With muted shadow he looks up
to the men in a motionless hay-wain.

Leale's sympathies are clearly with that 'sharp, vibrant' early joyfulness.
The men in the motionless hay-wain have the posthumous dignity of Fine
Art, and one suspects that he's as bored by completion as the dog is. He's
a provisionalist, committed to experiment and a modest amount of risk.
Large, finished canvasses are not for him, and *Leviathan*, his first full
collection although he's now into his fifties, has all the freshness of a
painter's (and musician's) sketchbook. His short poems, often two to a
page and still with plenty of white space around them, are packed with a
pithy, doodling wisdom. Many of them delight in ellipses and the
shorthand urgency of ampersands, but there's nothing diffuse about them
– they become the instances of their composition. Often it's as if the notes
for a poem have, surreptitiously, become the poem itself, and Leale knows
how to leave well alone. Only a thoroughly practised writer is able to resist
working his marginalia towards the centre of the page. Like the footprint
in wet cement which he observes in 'Marked Remains' his instinct is for
'disturbing a surface/casually/for ever' (the significant weight of a single
line given to that *casually*) and his playful linguistic displacements are of
a piece with his more overtly serious inventiveness – as in 'A Vegetation
to be Ready by the Parsnip':

Aubergine aubergine
Lettuce pray for the marrow
For no one radishes the end
We have all cucumbered our unworthy chives
With foul swedes
It ill beetroots us to publicly sprout pea
From the endive our fennels
None escapes the cabbages of thyme
Even the wisest sage comes to a spinach
Celery celery I say unto you
This is the cauliflower
When salsifiers all
Artichoke and kale.

Joyce-speak, Milliganese and Professor-Stanley-Unwinism all have a
share in such cleverness. In his darker moments, Leale acknowledges the
huge desolation of Leviathan – 'your irredeemable dark chanting
sounding within us' – and glimpses of intense loneliness keep surfacing
throughout his book, but his chief commitment is to the pleasure principle

of improvisation.

I find it difficult to ses what principle Frank Kuppner is committed to in *A Bad Day for the Sung Dynasty*. His own account of what he's up to can be quoted, for convenience, from a blurb which announces it as being 'characteristically self-deprecating':

> This work consists of 501 4-line observations and 10 4-line observations on the verse form, which is taken from the common usage of translators of Chinese poetry, provoked by looking at the illustrations in Osvald Siren's *Chinese Painting: Leading Masters and Principles* (London, Lund Humphries, 1956-8), and feeling certain that the whole story was not being told. Many of them are supposed to be funny.

Supposed to be? Whether that's an invitation to laughter, or the Emperor's command, is not quite clear. Perhaps it's all part of the self-deprecation. Perhaps it means that if you're not laughing – or smiling inscrutably – you must be in league with those Li-po-faced reviewers who can't take a joke. But it is difficult to take one at such length. The 'whole story' strikes me as adding up to an enterprise in cod-orientalism, as if a stand-up comic poet from the Versewaggon had hit upon the idea of doing a tour of the classiest Chinese restaurants. There's plenty of dead-pan wit and wisdom, much of it by courtesy of willow-pattern:

> It is a hard thing, deliberately to choose a cave
> Inaccessible halfway up a cliff to meditate in,
> And then glance down one morning in a state of
> comparative bliss
> To discover a sea-level below, rising alarmingly.

True. Many of these narrative vignettes – touching on themes of politics, art and philosophy – take a delight in the thought-provoking properties of bathos:

> In paradise, the collection of Buddhist sages,
> Sitting in groups below stupendous pagodas,
> With an expression of serenity on all faces,
> Try to ignore a recent, unusually durable fart.

A handful are genuinely haunting, particularly those which survey the landscape. They have a cryptic mysticism about them and are cloudy with a nice whisper of immanent knowledge withheld – 'The host and the stone smile knowingly at each other' – but, *en masse*, to take a metaphor from over the way, you can't make Mount Fuji out of 501 mole-hills.

8
Responsibilities
February 1985

Seamus Heaney: *Station Island* (Faber & Faber)
Seamus Heaney: *Sweeney Astray* (Faber & Faber)
Peter Porter: *Fast Forward* (Oxford University Press)
Geoffrey Grigson: *Montaigne's Tower* (Secker & Warburg)
Dunstan Thompson: *Poems 1950-1974* (Paradigm Press)
Michael Riviere: *Selected Poems* (Mandeville Press)
Craig Raine: *Rich* (Faber & Faber)
Blake Morrison: *Dark Glasses* (Chatto & Windus)
Andrew Motion: *Dangerous Play* (Salamander Press)
David Harsent: *Mister Punch* (Oxford University Press)
Florence Elon: *Self-Made* (Secker & Warburg)

WHEN ASKED THE reason why he wrote poetry, Louis MacNeice's answer was characteristically plain-spoken. 'Because I get restless when I'm not writing it'. Many poets, I suspect, know that feeling of restlessness only too well, but only too often their response to it merely occasions the occasional. The gap between urge and compulsion, inclination and necessity, widens to a gulf which receives poem after poem whose feeble, *willed* life is spent long before it hits bottom. You can see it lying there, imprinted, but you'll wait for ever for the echo. More than likely, although it never became a recognisable shape, it tried to be *about* one. How many poets, in search of material, have gone to the cupboard in which they keep their pet numinous objects, or simply toyed with the properties immediately to hand – the dolour of pad and paperweight, the misery of manilla folders etc. Desk Death.

These thoughts are prompted by a fine sequence of six short poems in Seamus Heaney's new collection *Station Island*. Resisting the application of what I've just been describing, it's called 'Shelf Life'. At a glance it appears to be a random hoard of oddments, including a granite chip, a smoothing iron and a snow shoe, which radiate a conveniently talismanic glow – the kind of clutch a lesser poet would work up into a mildly resonant, emblematic repository of his modest preoccupations. Sufficient unto a working day. What Heaney has done, though, through an intense act of concentration in which inclination, ambition and memory combine and conspire, is to hold a dialogue with himself in which the items become intermediaries. They keep their own small shapes but they are intimate with his large concerns. '*Seize/the day*' commands the granite chip, anticipating the words of James Joyce who appears as the final familiar ghost in the much more theatrically self-communing central section of the book – of which more in a moment – and tells Heaney not to be so earnest: 'let others wear the sackcloth and the ashes./ Let go, let fly, forget./ You've listened long enough. Now strike your note.' Or again, in 'Old Pewter' – 'I love unshowy pewter, my soft option/when it comes to the metals', contemplation of the object becomes subjective in its precise definition of a temperament, this time anticipating (with a crucial pun) Heaney's

later claim that 'I have no mettle for the angry role'. Unshowy, soft –
though never soft-centred –, alert to the hidden sources, a diviner who
once pointed out his delight in the accidental rhyming of *word* and *stirred*
and who rhymed 'to set the darkness echoing', Heaney has the great gift
of being able to present himself as a poet on active duty so that however
occasional the event that concerns him, or however fugitive the feelings
that occasion the words, the resultant poem is one more witness to
necessity:

> Anyhow, there I was with the wet red stone
> in my hand, staring across at the watch-towers
> from my free state of image and allusion,
> swooped on, then dropped by trained binoculars:
>
> a silhouette not worth bothering about,
> out for the evening in scarf and waders
> and not about to set times wrong or right,
> stooping along, one of the venerators.

Although defining how he might be seen through the lenses of those
'trained binoculars' which are to be found on any border where politics
draws the line, the last two lines of that quotation from 'Sandstone
Keepsake' are far from being ironic. Heaney is indeed 'one of the
venerators'. He cherishes his free state of image and allusion. It is where,
as he puts it in 'A Migration', 'quick and silent/the deer of poetry' stands
'in pools of lucent sound//ready to scare'. It is 'The Birthplace' where

> We come back emptied
> to nourish and resist
> the words of coming to rest:
>
> *birthplace, roofbeam, whitewash,*
> *flagstone, hearth,*
> like unstacked iron weights...

The nourishment comes before the resistance. In fact, it gives birth to the
resistance as an inner check to avoid the temptation of nostalgia and
sentimentality. This is one kind of responsibility – the inherently poetic –
and it is second nature to a poet of Heaney's quality. In short, it is the
note Joyce's ghost urges him to strike.

Which brings us to 'Station Island'. Yes, it is an important sequence,
though it seems to me to be written rather too much in the knowledge that
it is so. Its twelve sections (five of them in the terza rima of Dante's *The
Divine Comedy*) are set on Station Island on Loch Derg in County
Donegal where Heaney, in an uneasy spirit of penitential vigil, encounters
a succession of ghosts including William Carleton, Patrick Kavanagh and
– most poignantly – his second cousin, victim of a sectarian killing. He

has sought them out as an exercise in expiation, and they are quick to turn shelf life into Self Life. The ventriloquised self-accusations range from gentle recrimination to out-and-out castigation. They raise questions of responsibility to past, present and future, to the race, to the unresolved tragedy of historical circumstance. They are interspersed with sensuous recreations of a Catholic boyhood ('I was back among bead clicks and the murmurs/from inside confessionals') – the seed-time of Heaney's soul – which while they may lack the dramatic impact of the more portentous encounters nevertheless keep in view the instinctive Wordsworthian strain in Heaney, linking him too, of course, to Kavanagh: '*For what is the great/ moving power and spring of verse? Feeling, and/in particular, love'.* As a whole, 'Station Island' is never less than sonorous. It is a deeply considered work, an application and extension of Heaney's troubled sense of responsibility to a wide and densely-textured canvas. To return to 'Shelf Life' after reading it is to experience an added dimension of richness in the more successful, if less ambitious, poems which make up the first section of the book.

The third and closing section of *Station Island*, is a series of poems voiced by Sweeney, the legendary Irish King who was turned into a bird because he cursed St. Ronan. It runs parallel to Heaney's own excellent translation of the mediaeval work *Buile Suibhne*. In his introduction to this translation, Heaney writes: 'insofar as Sweeney is also a figure of the artist, displaced, guilty, assuaging himself by his utterance, it is possible to read the work as an aspect of the quarrel between free creative imagination and the constraints of religious, political and domestic obligation'. Not surprisingly, then, the poems in 'Sweeney Redivivus' seem caught between the instincts of section one (the 'free state of image and allusion') and the imperatives of section two. There are marvellous moments in them, such as the opening of 'The First Kingdom':

> The royal roads were cow paths.
> The queen mother hunkered on a stool
> and played the harpstrings of milk
> into a wooden pail.
> With seasoned sticks the nobles
> lorded it over the hindquarters of cattle.

but there seems a simultaneous drive to force them into straight-jackets of syntactical obscurity which, perhaps, embody those very same 'constraints of religious, political and domestic obligation'. Obligation, that is, at odds with observation.

Despite all reservations, I find *Station Island* an immensely impressive book, and regret the need to rush into print about it. I should prefer, for a while, to remain turning over in my imagination this palpable image of Heaney's poetry: a deer caught in the thicket of circumstance, the agile companion of that 'wood-kerne/escaped from the massacre' (though always within ear-shot of it) who goes on weighing his responsible *tristia* in a language of rare intelligence and beauty.

Peter Porter weighs his *tristia* in the strict balance of a deceptively conversational verse, and seldom finds them wanting. His many ghosts and responsibilities are in the modulations, the finely-tuned machine of a habitual melancholy. Like the later Auden – whose arch lexicon he sometimes dips into at the most unlikely moments ('I could outlive my wife/but never be natured into the space/which she proprietored') – he spends a lot of time talking to himself within hearing of God and the gods with their interchangeable upper and lower casings. At one point in his new collection he quotes Thomas Hardy, a fellow ruminator predisposed to stoicism, – 'Tragedy is true guise' –, and much of *Fast Forward* is concerned to exemplify 'that Augustinian fairness which gives us metaphors/Appropriate to our condition'. Although many of these metaphors – as they have always been in Porter's work – are drawn from contemporary life and often sparkle with a knowing metropolitan wit, they serve a sober classical temperament which keeps surfacing in a series of monitory statements, variations on his central theme that we are 'doomed to claim/all that we envisage'. However fast the tape runs forward, the world's 'terrible moments return as jokes'. In fact the cassette, like digital time, is an illusion. Experience does not run forward and backward at the touch of a button, even though in our global nightmare 'the fire has crept into a governed switch'. Porter binds his readers onto the age-old loop of desire and its consequences, the recognition (Hardy again) that jokes anticipate the consummation of their own terrible moments:

> tee-shirts at Paphos
> Are printed with postures of fucking
> And the silent amphitheatre sings to the sea.
>
> Waves which bore the Greeks round the world
> Have sunk now to evenings in theatres,
> More like Noh Plays and The Gang Show
> Than Tragedy, capital T...

Porter is a much-travelled poet, and everywhere he stops off reinforces his convictions. Even his *trouevés* become sonorities. At 'Santa Cecilia in Trastevere' '"This not/unpleasing Eighteenth Century church" (I quote)/ enfolds a darkness round our lightest step'. One suspects that he knew it would – which was why he went in. 'The urn below the soil...is for geographers of finished love'. While often seeming to envy those 'secure in perfect night' or 'enjoying eternal rest' with an almost Sophoclean relish, Porter is always lured back to the ambiguous delights of unfinished business, just as

> Our learning told us that the gods came down
> Not to impose their rule on croft and creek
> But to take holidays away from dark
> In this domain more beautiful than theirs...

I finished *Fast Forward* with the sense of having been in the company of a crepuscular temperament which nevertheless celebrates this beautiful domain, 'creation's plain tenure, the warrant of birds'.

Another of the venerators is Geoffrey Grigson, and celebration of creation's plain tenure in all its variousness is the chief impulse of his poetry. His insistant, often combative lyricism seizes every opportunity for 'loving/in words', for the demonstrative affirmation of being alive in the shadow of mortality. As he's grown older – he'll be eighty this year – his relish for the natural world, his capacity for amazement and his sense of sheer 'bloody wonder' has increased to a pitch where seeing and feeling have become a kind of instant utterance – brief, packed and memorably vivid. In the title poem of *Montaigne's Tower* he hopes that it was here 'that Montaigne wrote' because the view so exactly corresponds to his own perspective:

> He looks down, with feeling he sees again
> How exceedingly sweet is this meadowed
> Small valley below and how half-redding
> Vines in such a light cast straight
> Black bars of shadow in row after row.

Those black bars, given an added resonance by his awareness that he has been standing inside a tower, are, in fact, cast by nature herself. Where Grigson is actually standing is, if course, in the prison of his days which have taught him – in the words of his admired Auden – how to praise. Poem after poem shows him watching the play of light and darkness on loved scenes and objects. In 'Swallows at Sparrowthorn'

> Watching late in June earth's green hair
> Lazily tosssed by intermittent winds
> In sunshine, after rain,
> I say inevitable pleasure again
> Drives out inevitable pain.

The pain is often in the physical process of aging. Grigson imagines Montaigne 'going/Slowly as if arthritically outside' but it is hard not to sense that pain as his own, and in a marvellous poem, 'Elegy for Extra-Homes', a more elderly man (Montaigne was, after all, only 59 when he died) is absorbed in his own dark thoughts while nature goes on teeming around him:

> And cleavers, how insistently cleavers
> Climbs in all corners. He's been cut into. He can lift
> Nothing. She must lift all. He sleeps after eating. Hell,
> Sole Hell he fears now, is horrible dying, asking, asking

> Well, was it worth it? "It" is that consequential, oddest
> Of accidents. "It" equals living, is all he recalls,
> All he's forgotten...

The answer Grigson's poetry gives is to relish that 'consequential, oddest/ Of accidents' – Yes it was, yes it is, worth it –, to call a poem 'Alive', to make it a list of affections and to say (with that touch of the short fuse which is so unmistakably his) 'Accuse me of making a list./Very well, I make such a list...//...And my old list is alive; and continues'. Accuse him who dares!

I wonder how many modest, authentic poets owe, perhaps, their surviving singletons to Grigson the anthologist. In a field where so many compilers are content merely to gather other compilers' flowers, he has made the most unlikely corners his own as well as finding unexpected rarities out on the common, and we are so much the richer for it. His latest, *The Faber Book of Reflective Verse* is, he announces, likely to be his last. If he has successors, let them consider Dunstan Thompson's *Poems 1950-1974*. Thompson, who published in the 40s and early 50s, virtually ceased to appear in print after the mid-50s but continued writing for a further twenty or so years. As the recent re-emergence of the excellent E.J. Scovell has demonstrated, such silence can eventually prove golden. Thompson's posthumous collection is a bulky one, and much of it is, it has to be said, an unimpressive mixture of stodge and gossip, but a number of its shorter lyrical pieces contain beautiful cadences and a few of them are immaculate. 'In the Church at Ticehurst' has gone straight into my commonplace book:

> Here lyeth the body of Adrian May,
> Second Son, and Gentleman.
> Sepulchral images of clay
> Call in the youthful summer day.

> But there is nothing here to say.
> He died when he was young. Begin,
> Dissembling Flowers, to array
> Cold autumn come to early May.

> Yet stay. What Greek would turn away
> From one so fortunate? To win
> In spring is grace enough. This May
> Needs no winter in which to pray.

And another poet of modest excellence who has published little, late, but puts many more established reputations to shame, is Michael Riviere. Let any anthologist who seeks the good, whether or not it is *representative* or *significant*, go to his *Selected Poems*. Here is 'The Greek Chapel', which carries an epigraph from Erasmus: '*Christianity is a folly that is superior to wisdom*':

> Can this, then, be the gate?
> Through this small barn, or stable,
> This flaked iconostasis,
>   Does 'eternity' wait, –
> With these wicks in the tray
> To light one on one's way?
>
> Hard, finally, to choose:
> Life, or oblivion;
> To get up, or sleep on.
>   Only a fool would lose
> His last Good-night, and stand
> Here with a light in his hand.

Grigson has done much to shape the taste by which poems of this kind and quality can be admired and cherished in a literary climate only too ready to stifle them.

It is much easier to dazzle, as Craig Raine has found out. He is a poet who is cunningly aware of his prodigal talent, and in his new collection, *Rich*, he's continually stepping back and admiring his poems with a knowing delight in their fluency, their surfaces, the texture of their compulsive transformations. His talent, defined in the title poem, is for 'transforming the world/like the eye in love' but these transformations are so often an end in themselves, and the eye can all too easily appear to be in love merely with its own seeing. The poems in *Rich* are full of types of the artist observing what he's done. In 'Placebo' – part love lyric, part aesthetic adventure – Raine announces:

> Suddenly like Matisse
>
> In a three-piece suit
> and consultant's white coat,
> I take infinite pains
> to keep this model alive...

Here, on the one hand, is the colour, the energy, the brightness of the art (Matisse being one of the great colourists) but here too is the immaculate contriver, the dandy in his three-piece suit with a touch of the clinician about him. Raine's poise – his being the artist always *demonstrating* his skill – is one of the most striking things about him.

Like 'Placebo', 'A Free Translation' is another aptly titled poem.

Raine is certainly free with his translation, where everything can become anything else ad infinitum. For him, poetry is not what gets lost in translation but what gets found in it. In this particular poem there's another type of the artist, or rather the magician. While doing the washing-up (the mundane becoming the marvellous for him even at the sink) he considers his fingers:

> Rinsed and purified
> they flick off drops
> like a court magician
>
> whose stretching fingers
> seek to hypnotize
> the helpless house...

Again, what is striking is the cunning self-definition – those dapper, per-suasive coups of imagery he keeps pulling off: 'the pagoda/of dirty dinner plates', the dustbins' 'coolie hats' etc. Raine is the court magician of a post-courtly world. Several of the poems delight in a boudoir eroticism, and Sir Walter Raleigh makes at least two separate appearances in the book, but one always comes back to this awareness of 'hypnotizing the helpless house', of being the performer. Raine's domestic interiors become little theatres of effect where he's absolutely in command. One audience gasp after another.

As the middle section of *Rich*, Raine has published an affectionate autobiographical study originally delivered as a lecture. In it he describes his father's genius for story-telling. 'My father would gather me up and rub his bristly face against mine, saying "Gnaggle, gnaggle, gnaggle". Prodigal mimesis from which I've learned'. He has learned it from James Joyce, too, and he's certainly the prodigally gifted son, but there are times when I find myself begging for the relief of a little parsimony.

Blake Morrison has been an assiduous apprentice, publiciser and critic of Seamus Heaney and Craig Raine, and there are moments in his first collection, *Dark Glasses*, when he achieves an almost uncanny fusion of their mannerisms. Here he is addressing 'A Child in Winter':

> your home's the cradle
> of a snowy hillfort
> with pink turrets
> and underground springs.
>
> Daylight bores you: all night
> you otter in our bed until
> we wake to find you with us,
> hands folded like a saint...

More of Heaney there, perhaps, (I like the infant otter already developed into a *verb*), while the opening of 'Grange Boy' corrects the balance:

> Horse-chestnuts thudded to the lawn each autumn.
> Their spiked husks were like medieval clubs,
> Porcupines, unexploded shells. But if
> You waited long enough they gave themselves up –
> Brown pups, a cow opening its sad eye,
> The shine of the dining-room table.

This poem, like others in the book's first section, is a low-key dramatic-monologue-cum-narrative fiction, and its speaker in recollecting the personal and social experiences that have led up to his uneasy acceptance of responsibility for the family estate introduces perspectives familiar from the poems in Douglas Dunn's *Barbarians*: 'One morning they began without asking'. There are touches, too, elsewhere, of Peter Porter – whom Morrison clearly admires – both in 'Our Domestic Graces' ('Elected at last – guest musicians/At the garden party of the gods') and in the early-Audenesque satire of 'Transfusion': 'It is as we had always suspected:/God exists. Our scientists detected...' etc.

I don't dwell on these echoes merely to suggest that Blake Morrison has not yet achieved a distinctive voice. In a way, he has, and it is a compendium of the Zeitgeist. He is an extremely intelligent writer who inhabits the house of contemporary art and knows every mark on the wall-paper, every knot and whorl of the stripped pine. Move outside, and the rinsed landscape of his title poem is representative: 'This Norfolk skyline, vast and open-hearted,/Levels with its questioners, or seems to....//There are footlights on the dipped horizon,/As if the ones whose plot we are a part of/Were on the brim of coming clear.' Always on the brim. Morrison's is the current aesthetic of being 'none the wiser', of defining the immanence of meaning in the ambivalent or withheld gesture: 'something cries out to be resolved./The pen moves off with its search parties'. When a phone rings, it is 'perhaps for you' and sets up frissons of speculation. And by the end of the last section of Morrison's long poem 'The Inquisitor' the whole point seems to be that we are still none the wiser:

> There are no ends, though, and no answers, for this
> Is secrecy, whose art is to withhold
> The logic it is richer not to know.

This is what it is all about, a teasing obliquity, the International Plot as metaphor for the impossibility of *knowing*, sex as the ambiguous area where secrets are variously hoarded, shared and betrayed. A significant encounter somewhere in Europe, London or Norfolk with portentous clouds of History riding above. A hinterland of domestic and political intrigue. Reading 'The Inquisitor' I was reminded of *The Ploughman's*

Lunch, very much a 'film of our times'. *Dark Glasses* is a not unimpressive book of our times. But you can't see the eyes.

Despite his preference for obliquities and narrative procedures similar to Morrison's, you can see Andrew Motion's eyes from time to time. They are intelligent, mellow, neo-Georgian and circumspectly sad. By far the best poems in *Dangerous Play*, a handsomely-produced selection of his work over the past ten years, are the poignantly direct ones of sections four and six, set either side of a prose account of his childhood. They are full of a gentle, generous, elegiac candour, whereas much else in the book seems *voulu* despite Motion's ambition, and his talent for orchestrating voices from the various social milieux about which he has read. The title poem, for example, is an imaginative response to James Fox's marvellous sleuthing enquiry into the murder of Lord Errol. *White Mischief*. It's a kind of inside job, an inventive, slightly exploitative voyage into a rich world reconstructed by another writer. Motion's narratives are loaded with an air of complicity and the ghostly presences of secret sharers:

> It's as if I were dreaming
> And could not control what I saw. As if I might find
>
> his face had been changed into one that I know,
> or into my own, and could never be altered back
> to a stranger's again...

Mon semblable, mon frère – gazing back through a gauzy net of shifting images and snatches of dialogue which gently rises and falls against a beautifully painted backdrop of exile. I admire Motion's professionalism, accomplishment and high polish, but miss the 'compelling drive' announced by his publisher.

With David Harsent's *Mister Punch*, though, we're into compelling overdrive. This remorseless sequence of libidinous grand-guignol with its obscure hints of redemption is prefaced by Jung's statement that 'the wounded wounder is the agent of healing' and no doubt exemplifies the double-edge of another of his remarks that 'the unconscious of man can reach God knows where'. The loaded, controlled tension of Harsent's language is brought to bear on a series of violent cameos, inevitably reminiscent of Ted Hughes' *Crow*, in which his wounded puppet plies the stick and, indeed, a whole armoury of bestial psychic equipment on behalf of our shadow-selves. It's a *tour de force*. Punch travels, lusts, acts out voyeuristic fantasies, falls to his devotions – 'I held myself in contempt; Lady,/I flogged myself with inventions' – and appears to end up uneasily at peace with himself inasmuch as we leave him with a 'limp dick'. Only a temporary malfunction, though, surely, since the whole point of Mister Punch is that he beats the devil, banging his way out of all constraints:

> Punch, in the crowd with his stick,
> is rabble-rousing
> as ever. His claque are baying; their sharp
> snouts mark them out,
> their whisky smell. He whacks
> legs and grins invisibly.

Whack on. Whacko.

The poems in Florence Elon's first collection, *Self-Made*, display a cautious, twice-bitten drive towards accuracy. Her ironies sit lightly on a deeper solemnity, just as, in her 'Epithalamium for a Second Marriage', after pointing out that 'I've heard this show before' she ends on a note of tentative affirmation: 'What I feel/is new and might last'. Many of her poems concentrate on themes of family, European ancestry, and the making of an American self. They are often plain-spoken to the point of seeming rather characterless in their honest attempt to define personality:

> I am the last one of my friends
> in order of 'American':
> each born of people born elsewhere,
> grand or plain parents
> immigrating from foreign lands,
> Italian, Russian, French, German;
> mine were the last to come.

To discover and celebrate their legacy is Florence Elon's main concern, and it would seem that she is learning all the time. When 'In the New World' first appeared in an anthology eight years ago, her mother donned 'fur caps, high boarskin boots,/brocaded gowns of her Hamburg youth'. Now, in the same poem, the same clothes recall a youth spent in Moscow. What's in a city? Or a fashion?

9
Implications of Mortality
July/August 1985

Douglas Dunn: *Elegies* (Faber & Faber)
Gavin Ewart: *The Young Pobble's Guide to his Toes* (Hutchinson)
Peter Redgrove: *The Man Named East* (Routledge & Kegan Paul)
Charles Causley: *Secret Destinations* (Macmillan)
David Scott: *A Quiet Gathering* (Bloodaxe Books)
U.A. Fanthorpe: *Voices Off* (Peterloo Poets)
Jean Earle: *The Intent Look* (Gomer Press)
Duncan Forbes: *August Autumn* (Secker & Warburg)

ANYONE WHO HAS suffered personal loss is left, at bottom, with the plain facts. For Douglas Dunn these are that in March 1981 his wife, Lesley, died from cancer of the eye – a particularly bitter irony given that she was an artist of great sensitivity to light and its conversation with lovingly chosen objects – and his new collection, *Elegies*, which confronts their shared life and her death in a sequence of remarkable poems, is a heart-breaking book. It is also utterly without self-pity, a celebration of a rich and affirmative marriage. The entire volume is, of course, shadowed by a remorselessly familiar story which in this case begins in hospital with 'the mind sliding against events/And the antiseptic whiff of destiny' and ends with intimations of a new life contingent upon the old:

> She spoke of what I might do 'afterwards'.
> 'Go, somewhere else.' I went north to Dundee.
> Tomorrow I won't live here any more,
> Nor leave alone. *My love, say you'll come with me.*

However it is precisely because she does so vividly come with him into the making of these poems – their apprehension, witnessing and recollection – that the maudlin note is never struck. There's not a hint of Hardyesque guilt or Tennysonian gloom, not the slightest suspicion that death has provided the occasion for rhetoric. The poems seem an exact transcription of what was there in the relationship. In no sense at all are they compensatory. *Elegies* is the record of 'moments of me/And moments of my love and me together,/And her moments, her secret visions in them' and it is a measure of Dunn's achievement and imaginative generosity that it is *her* moments, in life and death, which most vividly inform the collection. The book is a gift to Lesley, written with the wit and clear, unsentimental intelligence she so obviously approved of, and, as it were, offered to the reader over their shoulders by private invitation. What gradually emerges, throughout the sequence, is the portrait of a woman who 'refused all grief, but was alight/With nature, courage, friendship, appetite'. When Dunn does employ conscious literary artifice, even pastiche, it seems part of a serious game the couple might have played together, a mode of heightening the pleasures of living in the knowledge that 'art is love':

> My lady loved to cook and dine, but never more
> Across starched linen and the saucy pork
> Can we look forward to *Confit de Périgord*.
> How well my lady used her knife and fork!
> Happy together – ah, my lady loved to sport
> And love. She loved the good; she loved to laugh
> And loved so many things, infallible in art
> That pleased her, water, oil or lithograph,
> With her own talent to compose the world in light.

In 'Anniversaries' there is a direct allusion which combines John Donne's 'The Anniversarie' and 'The Relique': 'That day will still exist/Long after I have joined you where/Rings radiate the dusty air/And bangles bind each powdered wrist' but such referential hyperbole is set up only to be brought down to common earth, and Lesley's own words – 'Write out of me, not out of what you read' – echo throughout *Elegies*:

> I shiver in the memory
> And sculpt my foolish poetry
> From thwarted life and snapped increase.
> Cancer's no metaphor.
> Bright rain-glass on the window's birch
> This supernatural day of March,
> Dwindled, come dusk, to one bright star,
> Cold and compassionate.

Cold, there, does not mean *unfeeling*. Quite the reverse. It is implicated with the compassion, and it has to do with the unflinching directness of Dunn's attention to detail – all those 'objects implicated in my love'. The recurring images of light are never soft at the edge. They are the essence of concentration: 'Writing with light, the heart within my eye/Shines on my grief, my true contemporary.' And in the poem which has haunted me most, 'Sandra's Mobile', light and movement combine in a single object given and received with love. The moment of death is neither dark nor desolate. To borrow a line from another poem, 'the air was the fingertips of loneliness' but here it is the poet's own breath, and in touching the three seagulls it is quite simply the kiss of that continuing life which the entire book celebrates:

> A constant artist, dedicated to
> Curves, shapes, the pleasant shades, the feel of colour,
> She did not care what shapes, what red, what blue,
> Scorning the dull to ridicule the duller
> With a disinterested, loyal eye.
> So Sandra brought her this and taped it up –

Three seagulls from a white and indoor sky –
A gift of old artistic comradeship.
'Blow on them, Love.' Those silent birds winged round
On thermals of my breath. On her last night,
Trying to stay awake, I saw love crowned
In tears and wooden birds and candlelight.
She did not wake again. To prove our love
Each gull, each gull, each gull, turned into dove.

For Gavin Ewart, mortality is the encroaching scent of a spiked bouquet. His new collection is a generous, bumper fun-book, full of skilled variations, but the fireworks of his clever versification dazzle against a darkening sky. 'With each new book the old poet thinks:/Will this be the last?/...Cram the poems in like a herring glut –/two, three to the page!' *Carpe diem* is the persistent theme, and although, apparently, 'no sensible person would ever want to be young again' *The Young Pobble's Guide to His Toes* is all for ensuring that one's pedal extremities are not bitten off before time, or that they don't go stiff prematurely for lack of dancing the night away:

The moral shines bright as a mermaid's hair.
Count them and keep them while they're still there!

Or to put it another way, there's no pobble like an old pobble. Ewart seems to regard old age as a condition which counts its blessings (all ten of them) even while contemplating 'liver-spotted hands', and he relishes every opportunity for making the same mistakes as ever. He's a celebrant of human fallibility, and a discreet folly is what he's after. Why should old men not be bad and still a little dangerous to know?

In the typically entitled 'The Heel Has Come Full Circle' what appears at first to be a merely silly piece of occasionalia about Malcolm Muggeridge's religious conversion gathers conviction as it closes in on 'that great actor,/like a sage with a tome,/full of faith, froth and foam'. Not for Ewart the sage's cope, and his tomes are happily whatever comes to hand. Milton or a Menu. Many of the poems carry epigraphs from his miscellaneous reading, and footnotes direct the reader to catholic sources with the smallest possible *c*. Appended to a parody of McGonagall, for example, is the information that '*The first two lines of this poem are genuine food advertising of March 1984 in a London take-away/eat-in restaurant*'. Like a latter-day Pepys (Pepys being one of his heroes who inspires several of the poems in the book) Ewart is a Londoner who gets around:

London is good and bad, a teasing monkey
(remembered from a kids' book with a moral),
and not for worship in such all-out postures.

Those all-out postures refer to the love particular poets have had for the places with which they have become identified, such as 'Norman Nicholson alone in Millom', but Ewart is a Town Owl and there's a drop of the metropolis in most of his work. His seemingly effortless quadruple and quintuple rhymes are more Cole Porter than W.S. Gilbert, and belong in a night-club. Even his more book-ish parodies are a species of literary floor-show. Yet at the same time, and again like Pepys who in another of the footnotes *'saw the limbs of some of our new Traytors set upon Aldersgate, which was a sad sight to see; and a bloody week this and the last have been'*, Ewart peddles the broadsheets of a national conscience. Naughty Samuel was also Mr. Pepys, and Mr. Ewart is often there behind the carnival mask of Bad Gavin:

> At Death we're shouting 'Gotcha!',
> we're perfect shining knights –
> no diplomatic botcher
> has any bleeding rights...
>
> How grand for circulation
> and for the Tories too,
> a floor show for the Nation,
> and free for me and you!...
>
> We know there's news in 'traitors'...
> and as the hot war nears
> like stripshow fornicators
> we roar it on with cheers...
> we hope it lasts for years!

In *The Young Pobble's Guide to His Toes* there's something for everyone except for Prunes and Prisms, and there's a handful of really fine poems as well.

If, for Gavin Ewart, the flesh is pleasurably weak, for Peter Redgrove the spirit is more than willing. 'One who is everywhere at once must be joyous' he writes at the end of 'The Happy Ground', a poem which appears in a small volume from the Taxus Press but does not reappear in his full collection *The Man Named East and Other New Poems*. 'The Man Named East' itself, though, begins with a bit of reconstitution: 'The dew, the healing dew, that appears/Like the dream, without warning, hovering on the blades' has its origins in 'The Happy Ground' where 'the dew, healing dew//Appears suddenly in its completed form/On all the grass-stems in the million meadows'. This observation of what seems to be Redgrove's working method is merely offered to point up how his poetry traces itself back to the source. There is a ground beyond the Happy Ground but it is immaterial whether it comes before or after. Redgrove's is the rhetoric of Unity, and his poems are a concentration of autochthonous forces. Which poem a phrase or image comes from is incidental. One stanza is so many lines of palpable spirit dissolving into the next, and the text is the numinous meaning of sensation. 'I stand by the small stream which contributes' he says, and there's a serious pun in that second verb. For Redgrove everything is contributory and contributary, an expanding universe, a holy flux of luminous and cleansing simplicities where even the smallest trickle flows into some kind of cosmic lake of revelation, so that 'I bend/My ear to the water and now I find/ Underspeech...'. What he hears is not some pantheistic still sad music but the laughter of a comedy bent on reconciliation. His imagination dodges all such labels as *surrealist, fantasist, absurdist*, and it's some kind of tribute to his hypnotic powers that lines such as

> All men on earth are brothers, under heaven

> Where Lear-shaped fathers scatter their botany, their seed
> Out of the sky, the great conjuring pisstrick

seem, at the time and in context, neither banal nor trivial. With linguistic sleight of hand, they unite the Royal Baths and the Tap Room in a gush of affirmation. Only when considered in isolation do they give themselves over to parody or to the embarrassing pretentiousness of some of Redgrove's imitators who lack his sense of humour. In poetry, a guru without, at the very least, the suspicion of a grin is hard to take.

Redgrove has become a master of the hyperbolic simile – 'Sliding down the girl's face/A long convoy of tears/Shining like lorries through the night' – and one long poem of his contains enough metaphorical fodder to keep a mini-Martian provided for a whole slim volume, but for him accuracy of sensation is a means of penetrating beyond appearances; it is seldom an end in itself. His cultivation of the senses' innocence is no mere part of an aesthetic strategy. He would regard it as a way of 'becoming'. Even a visit to the barber is a laying on of hands, as in one of the book's most conventionally autobiographical pieces, 'The Proper Halo':

> The oil shivers in the barber's palm,
> He puts the plump bottle down, and that hand
> Descends swooping on the other; they rub together
> Like mating birds and as they fly to my head
> I see they shine. His rough fingertips
> Massage my scalp like the beating of a flock
> Of doves; now it is my hair that shines
> And stands up as though an ecclesiastical charge
> Were passing through me; I laugh!...

I laugh too. Somehow there seems to be no choice, and certainly the charge in Redgrove's work is considerable. At the very least it tickles, and often it induces the shock of recognition.

Though his more circumspect method is very different from Redgrove's prodigal abundance, Charles Causley's poetry can also be seen as a search for unity of being. His latest collection carries an epigraph from Martin Buber: 'All journeys have secret destinations of which the traveller is unaware' and, as I read through *Secret Destinations*, I found myself responding with a quotation of my own from a poem by R.S. Thomas: 'It is too late to start/For destinations not of the heart'. Much of Causley's recent work is, at first glance, travelogue of a high order. It gives vivid accounts of dramatic scenery in Portugal, Greece, Canada and Australia while at the same time celebrating new acquaintance and established friendships. It's detailed, populated, and full of an intense gratitude for companionship. Implicit in every arrival, though, is a departure which intimates a deep concern for those left behind:

> Today
> I see the naked-footed children trawl
> The dam for yabbies, and I watch you clinging
> Together, minute-long, before I'm driven
> Back to the airport. And it is as though
> You fear – one, both of you – another kind
> Of fire within this Eden, or blood broken
> Under the hard sun. The incurious blue, still burning
> Over the homestead roof. The sprinkler turning.

A sense of the fragility of personal relations – and their precious importance – is set against a backdrop of wounded landscapes. Home being where one starts from, Causley looks out from Launceston Castle on a 'quarry's old wound' and notices how 'poppy, valerian/Bleed by the lean lake-side', but it's the same at Trephina Gorge in Australia where 'the gorge opened its wound of rock' or at Gudow where 'a parapet bleeds red sand'. In this context, where his surroundings seem an image of his disquiet, the traveller becomes the human spirit in search of healing, the wounded surgeon operating on the body topographic:

> And underneath our jaunting tongues is this:
> How both of us came, hand in cooling hand,
> To the stone centre of the wilderness.
> Drank from a single cup. Shared fortune; bed.
> Pretended not to notice how love bled
> Into the eager sand. Lay, heart on heart:
> Yet never slept so cold, so far apart.

'Jaunting tongues' in that first line is a beautifully judged phrase. It acknowledges the naive enthusiasm of a tripper merely passing through and chattering about the itinerary, but it is followed immediately by intimations of the sacramental, so that *tongues* takes on an altogether more powerful resonance. What follows is no dissolution into vague spirituality, though. There's pain at the still centre, and 'Gudow' ends, as do so many of the poems in *Secret Destinations*, on a note of intense personal loneliness. Causley is a companionable poet but he is, in some ways, a desolate one. He knows where all the ladders start, and in 'Returning South' it's in the rag and bone shop of his own pocket:

> Unjacketed,
> I chuck cash, keys on the still-falling shelf.
> Unpack shirts, socks. *Dear Christ, what's this? Myself.*

All the themes which have distinguished his earlier work are still evident, most notably that of hurt innocence (there's a fine new translation of Rimbaud's 'Sleeper in a Valley' – he was bound to get round to that in the end) and he has not altogether abandoned the ballad form for which he is best known. However, what makes *Secret Destinations* so impressive is its direct, personal candour, and a kind of stubborn craftsmanship which has only recently become a sustained element in his verse. A number of the poems are written in stanzas both weighty and spacious. The book begins with a series of family portraits, and is informed throughout by the example of Richard Bartlett, Causley's 'shadowed grandfather/...stone cutter, quarreyman' who died when a slate fell on him and split his skull. At the moment of his death, Bartlett was about to split a stone, 'trying to find/A place to insert the wedge'. The analogy is obvious, but Causley refrains from making it immediately. He pays Bartlett the tribute of a full and moving biography before closing the ninety-year-old local paper in which he has been reading about him and observes himself as a poet attempting to match those virtues of painstaking craftsmanship by which his ancestor lived:

> I close the paper,
> Its print of mild milk-chocolate. Bend to the poem,
> Trying to find a place to insert the wedge.

The wedge inserted by David Scott in his excellent first collection, *A Quiet Gathering*, is the Latin word *quodlibet* and all that it implies of emotional and verbal scruple:

> It would be a good title.
> It pleased Duns Scotus
> and we share initials.
> All those airy questions packed
> into the neat hutch of a Latin word;
> quodlibet: exactly separating this from that.
> It got to such a pitch with him,
> and I know how he felt,

that his stomach would not settle
for less than the essence of a thing.
The pleasure of getting it right
meant he could draw the blankets
round his chin, and sleep tight.
The converse I find is true,
tossing this way and that,
sorting out which, if any,
of the possible conditional clauses, will do.

Despite the claim, or apologia, made in those last four lines, Scott is closer to his delightful characterisation of Duns Scotus than he would seem to allow. The conditional clauses *are* sorted out, and the pleasure of his verse has much to do with how right he gets the essence of a thing or of an experience. There's nothing complacently snug about these immaculate poems but they fit their subjects perfectly. They are full of gentle, contemplative intelligence and a tenacious modesty. Scott is an Anglican priest in a small Cumbrian parish, and one of his most striking gifts is for hinting at a significance in the smallest detail. He has a patient, parochial eye which gazes long enough at the incidental to discover its central importance. For example, in 'David Livingstone on the eve of discovering the Victoria Falls' he catches the magnitude of the event and the simple acknowledgement of basic human needs in a single sentence:

On these nights of clear skies
he is grateful for his warm shirt,
its Scotch wool; at the end of the night,
this noise.

Though working within a small compass (and most of the poems are very short) this is imagination of the highest order. In a moving tribute to a dead friend, Scott writes 'you sat still; and had a private voice/which only carried as far as it needed'. At a glance, this might be seen to suggest a limited scope of influence but, of course, it does no such thing. It means that, as is the case with Scott's own poems, the response was acutely sensitive to a core of privacy at the centre of every occasion. Many of the poems are hushed interiors. In 'The Seamen's Reading Room, Southwold' Scott takes pleasure in observing 'outdoor furniture/inside' and in 'On Visiting Keats House' 'our Duffle coats, when we leaned/on the glass to read this letter to Fanny/gave a slight tap of toggle. We read,/with eyes only, a postscript full of dashes/and torment'. Again, as with the portrait of Livingstone, the slight and the momentous are heard and seen together. The toggle and the torment. It's this quiet attentiveness that entices rather than demands the reader's own attention. Nothing, however small, is overlooked just in case it can offer illumination. Perhaps there are occasions when, like Baron Von Hugel in another of the poems, David

Scott seeks to reassure himself 'that directing a soul/ is not only a matter of angel's talk, it is/also the knack of catching the evening post', but he shouldn't worry. Catching the evening post is what his scrupulous, affectionate poetry does best.

U.A. Fanthorpe's third collection is much the same mixture of wit, compassion – and a dash of disdain – as before. *Voices Off* speaks for the supporting actors in life's cast list. Some of its most entertaining poems, as in the previous books, are dramatic monologues given to walk-on parts. Or, in the case of 'The Person's Tale', a walk-in part where Coleridge's celebrated scapegoat becomes hot under his stiff collar when he considers not only his posthumous reputation but the damage done to 'the proud name of Porlock' as well:

> Prepared for any
> Extreme office, I presented myself
> Before Mr. C–. *Sir*, said I, *I am here.*
> *The very man,* quoth he, clasping me in
> A distasteful embrace. *Most reverend sir –*
> Then for two hours detained me at his door
> With chronicles of colic, stomach, bowels,
> Of nightly sweats, the nightmare, cramps, diarrhoea...

This is one of the most sustained voices. Others include an ambitious local poet ('Betjeman now – /He rhymes too far apart. I'd have 'em close/Like church bells. I'm ready for publication'), some hilariously recognisable entries in a church visitors book ('Super! Fantastic! Jesus Lives! Ace!') and a group of students having difficulty with Yeats ('Married a median/Who believed in automatic writing'). U.A. Fanthorpe is good at this kind of thing. She's a clever mimic, and one can forgive her an occasional lapse into snide, slightly patronising exasperation. Sometimes her targets are a bit too easy, though, and there's an embarrassingly breezy piece of fun-poking at the expense of Royal Family addicts: 'With a Grundy here and a Gloucester there/Here a chukka, there a chicken, here and there a corgi' etc. She shouldn't be wasting her time with this kind of thing. There are others who can do it much better – if indeed it's worth doing at all.

Much more impressive are those poems on which, surely, her growing reputation rests. These are evocations of particular places, rooted in history, which have become palimpsests and where the 'voices off' are the echoes of past generations heard in the fragments that remain. Or portraits of that submerged population group which her work as a hospital clerk have occasioned – the best of these, in this collection, being 'Visiting Mr. Lewis in January' and the excellent 'Patients' in which the 'true patients' are not 'the official ones, who have been/Diagnosed and made tidy' but 'us/The undiagnosed':

What drugs
Will help our Matron, whose cats are
Her old black husband and her young black son?

Who will prescribe for our nurses, fatally
Addicted to idleness and tea? What therapy
Will relieve our Psychiatrist of his lust

For young slim girls, who prudently
Pretend to his excitement, though age
Has freckled his hands and his breath smells old?

When U.A. Fanthorpe speaks in her own voice for the undiagnosed –
those who, like Dickens's Mrs. Gradgrind, might well say 'I think there's
a pain somewhere in the room but I couldn't positively say that I have got
it' – she is at her sympathetic best, and quite free of that knowing,
ever-so-slightly superior ring-mastery with which she gets her little men-
agerie of performing voices to jump through the hoops of their own
innocent pretensions.

'There is a stillness around objects' writes Jean Earle in a poem from
her second collection, *The Intent Look*, and that stillness serves both to
isolate those objects as they appear in her work and to insist on their being
part of a pattern as coherent as it is mysterious. In this she often reminds
me of Edwin Muir with his gift of mythologising the domestic. At times
her scenes are finely attuned to the sinister and threateningly ambiguous
('Up the garden, a dog steals raspberries,/With smiling teeth') while at
others they are offered 'like bundles children carry or clutch in sleep,/Full
of sustaining treasures'. Always, though, they reveal an acute, pained
sense of the long perspectives, an awareness of how briefly we occupy our
little space. In 'A Neighbour's House' the previous inhabitant, 'a tall old
woman/Of a stripped serenity' still seems its owner in the poet's imagination even though a newcomer is already knocking down walls and making
it over:

Young man, I wish you every good.

It is not your property
I take over to inhabit secretly –
But the outworn life,
Willed to me by deeds not of this world.
To do with hands round cups
Brimmed with our common fears.
To do with looking at what life is
Together.

Catching one long breath.

Jean Earle is in her seventies, and 'our common fears' are her private ones

('Forgive me. My nature asks/This lonely question'). These fears, and mortal questions, ambush her with a desolating immediacy which is somehow all the more sharply felt for its being experienced in a commonplace setting or action:

> Oh, my sweet dead – the cakes.. the cakes!
> All news discharged to the faint, receptive sheen
> Of your listening eyes. Then, for the first time,
> I knew that you were dead at last, and I –
>
> Healed?
>
> It came upon me with the emptied teapot
> And the westering sun. I had no plans for you
> Beyond the afternoon.

The pleasures and limitations of a nicely observed domestic poetry are everywhere apparent in Duncan Forbes's first collection. Despite some ambitious moments, *August Autumn* keeps stepping aside to acknowledge that there's a world elsewhere while at the same time seeming to shrug off more awareness of it than is decent:

> The sky is endless and there is no sky.
> All resurrections are deciduous
> Or so the birdsong and the leaves imply.
> Well, in again to cake with chocolate eggs,
> Then *Murder On the Orient Express*.

That 'well' is just too all-embracingly sensible like the Wellingtons and windcheaters which Peter and Jane wear in 'Sheltered Upbringing' while they help daddy garden:

> He clips the privet and they feed the bonfire.
> Soon they will plant potatoes in its embers
> And eat them, hard and gritty, after tea.
> At dusk they listen to their bedtime story:
> *Henry The Green Engine* who was immured
> For disobedience like Antigone.

Of course Forbes intends a gentle mockery, and he is in fact very good at taking a detached, affectionate look at the continuity between his own middle-class childhood and his present family life marked out by Jackdaw Folders and the Reverend Awdry. He's even better in a handful of poems about the death of his father-in-law where the ironies are in the situation itself rather than in his manner of perceiving it. Here his plain, unequivocal candour is very moving:

> And where your father read our banns
> Is an empty step where his coffin stands.

The same black fleet of cars on hire
Brought him and the bridal party here

And he found it difficult not to cry
As I do, biting back tears, today

At this sad marriage of love to grief,
This funeral of a married life.

This points to the poet Duncan Forbes may become if he manages to stop hiding in the shelter of witty circumspection.

10
Conceit and Concern
January 1986

Roy Fuller: *New and Collected Poems* (Secker & Warburg)
Norman MacCaig: *Collected Poems* (Chatto & Windus)
Michael Longley: *Poems 1963-1983* (Salamander Press)
Jeni Couzyn: *Life by Drowning* (Bloodaxe Books)
Jeni Couzyn (ed): *The Bloodaxe Book of Contemporary Women Poets* (Bloodaxe Books)
Anne Stevenson: *The Fiction Makers* (Oxford University Press)
Anne Stevenson: *Black Grate Poems* (Inky Parrot Press)
Richard Murphy: *The Price of Stone* (Faber & Faber)
Peter Reading: *Ukulele Music* (Secker & Warburg)
John Gohorry: *A Voyage Round the Moon* (Peterloo Poets)
William Scammell: *Jouissance* (Peterloo Poets)
Tim Dooley: *The Interrupted Dream* (Anvil Press)
Faber Poetry Introduction 6 (Faber & Faber)

FOR SHEER WEIGHT, the book of the season must be Roy Fuller's. To begin his *New and Collected Poems* at the beginning is, as Randall Jarrell once remarked of another poet, like receiving Auden's carbons for Christmas. All the familiar thirties land-marks line themselves up for the next decade, simplified by their familiarity. 'The objects are disposed: the sky is suitable', the airman's in his heaven and all's wrong with the world. It's a 'wounded land'. Offshore an explicitly phallic lighthouse stands 'aloof with rolling eye'. Practising its surreal deceptions 'the false clock is ticking on the mantelpiece' while the dead practise their 'executive gestures'. The intelligentsia feels 'generalised compassion' and the poet, thinly disguised as a somewhat routine crime-writer, is by now all too accomplished at springing 'the necessary surprise'. The necessary murder hangs guiltily in the air. Choice has become a recession of closing options and, such as it remains, is presented to fellow combatants from a dais in the Briefing Room. We're at real war now. Up go the didactic, unarguable lines on the Commander's blackboard, and his baton points them out: 'Now man must be political or die:/Nor is there really that alternative'. And so on. The more strident the public certainties, the greater the personal confusion for Fuller caught between 'the illusory and real'. He writes, for the duration, as a contemplative on active service with a job to do, but although he wears an officer's uniform his 'only rank is consciousness', that hinterland where every man is his own private:

> Even the road conveys the sense
> Of being outside experience;
> As though, this winter night of war,
> The world we made were mine no more.

So, gradually, a characteristic, individual voice emerges. Having removed the Auden shorthand from his notebook, Fuller begins to develop his natural bent for well-read, scrupulous meditations on the residual ills of the mid-twentieth century often accompanied (or prompted) by a catalogue of his own anxieties and discomforts. In a poem on the death of André Gide in 1951 he reads the news, typically after a night of insomnia, then goes on to contemplate a future in which

> Whatever routes the intellectuals haunt
> Around the action of their times will want
> The practical travel notes of Gide...

Although he remained loyal to Auden long after he stopped using Macspaunday travel notes, and although he has indeed paralleled the master's rapid aging by carefully contriving a persona of premature crustiness and mock-bufferdom, Fuller's particular brand of wry, ironic angst has become very much his own. It is his strength and his limitation. Despite disclaimers as to the power of poetry to change the world, there's always the sense when reading Auden that history is being made, that his work is somehow an active part of the zeitgeist, making – as Fuller claims for Gide – 'an alteration in the epoch's tense'. His come-and-go obsessions with psychoanalysis and fashionable rigmarole in the thirties and early forties seem less a peripheral dabbling than a kind of cultural urgency. Fuller, on the other hand, has inherited the shift that this urgency brought about, and his continuing achievement has been to modify it according to his more modest lights as a poet acutely sensitive to historical and social change. His poems really do make nothing happen, and that is what they are ruefully but resolutely about. Built into them is the awareness that they are civilised footnotes to a destiny already shaped elsewhere, and their rhetorical flourishes often amount to an honourable, resonant shrug:

> Anticipate the ice-age as you can,
> Anticipate the burning should it come,
> Live with your death, your species' death – with craft,
> That on this globe, and those unknown and past,
> The gases and the carbon spirals clasp
> A spirit fearful but immortal somewhere.

Fuller recognises in himself one of those intellectuals who, in the words of the Gide poem, 'haunt/Around the action of their times', and his best work emerges from the accuracy with which he analyses various shades of political conscience and personal inertia. Like Brutus in that fine poem 'The Ides of March' he often considers every angle of the moment when one might be 'about/To cease being a fellow traveller' but inevitably Brutus's final, fateful greeting to the conspirators ('Good morning, comrades') is not for him. Instead, in his sonnet sequence 'The Historian', he establishes a characterisation and setting which is to become, increasingly, his starting point:

> The scene my study: Faustian locale!
> I speculate on my lack of energy
> Before the tempting foolscap, and decide –
> My theories staggering, my learning sound –

That I am sickening for a minor ill;
And wonder how in my solitary life,
I caught the bug. Unquestionably I ache.

It's all there in that stanza: the curious lack of energy with its hint that it might be a symptom of the times but nevertheless about to be transformed into a full-stretch of thoroughly accomplished craftsmanship, the ambiguously *staggering* theories of a writer confident of his learning but unable not to doubt its ultimate value, the Faustian locale with its nervously jokey glance at the moral consequences of ambition, and the premonition of 'a minor ill' which of course anticipates the inescapably major one which calls everything into question. In those early days of easy Audenesque gestures, it was a stage-prop horizon which appeared 'like an illness' but increasingly in Fuller's work, however full of ranging speculation it may be, the key-note is a personal one. He prefaces a set of memorial poems with an epigraph – again from Gide – which states plainly that 'Illness is to reconcile us to death', and in a sense most of his recent work has haunted around that sentence. The older he gets, the wittier and more self-deprecatingly occasional his observations become:

My briefcase falls open in the street. Displayed:
Aspirins for migraine, chocolates for my wife.
Despite my 'Oh bugger', strangers come to aid
The old boy picking up his bits of life.

But, despite the 'Oh buggers' that find their way into his verse as the quotidian gets him into muddles and not much seems to be in the right place any more, 'the young boy still continues on his foolish course' open to new experience and experimenting with a variety of forms even if, rather too wilfully, most of them tend towards the elegiac. Or perhaps that very wilfulness is a ruse:

I must return
To the usual perils of longevity
In the man of letters. Being out of date
And out of print, and feeling orphaned, I
Can't help a grin at my self-pity.

Few poets have aged with such spry acceptance as Roy Fuller, or with such emphasis on the aches and pains. There's seldom less than a gleeful relish in his complaints. His 'gerontic pacings' are a distinctive dance to the music of time, and now that he is so handsomely and bulkily in print may his grin widen as he slips out to buy the aspirins and chocolates.

Perhaps at the same time he might like to buy an un-birthday present for his fellow septuagenarian Norman MacCaig. If so, MacCaig's poem 'Request' offers him the choice of 'a box of telepathy,/a bottle of clairvoyance,/and a gift of tongues'. And if it weren't such a clear case of carrying scotch to Edinburgh, he could simply combine all three by presenting the old wizard with a copy of his own *Collected Poems*. It's a huge crate of a book of bottles, boxed as a gift, packed and fluent, full-measured and effervescently spirited. MacCaig has been corking his miniatures since 1955 and shows no sign of closing the still. Each page should carry a health warning for the prosaic: 'These poems may seriously affect your balance'. They are full of the drunkenness of things being various but they also recall Richard Wilbur's comment on verse craftsmanship that 'the strength of the genie comes of his being confined in a bottle'. Despite its celebration of abundance, MacCaig's restless, playful, wise imagination seldom runs over. It filters carefully into each poem, drop by drop, glinting with a purposeful intellectual mischief – questioning, puzzling over natural phenomena and thriving on its own inexhaustible draught of correspondences. In a short progress-report-cum-apologia 'Still Going' – and I'm only half-prepared to believe he's innocent of the pun in that title – MacCaig writes:

> I won't give up being deceived by landscape's
> Likenesses and incorrigible metaphors.
> They swish long currents in my mind – fancy
> A stagnant mind: a crystal of braincells.

That 'fancy' is typical. At one and the same time it's an invitation, a philosophical brain-teaser and an exclamation – 'Fancy that!' Few poets are as adept as MacCaig at appearing utterly amazed by appearances. 'Things' he seems to be saying 'are not only more various than we suppose but more various than we *can* suppose'. He delights in giving vivid utterance to intimations of unity while insisting on their tantalising evasiveness:

> A flower as possibility, burning with more
> Ambiguity than a flower's, melts and grows
> In the foregarden of my mind; and never
> Its lapsing selves are narrowed to a rose.
>
> How give to you, with only this to give,
> One flower that would be one and include
> (Even though it should die) in its strict sculpture
> All the wild roses in the wilder wood?

MacCaig's kind of speculative inventiveness is bound to seem whimsical on an off-day, but he's so disarming that you're never quite sure if the day's his or yours. What is beyond doubt, though, is that he is a master of the metaphor as direct statement where cleverness and feeling combine in a hauntingly plain-spoken accuracy:

When the door
scraped shut, it was the end
of all the sounds there are.

You left me
beside the quietest fire in the world.

I thought I was hurt in my pride only,
forgetting that,
when you plunge your hand in freezing water,
you feel
a bangle of ice round your wrist
before the whole hand goes numb.

I first heard those lines on the radio twenty years ago. I have been able to quote them from memory ever since.

Michael Longley's *Poems 1963-1983* begins with 'Epithalamion' and closes with 'Rune', thus conveniently indicating the points of celebration and inscription between which his immaculately sensitive work negotiates. Of the prominent Ulster poets, he's he most adept at assembling the shards of a culture into firm, inclusive keepsakes. He has become a remedial poet. His spells are curative. Seamus Heaney may contemplate his shelf-life of significant objects, but Longley fragments his into verbal nuggets which he rolls in his palm, listening to them click as they catch the light. For him a characteristic poem is a close-up of ear and eye – enigmatic, allusive, at best piercingly unsentimental:

I make my peace with murderers.
I lock pubic hair from victims
In an airtight tin, mummify
Angel feathers, tobacco shreds.

All that survives my acid bath
Is a solitary gall-stone
Like a pebble out on mud flats
Or the ghost of an avocado.

This exquisitely naked miniature in which violence and sweetness, sententious statement and intimate detail, are locked together within eight lines as airtight as that tin itself, was originally entitled 'Love Poetry'. It how appears in the 'New Poems' section of Longley's collection as 'Love Poet', shifting attention from the genre to the personal. This is instructive. Paradoxically the more oblique and runic Longley's method has become, the more intensely felt has seemed the pressure of emotion. For him the cryptic is revelatory. The earlier, expansively formalist poems – occasional celebrations, verse epistles, tributes – though accomplished enough and advertising an approachable, decent, thoroughly civilized poet, seem impersonal by comparison.

Jeni Couzyn is another poet who has shown a keen sense of natural magic and ritual. Much of her best work has been in the form of secular spells and domestic incantations, often sharply up-to-date in their reference but cunningly primitive in their folk-lore cadences, their repetitions and parallelisms. The poems in the earlier sections of *Life by Drowning*, although they often lapse into unexceptional sub-Lawrentian pieties ('For love is an opening, an outward thing/but the need for love is a hunger that no food will fill'), are impressive. They can be fierce and tender in a swing of moods which combines artfulness and intuition:

> I was believed!
> Something fell from my face with a clatter –
> my punishment was over
>
> and in that moment
> fell from my mother's face a particular smile, a kind of
> dear and tender curling of the eyes
>
> fell.

This is beautifully paced – the verse movement which falls into 'fell' – but Jeni Couzyn has always tended towards the exclamatory, and consciousness of a mission seems recently to have hardened her art into what reads like crudely simplified transcripts of an appeal to sisterhood. Her rhythms have become strident, and there is too much stuff like this:

> Infinite! That surely is the secret name
> the unimaginable, the immense mystery!
>
> No. That is the sacred name for Within.
>
> Is it Nothingness?
>
> It is not. That is the lie of Reality.
>
> Truth?
>
> Truth is what it says.
> Truth is the name for itself.

Such vacuous rhapsodising could only have been written by an admired poet who is listening to the hush of her audience, an audience which believes her to be writing from what Elizabeth Barrett Browning called 'the depths of womanhood'. This is a phrase which Jeni Couzyn picks up in her interesting introduction to the *Bloodaxe Book of Contemporary Women Poets*. Here she expresses her debt to that true poet Kathleen Raine, whose influence can clearly be seen on a number of the poems in *Life by Drowning*, and praises her for having 'steadfastly refused to be drawn into the spiritually impoverished cul-de-sac of "clever" poetry that has dominated literary fashion in Britain for most of her writing life'. The trouble is that Jeni Couzyn now seems to be prescribing too conscious an antidote to what she sees as cleverness, and in this she is being untrue to her talent. 'The message of the men is linear...//But the message of the women is love,/has always been love...'. Messages, messages. I don't want a poem to tell me this ten times over. There was a singular time when Jeni Couzyn's poems managed to prove it.

Anti-cleverness is a theme in Anne Stevenson's autobiographical contribution to the Bloodaxe book. 'Much of what passes for poetry these days seems to me trivial, self-regarding games-playing: cleverness for cleverness's sake – or for the poet's sake. But I no longer want to play the literary game. I had enough of that in Oxford'. She's settled into a Durham village now, so it's therefore perhaps time for some vale-dictions. Nevertheless I'm puzzled and disappointed to find her devoting the last eleven pages (rather a lengthy postscript) of her otherwise excellent new collection to a whimsical appropriation of Villon in her 'A Legacy: on my fiftieth birthday'. The less said about this the better, but something must be said. It's witty, I suppose, nice for her family and friends, and full of in-references for the fashion-mongers, but who really cares that she intends to leave

> To Andrew Motion, any fame
> That to my thin books may adhere
> Like sheep's wool to a barbed-wire name.
> Further, my reputation for
> High-flown frigidity to Fleur
> Who in the Oxford lists has been
> The lady aptest to prefer
> The acid to the saccharine.

Tart and affectionate enough but – for all its playful self-effacement – too much a symptom of the cleverness it purports to be saying goodbye to. For an apparently voluntary exile Anne Stevenson still seems addicted to court news.

That's less than half the story, though. Almost without exception, the rest of *The Fiction-Makers* is absorbing. In a tribute to Elizabeth Bishop, 'Waving to Elizabeth', Anne Stevenson has her admired poet say 'This high smooth sea's more quiet than the map is,/though the map, relieved of mapmakers, looks imprisoned and free'. Here an American ghost meets and merges with a British one as those last three words recall Edward Thomas's wish to stand 'fixed and free' in a rhyme. *The Fiction-Makers* is preoccupied with map and sea, form and flux, the shifts of perception and memory, and with states of being locked in and out of language. Like Bishop and Thomas in their different ways, Anne Steven-son is becoming a haunted but companionable solitary for whom land-scape, the otherness of animal nature and the intimate habits of friendship both accentuate and alleviate her sense of isolation. Other moving tributes to dead friends – Frances Horovitz and Anne Pennington – have a clear beauty as she notices the things they would have noticed and remakes their own fictions. Language locks her into a loving circuit of celebration. When she's locked *out* it's by the inescapably human humdrum, the domestic, but with an engaging wit she manages to celebrate this too. Prompted by affection for a noisy son practising his drums upstairs

> The woman in her burrow
> looks up to him, boasting and fussing.
> But her mind broods lonely
> on the sands by a tidal river.

That burrow is Anne Stevenson's well-earthed cave of fiction-making and the more she holes up in it the more attentive she becomes to the idea of a real world beyond it. In 'A Prayer to Live with Real People' – one of a sequence of 'Black Grate Poems' (also handsomely available from the Inky Parrot Press with delightful illustrations by Annie Newnham) – she prays to her household gods to save her 'from Habitat and snobbery and too damn much literary ambition'. *The Fiction-Makers* shows her settling into a 'new life' with all her ghosts around her. Most of them are on her side, as real as the locals she wants to adopt. If she can completely kick the poetic Habitat habit, the inverted literary ambition with its eye cocked towards fashion which still shows in 'A Legacy', her next book should be better still.

Richard Murphy's work is an interesting blend of the sensuous and the austere. *The Price of Stone* is an elegant, highly crafted collection, full of contrivance and patches of very fine writing. It doesn't leave a poem unturned, but too great a sacrifice of material to the demands of construction tends to make a stone of the art. Although the first half of this book contains some fine lyrics, Murphy keeps getting weighed down by artifice. In 'Stone Mania' he writes of 'the house whose construction has kept us entirely apart'. This is addressed to a loved one who has had to pay the price of the poet's 'passion for building in granite' – a passion which throughout the collection he insists on exploring as a metaphor for the craft of verse – but it also draws attention to a procedure which keeps him apart from his reader as well. One keeps watching for the next appearance of 'a wise old mason', 'the stonework of my heart', 'each random stone made integral' etc. and rather distantly admires the rhetorical expertise.

The entire second section is a sequence of fifty sonnets in which Murphy traces his lineage and growth as a poet by means of giving a voice to buildings which have had significance in his life (birth-place, school, a friend's cottage and so on). There's a lot of indomitable Anglo-Irishry in this. It's an extremely enterprising project, packed with cunning effects which keep drawing attention to their own literary ingenuity – 'to renovate my structure', 'plucking lost tunes from my structure', 'made me sound in my ruins', 'he restored my site'. 'Much as you need a sonnet house to save/ your muse...' begins 'Carlow Village Schoolhouse'. That sounds rather desperate. It's as if the schoolhouse may have Murphy's number. At times, along the way, as yet one more building bent the ear, I felt that I needed another sonnet like a hole in the wall. It's all so literary, consciously poetic and rather *vieux château*. Yet what a powerful descriptive gift Murphy displays when he's not labouring on the construction site. In 'Morning Call' two girls are

> Lovely as seals wet from fishing, hauled out on a rock
> To dry their dark brown fur glinting with scales of salmon
> When the spring tide ebbs. This is their everlasting day
> Of being young. They bring to my room the sea's iodine odour
> On a breeze of voices ruffling my calm as they comb their long
> Hair tangled as weed in a rockpool beginning to settle clear.
> Give me the sea-breath from your mouths to breathe a while!

The second book of Peter Reading's latest collection, *Ukulele Music* is entitled 'Going on'. And on and on as the ship of ghouls goes down:

plīnkplĭnkă| plīnkplĭnkă| plīnkplĭnkă| plīnkplīnk| plīnkplĭnkă| plīnkplīnk
plīnkplĭnkă| plīnkplĭnkă| plōnk| |plīnkplĭnkă| plīnkplĭnkă| plōnk

How scrupulously he observes the caesura as all around him lose their heads very nastily. With what sardonic relish he catalogues the tabloid horrors of our time – and of all time, H.Sap. being what he is. Giving the two fingers to 'poetry wallahs' in mockingly accomplished classical metres, he has made a considerable and deserved reputation for himself as a writer who ransacks the columns of historical documents, foreign correspondents and, above all, 'last week's dailies before they're/screwed up to light the Parkray'. His imagination is thrilled by the worst to be found in newsprint, and he's brilliantly in control of the end of his tether. Call his poetry compassionate after its terrible fashion and it answers plinkplinka. Call it callous and not a little voyeuristic and it calls back C'est La Vie. Plonk plonk:

> 'Life is too black as he paints it' and 'Reading's nastiness sometimes
> seems a bit over the top' thinks a review – so does *he*.

> Too black and over the top, though is what the Actual often
> happens to be, I'm afraid. He don't *invent* it, you know.

I know he don't. I'd have to be suffering from a very acute case of Podsnappery indeed to think for a moment that he did. What troubles me ('Hooey and hooey and tosh' or not) is just that Peter Reading makes an aesthetic of cruelty while loudly disclaiming any moral consequences for his skill. He's an on-stage dandy of destruction, slashing his lurid, undeniably authentic canvasses with so much vigour that the act becomes self-generating. There's little doubt that he's going to go on playing to full houses. The danger is that he'll become an institution. 'Let's go and see Peter Reading tonight'. If that happens I'm not sure that it won't be down to him. With his ever increasing brilliance of organisation and the same awful material, he may just be becoming too spectacular for our own good.

John Gohorry's poems are often abrasive but always good-natured, and *A Voyage Round the Moon* is an enjoyable first collection by a bright-and-breezy realist. Playful, unencumbered by his considerable learning, wryly nostalgic though seldom indulging in false sentiment, Gohorry persuades us that intelligence brings its own rewards. He can sustain lengthy commentaries on art and manners with a robustness of rhyme and metre in the best Jonsonian tradition, and even comes close to pipping Pope at the post:

> Alma before her mirror sits
> applying the dear counterfeits
> that prolong youth and banish age
> to some unthinkable last page
> of Revlon's catalogues or hardly
> probable collapse of Yardley...
>
> *'let beauty paint her mortal parts*
> *with all the cosmetician's arts*
> *not to conceal the body's dross*
> *but show the soul in all its gloss*
> *infinity of light and wit,*
> *more truthfully because of it.'*

Clever though he often is – not in the 'Oxford poetry' sense but in the tradition of true scholarly wit – Gohorry's best poems achieve a gentle, unembarrassed candour. In 'Family Resemblances' he recalls how his father used to carry him, as a small child, on his shoulders. Now he carries his own son in exactly the same way and addresses the ghost of the one through the other, a familiar theme which Gohorry handles well:

My diminutive, dear, and alas dead father,
I carry you on my shoulder through the high ferns
of our afternoon walk, your stomach a two month laboratory
of scarcely perfected experiments, your eyes,
if the textbooks are right, still perceiving
conifers, oaks, and the clambering family
you are just beginning to know yours, but can't
name, bizarrely inverted. One of them climbs down
into the fork of a treetop, adjusting
a lens in her stomach, and lifts it down
to her eyes in some escapade that will capture
these seven others and yourself ranged like squirrels
on a massive, collapsed oaktrunk.

This mixture of scientific curiosity and private tenderness is typical of Gohorry's spirit of human enquiry.

William Scammell is another Jonsonian poet. His energetic wit is less cloistered than Gohorry's and in much of his work we find him with his sleeves rolled up in the School of Life:

Starved of my proper diet, I broke fast
and hungered round the city, swallowing down
a hundred films, plays, concerts: periphrast
by night, by day a cipher in the town.
In weeks I'd shed my background; see, at last
a haughty traveller on the underground!
storming the citadel, by very force
master of every modish intercourse.

Scammell has become a readable critic in the literary journals where his intercourse is refreshingly anything but modish, and in his third collection, *Jouissance*, there are some lively observations on the literary life, and particularly on the world of popular culture. A poem like 'Ancient and Modern' is a roll-call of yesterday's men and women who still cast their glamour on his imagination, but the best poem in the book is a very plain, very quiet one written in memory of Pete Laver who was curator of the Wordsworth museum and library at Grasmere and a good poet himself:

Pete dropped baldly on Scafell
walking one minute, dead the next
at an age neither biblical
nor glossed by any text.

It dins in our ears, crumples the eye.
It steals a day from its normal perch.
It grabs the legs from under pay
thinning a voice to fill a church

> where all's one voice, or would be, were
> there comfort in a shared defeat,
> anything new to be read in terror,
> wisdom in getting to your feet.

So much contemporary poetry seems polarised between the purveyors of mere conceit and the honourable possessors of grave, ineffectual concern. In his first collection, *The Interrupted Dream*, Tim Dooley leans towards the latter. He goes in for an Arnoldian sobriety laced with echoes of Larkin:

> What feels like a gasp out of the nineteenth century,
> a 'let us be true to one another' flung in unbelief
> at sea, signifies hope that small trusting creatures
> can learn or live sharing. We touch to that rhythm
> and glance indoors at the ephemera of love, collected.

Dooley's breadth of reading and consciousness take in internationalism – two sections of the book are prefaced with epigraphs from Neruda and Jaccottet – but his sensibility remains provincial. Like so many provincials he is nicely ironic about his position but it remains a rather lame one: 'Holding a glass of cider and a Penguin Mallarmé,/I pose for a leisured life while there is work to do'.

Faber's latest *Poetry Introduction* is worth getting hold of for the poems of Alan Dewar. He certainly doesn't waste a moment scribbling in the margins while there is work to do. His muscular rhythms and admirably compressed lines embody the industrial activity and landscape about which he writes. He's no elegiac observer of abandoned machinery. There's a heartening anger and political nerve in his work:

> Forget those time-softened mills,
> forget the quiet renewals
> spilling power through the race.
> Ignore the sadness, entropy
> of solar silence dimming
> on our bright panels. Look:
> sky is the black of absence.
> The firth is like mercury.
> Against the water, complex black
> steels and concretes cluster.
> Waste flares off, fierce worklight
> is fired at the groundplan.
> Roads bend in like lines of force;
> are gridded into service,
> spiralling round towers.
> Matt blocks absorb
> material, transform.
> Kiln of the great anarchy.

11
Seeing and Believing
November 1986

Louis Simpson: *People Live Here – Selected Poems 1949-1983* (Secker & Warburg)
Amy Clampitt: *What the Light Was Like* (Faber & Faber)
Gjertrud Schnackenberg: *The Lamplit Answer* (Hutchinson)
Frances Horovitz: *Selected Poems* (Bloodaxe Books)
Charles Tomlinson: *Collected Poems* (Oxford University Press)
Paul Durcan: *The Berlin Wall Cafe* (Blackstaff)
Edna Longley (ed): *The Selected Paul Durcan* (Blackstaff)
Hugo Williams: *Writing Home* (Oxford University Press)
Mary Jarrell (ed): *Randall Jarrell's Letters* (Faber & Faber)
R.L. Barth: *Forced-Marching to the Styx* (Perivale Press)

'IT IS GETTING harder and harder to write a poem. That is, I can start one well enough – but how to finish.' Only a confident poet risks making a statement like that in the secret knowledge that he will get away with it and deserves to; knowing also that as a direct witness to his commitment it is part of the greater risk of presuming to write poetry at all. In this case the poet is Louis Simpson, examining his craft in a marvellously candid working autobiography *Air With Armed Men*, published in 1972 and long overdue for reissue. What he goes on to say is worth quoting at some length:

> I used to be able to begin and finish a poem. I found that the poem was directed by certain external forces towards a certain end. But one day I found that ideas were better expressed in prose. No, it was more than that. I found that I no longer wished to please.
>
> The reader has certain stock responses to ideas, and certain responses – not very strong, perhaps, but operative nevertheless – to metaphor, meter, and rhyme. A poem that satisfies his stock responses is 'good'; a poem that does not is 'bad'. I find myself wanting to write bad poems – poems that do not depend on stock responses. I want to write poems that will not please. Recently I have been learning to write this new kind of poem. The most important change is in the content...
>
> Instead of statements which reassure the reader by their familiarity, or shock him by their strangeness – instead of opinions, there are only images and reverberations.
>
> I can never finish these poems. I wrestle with them and leave off when I am exhausted. Frequently, all that remains is a handful of phrases.
>
> The difficulty is that, to write this new kind of poem, which springs mainly from the subconscious, I must work not at technique, but at improving my character.

The scope and outcome of this discovery, re-direction of energies and experiment with the constituents of his character – the burden of memories, intuitions, and dreambound responsibilities he brings with him as an American of Jamaican and Russian parentage – can now be clearly seen in his *Selected Poems 1949-83* chosen from all his books to date and placed in groups rather than a single chronology. In a 'Note to the Reader', speaking still as the discreet but determined director of attention, he announces 'there is an opening section of "Songs and Lyrics" – in other sections the poems are centered around an idea. I believe that this arrangement shows the nature of my writing more clearly than has appeared up to now in separate books'. It does. In each section there's a movement from well-wrought formalism, those external forces moving towards a certain end in strict, often ballad-based stanzas with their echoes of Yeats and the early Auden, into a wider, more inclusive and populated world of deceptively relaxed fictions where the imagery of dream is continuously merging with witty social obervation. The shift is from the desk and its position of control, its single framed outlook on a narrow tradition which – as Simpson views it – has resulted in the poet sitting there, to the open road at the end of which 'we come to ourselves'. To move out into the open, to enlarge the range and sympathies of one's poetry, is to find that 'the land is within'. 'Deep, deep in the interior/The temple of the God is hidden'. As Simpson works away at this transformation, or *release*, the emphasis of poem after poem is on a celebration of the moment of setting out. He becomes his own imaginary traveller, and in 'As a Man Walks', for example, a visit to Australia serves to define all that is envigoratingly strange about his new sense of direction. It's a journey of the mind, an intuitive sense of trust in the adventure of what lies ahead:

> As a man walks he creates the road he walks on.
> All of my life in America
> I must have been reeling out of myself
> This red dirt, gravel road.
>
> Three boys seated on motorcycles
> conferring...
>
>   A little further on,
> a beaten-up Holden parked off the road
> with two men inside passing the bottle.
> Dark-skinned...maybe they are aboriginal.
>
> I might have been content to live
> In Belle Terre, among houses and lawns,
> but inside me are gum trees,
> and magpies, cackling and whistling,
> and a bush-roaming kangaroo.

People Live Here is the overall title of these Selected Poems, and increasingly Louis Simpson has striven to be in there among the people. As an epigraph to a section of his 1976 collection *Searching for the Ox* he quoted from Wordworth 'I have wished to keep the reader in the company of flesh and blood'. He knows that as a close observer with that 'nerve-tic irony' he must always be at a remove from the scenes he passes through, but he's engaged upon what he has called The Adventure of the Letter I, breaking down the self-absorbed identity of poet into fugitive fragments of experience and attempting to reconstitute them into something new and generously inclusive. He wants to create a Whitmanesque republic of the imagination in which he is both an invisible witness and the travelling representative of everything he can possibly get into a poem. The poet who could fuse lyric and argument in lines as powerful and beautiful as these from 'The Goodnight'

> The lives of children are
> Dangerous to their parents
> With fire, water, air,
> And other accidents;
> And some, for a child's sake,
> Anticipating doom,
> Empty the world to make
> The world safe as a room

decides they won't do for him any more. The tension in his work must cease to be set up by metre and rhyme. Instead, it must become the relationship between the poet and the voice of his ancestry in the process of becoming the Voice of America:

> To their simple, affectionate questions
> he returned simple answers.
> For how could he explain what it meant to be a writer...
> a world that was entirely different,
> and yet it would include the sofa
> and the smell of chicken cooking.

It's that passion to *include* and to respond to the world's passion to be included that has made Louis Simpson the poet he is – 'voices and shadows of desire/and the tears of things...Around us/Things want to be understood'. He's aware of the dangers of a romantic, hobo-ing sentimentality in this, and continually checks it. Sometimes it's fascinating to watch him mixing a limpid brew of simile and sententiousness, correcting himself and then making that correction the point of the poem:

> The fallen snow gleamed in the dark
> like water. Everything is a flowing,
> you have only to flow with it.
>
> If you did, you would live to regret it.
> After a while, passion would wear off
> and you would still be faced with life,
> the same old dull routine.

In fact, although he's finely tuned to 'image and reverberation', Simpson is addicted to a quotidian melancholy, and he gets many of his best effects by gathering a kind of numinous cloud around 'the same old dull routine'. He fills a poem with people and objects, hints at the desolation lying always just beneath the commonplace, then dissolves it in a wistful evanescence – 'The shadow of the word/flitting over the scene,/the street and motionless crowd'. His ironic urbanity is not always enough to allay the suspicion that the effects come a bit too easily at times. What he has achieved is a distinctive cosmopolitan *poésie de dèpart* with an American accent, a carefully contrived conversational poetry which can be enjoyed at many levels – for the resonance of its dream-images, its engaging anecdotes, wry proverbial wisdom and abundant delight in the pattern of inconsequence which make up the randomness of human behaviour. It certainly does not rely on stock responses. It relishes the necessary, complicit agility of its readers. With its central metaphors of the unreeling road, the journey ('I am going into the night to find a world of my own') and the poet surprised by unexpected, welcome shafts of sympathy ('Who lives in these dark houses?/I am suddenly aware/ I might live here myself'), it is a poetry which lives in the imagination as a distinctive landscape of shifting perspectives and unfinished conversations but not as firmly in the memory as those earlier 'finished' poems based directly on Simpson's experience as a rifleman in the Second World War, his Jamaican childhood and the shaping energies of metre and rhyme. In fact, that declarative last line of 'Love, My Machine' – 'I am going into the night to find a world of my own' – while it anticipates the direction his later work is to take, serves also as an echo (already fading) of the remarkable compassion and authority of 'My Father in the Night Commanding No', one of the finest poems written since the war and – for all his admirable openness to experiment and risk – representative of Simpson's truest gift. That gift is for plain, heart-breaking candour and for conveying the helpless wisdom of a child's-eye-view through those very statements which he came to mistrust. Though a consistently fine poet who knows that 'restlessness is a sign of intelligence', his reputation is most likely to come to rest on lines like these:

> And yet my father sits and reads in silence,
> My mother sheds a tear, the moon is still,
>   And the dark wind
> Is murmuring that nothing ever happens.

> Beyond his jurisdiction as I move
> Do I not prove him wrong? And yet, it's true
>   *They* will not change
> There, on the stage of terror and of love.

> The actors in that playhouse always sit
> In fixed positions – father, mother, child
>   With painted eyes.
> How sad it is to be a little puppet!
>
> Their heads are wooden. As you once pretended
> To understand them! Shake them as you will,
>   They cannot speak.
> Do what you will, the comedy is ended.
>
> Father, why did you work? Why did you weep,
> Mother? Was the story so important?
>   *'Listen'* the wind
> Said to the children, and they fell asleep.

Anyone unmoved by these lines, as Randall Jarrell once wrote of a passage by Whitman, would boil his babies up for soap.

If Louis Simpson's American landscape is the workaday broad-cloth of common experience lit by a gentle glow, Amy Clampitt's is a glittering brocade. Like the kingfisher which provided the title of her first book, her style is darting and iridescent. She's a mercurial poet who delights in the intricacies of syntax and metaphor in a permanently surprised and rather nervy way, and her outlook is a kind of coastal gaze with the sunlight in her eyes and with the hinterland of tradition, wide American spaces and complex European culture behind her. *What the Light Was Like,* her second collection, opens with 'A Baroque Sunburst' which

> struck through such a dome
> as might await a groaning Michelangelo,
> finding only alders and barnacles
> and herring gulls at their usual squabbles,
> sheds on the cove's voluted
> silver the aloof skin tones
> of a Crivelli angel: a region,
> a weather and a point of view
> as yet unsettled, save for the lighthouse
> like a Venetian campanile, from whose nightlong
> reflected angelus you might suppose
> the coast of Maine had Europe
> on the brain or in its bones, as though
> it were a kind of sickness.

There are eight closely packed pages of notes at the back of the book, providing not so much an explanatory aid as an additional pleasure in themselves – a kind of supplementary anthology full of incidental, lightly-worn scholarship – and amongst them she quotes Heraclitus on the permanence of change: 'It is not possible to step twice in the same river'. This, it seems, is what fascinates her to the point of obsession and operates as a principle in her poetry. She's preoccupied with the play of light, water and air, and with her own pocket of time as a bubble in the flux, and the movement of her verse is correspondingly vivid in its fidgety animation. It is somewhat similar to the small child in her poem 'New Life' who 'sees/the world moving past so fast, he delivers daily/not slow words but quick, predicated word clusters'. That fascination with the natural world, with the restless intelligence in things, plays through her packed, weaving, chiming sentences which are also characterised by an overlay of philosophy, theology and world myth in all of which she is clearly very well-read:

> the spruce
> has no taproot, but to hold on
> spreads its underpinnings thin –
>
> a gathering in one continuous,
> meshing intimacy, the interlace
> of unrelated fibres
> joining hands like last survivors
> who, though not even neighbours
>
> hitherto, know in their predicament
> security at best is shallow.

That phrase 'a gathering into one continuous, meshing intimacy' echoes throughout the book. In another poem a cat's eyes are described as a 'whole green-gold,/outdoor-indoor continuum condensed/ to a reproachful pair of jewels' – ornate but dangerous – and it is because she is so preoccupied with change that she keeps going back to the taproot. Rootedness of plants, places, people is emphasised along with a chilly fear of the infinite spaces. 'Oh we know nothing of the universe we move through', 'There is no safety'. In fact there is something fearful and vulnerable, even rather shrill, in the lissome liveliness of Amy Clampitt. In 'The Reedbeds of the Hackensack' which she describes as 'a last ditch effort to associate the landscape familiarly known as the Jersey Meadows with the tradition of elegiac poetry' she alludes to the Sumerian legend of Marduk, the god who built a reed platform on the surface of the waters and thus created the world – something made but frail, having 'the effect of unquenchable and universal yearning'. For all the brilliance of her metaphorical observations of the natural world, the finest moments in *What the Light Was Like* concern personal loss, home being where that unquenchable and universal yearning starts from. They can be found most movingly in the collection's central sequence 'Voyages: A Homage to John Keats' which, in eight fine poems, explores Keats' growth and suffering in art and body (exemplifying what, in another note, Amy Clampitt calls 'the powerful way in which literature can become a link with time and places and with minds otherwise remote') and in 'Black Buttercups', a poem which shows even more clearly than any in her previous book how much she owes to her admired Elizabeth Bishop:

> I was ten years old.
> Not three miles by the road that ran
> among the farms (still less if
> you could have flown, or, just as unthinkable,
> struck out across country, unimpeded
> by barbed wire or the mire of feedlots)
> the legendary habitat of safety
> lay contained: the memory
> of the seedleaf in the bean, the blind
> hand along the bannister, the virgin sheath
> of having lived nowhere but here. Back there
> in the dining room, last summer's
> nine-year-old sat crying on the window seat
> that looked into the garden, rain
> coursing the pane in streams, the crying
> on the other side and it one element – and sits
> there still, still crying, knowing
> for the first time forever what it was
> to be heartbroken.

Gjertrud Schnackenberg is a younger American poet, of Norwegian descent, whose high reputation invites an enthusiastic welcome for her first collection to be published in Great Britain. Like Amy Clampitt's, Schnackenberg's work is intelligent, subtle, accomplished in its craft, and intensely bright. *The Lamplit Answer* dazzles, but its finest poems are careful, questing explorations, seeking an inner light although generously inclusive of the world outside. The work is musical in many of its references and much of its arrangement, and there's a certain amount of arabesque ingenuity to be applauded or endured depending on one's response to the kind of skill which insists on displaying itself as a salon performance. 'Sonata', for example, is organised in sections according to the form ('Exposition', 'Development' etc.) announcing itself rather too disarmingly about half-way through as the kind of lonely-love poem in which 'Analogies...sort of stack around/My what-is-life-without-you-here idea'. It's a demonstration piece, proclaiming its virtuosity point-blank in line one hundred and forty-nine where it announces with remorseless satisfaction that it has reached 'Line hundred forty-nine'. It is no doubt this aspect of Gjertrud Schnackenberg's poetry which has drawn praise from John Hollander whose own compulsive numbers game, *Powers of Thirteen*, appeared recently. There's something both engaging and resistible about such bravura performance, pages of sportive intimacy leading to a 'Coda' which is so disarmingly throw-away as to seem almost banal:

> But I dislike it too; I too can't bear it;
> I find it undurably conceited,
> Belligerent, high-handed, asinine;
> I too can hardly force myself to read it;
> Come home before I write another line.

This, though, is less than half the story. Gjertrud Schnackenberg has a profound sense of history, and like Chopin, the subject of her collection's first, remarkable poem 'Kremlin of Snow' which reconstructs the composer's first year in Paris from his letters and journals, her performances transcend the applause of an admiring salon and are haunted by an almost translucent spiritual intensity. 'Time, caught in the act of listening outside the walls of music' is how Chopin's great-aunt described a pose of his mother's, and Schnackenberg works this quotation into a poem which moves in on itself to become an intense improvisation on the music of time. For her, the essence of time is dedication to selfless action. 'How perilous is purity of heart' she writes in 'Imaginary Prisons', summoning – though in a book packed with references to philosophy and theology she never mentions him – the ghost of Kierkegaard for whom purity of heart was 'to will one thing'. The protagonists of several of her finest poems are rare individuals who have given the lamplit answer in their singleness of purpose, commitment to a vision, and radiant humility. Their gift, as she conveys it in a verse of haunting repetitions and great *claritas*, is to unite the worlds of human, animal and inanimate nature in an intimation of purpose which seems always on the point of revelation. There is nothing inflated about this, although attempts to describe its effect may seem so. 'The Heavenly Feast', a meditation on the life and death of Simone Weil in simple elegiac quatrains, has a lightness of being which is the movement of the poem itself, dancing to the solemn music of a child's song:

> You finally lacked the strength
> Even to lift your hands:
>
> *Father, I cannot stand*
> *To think of them and eat.*
> *Send it to them, it is theirs.*
> *Send this food for them,*
>
> *For my people still in France.*
> And turned your face away,
> As famished as the grass.
> Only the stones at first

Seem to have a part in this,
And the little height of the grass
As it gains a fraction-inch.
But hidden in the grass

As if the grass itself
Were giving out a cry
I overhear the finch
Begin her native rhyme

And toil to paraphrase
Her version of your words.

Something of the same lucid compassion informs the best of Gjertrud
Schnackenberg's autobiographical writing – those bitter-sweet, gamesome love poems apart – and she closes the volume with a poem 'Supernatural Love' which contains her title phrase and recalls her father whose
memory is another persistent presence in her work:

My father at the dictionary-stand
Touches the page to fully understand
The lamplit answer, tilting in his hand

His slowly scanning magnifying lens,
A blurry, glistening circle he suspends
Above the word 'Carnation'...

The daughter touches her own pages with the same sense of loving and
curious absorption, and an awareness of 'the obligation due to every
thing/That's smaller than the universe.'

A similar obligation and awareness is at the centre of Frances
Horovitz's work too but, whereas Gjertrud Schnackenberg delights in
contrivance and seeks refinement to the pure essence through the perfection of often complex forms, she pares her poems down to a minimum
of words, each weighed for its place in short imagistic poems of even
shorter lines. The effect is one of distillation, a pellucid lyricism of love
and nature, capable of surprising with a sudden stretch of great beauty
but contracting at times into a thinly disguised invitation to spot the haiku:

At night the valley dreamed of snow,
lost Christmas angels with dark-white wings
flailing the hills.
I dreamed a poem, perfect
as the first five-pointed flake,
that melted at dawn:

There's too much of a knowing formula at work in her method of
attempting to make description an active element of the world it describes. Her verbs tend to draw attention to themselves in a way that turns

statement into the captions for arty photographs ('a frail wind hurries the brown leaves', 'black trees/barricade the sky', 'a full moon slices the wood' etc.) so that at any moment animation is frozen in its tracks by the self-consciously poetic. Frances Horovitz's poems hover, shift, alight on a brilliant image, sometimes holding fast and engaging the imagination but often running the risk of evaporating in a mist of sentimental, soft-focus rhetoric ('desire is formless between us/we are enormous as stars').

Her strengths, though, are considerable, and her *Selected Poems*, edited after her tragically early death in 1983 by Roger Garfitt, is an impressive collection. It is perhaps unfortunate that the growth of interest in her work which Garfitt mentions in his editor's note has been nourished by memorial pamphlets and readings, however generous these have undoubtedly been. It does no service to a gift to enshrine it, and there is the danger that a poet whose work combines an attractive, vulnerable delicacy with a considerable mythologising power will herself become a myth – disappearing not into the poems but into the excessive claims made for them by a small circle of admirers. Frances Horovitz is a poet whose art witnesses to an abiding love and courage. It is marked by an intuitive sense of history and pre-history, great openness and generosity to her friends, and a fearful tenderness for her son ('Oh could I believe the living and dead inhabit one house under the sky/and you my child run into your future for ever'), but to suggest as one critic has already done that 'her voice is not that of the "age" but of the earth' is to make the kind of noise that provokes an embarrassing echo.

> A postcard from the mountains.
> 'Love to all', you write,
> disdaining particulars for the general mode.
> You love us all –
> such kindness numbs, appals.
> Where you holiday in packaged, glistening snow
> I would come as fire, as revelation beast,
> and fuse our bones to the unmelting rock.

A poet who can write as directly as this deserves not to be overrated.

In a short prose piece from one of the books now gathered into his *Collected Poems*, Charles Tomlinson writes 'One accords the process its reality, one does not deify it', and this might serve as a definition of his intent and achievement. He is the strict celebrant of process, insisting at all times on accuracy of observation as a moral obligation. Seeing is believing but it is also a discovery of self. '"Who is this?"/ they say, who should have asked/"What does he see?"'. 'What he saw/Discovered what he was' Tomlinson writes of John Constable, and in 'Portrait in Stone' he describes the process of sculpting as an act of synthesis and revelation:

> Face in stone and
> Stone in face:
> Compacted in this still embrace
> Neither displaces either.
>
> The eye that married them,
> Grown wiser with the deed,
> A twofold matrimony thus
> Makes mind and eye unanimous.

Tomlinson is always emphasising the integrity of the individual in the act of perception; the keener the eye, the clearer the spirit. 'What does the man/who sees/trust to/if not the eyes?' he asks in 'A Garland for Thomas Eakins', and in 'Face and Image' he insists

> For, still, we must
> in all the trust of seeing
> trace
> the face in the image, image in the face

'Self is clear/as what we keenest see and hear', and in the later poems particularly Tomlinson's visual concerns are augmented by an attentiveness to sound, a skilful internal rhyming which is related to his vision. As he writes in 'Words for the Madriglist', 'Hear with the eyes as you catch the current of their sounds' and in the close texture of a poem such as 'How it happened' from 'Four Kantian Lyrics' he shows what he means:

> It happened like this: I heard
> from the farm beyond, a grounded
> churn go down. The sound
> chimed for the wedding of the mind
> with what one could not see...

For all his delight in 'the profusion of possibilities', not least in America where the landscapes and 'all the mob of objects' have offered him new worlds for old – Tomlinson remains a rather austere poet. 'Art/Is complete when it is human'. Yes, but to appreciate his work one has to come to terms with a certain 'fecund chill' (the phrase is his, and exact) which lies at the heart of it, and which the strictness of the poems implicitly acknowledges. The human is complete only when his art demands his uninterrupted concentration. All incidentals are mere illustration, and

> Illustration is white wine
> Floating in a saucer of ground glass
> On a pedestal of cut glass:
>
> A static instance, therefore untrue.

Even if his poems are rather cold in their fluency, Tomlinson is never less than true to their imperatives. 'Look. Listen.' they command. He does, and we do.

Few poets could be less austere than Paul Durcan or more helplessly human. His art is turbulent, entirely open to accident, muddle and sheer bloody absurdity, and in his new collection *The Berlin Wall Café* he is by turns banal, heartbreaking, zany and compulsively readable. A kind of visionary troubador with his feet and show very firmly on the road, in the first part of the book he entertains with a stand-up comedy of scurrilous anecdotes, bizarre fantasies, and cod news reports, many of them aimed at targets of political and religious repression. 'Archbishop of Dublin to film Romeo and Juliet' is typical in its mixture of surreal invention and contemptuous relish:

> The Archbishop of Dublin,
> Inspired by the example of Saint Samuel Beckett
> –We were told–
> Will isolate Romeo and Juliet
> In separate refrigerators:
> Romeo in a refrigerator in Rome,
> And Juliet in a refrigerator in Armagh;
> From which they will commune
> By telephone. At the climax – of the film –
> Intercourse will take place by television link,
> Courtesy of Eurovision...

However, it's in the second part of *The Berlin Wall Café* that we find Durcan's real achievement. This is a celebration of domestic life occasioned by the end of his marriage. In a sequence of poems, most of them addressed to his ex-wife Nessa, he explores in retrospect his 'addiction to romantic love' which in the demands it made of their relationship has led Nessa to 'seek, instead, the herbal remedy of a sane affection'. The poems are full of grief and grim humour without reproach or self-pity. They often glance back at the institutionalised repression which gave rise to the satire in the book's first half, and set against it the liberation of an erotic love which Durcan now invests with the full weight of personal loss:

> Standing up naked on the kitchen floor,
> In the smog-filtered moonlight,
> You placed your hand on my little folly, murmuring:
> I have come to iron you, Sir Board.
> Far from the tyrant liberties of Dublin, Ireland,
> Where the comedy of freedom was by law forbidden
> And truth, since the freedom of the state, gone underground.
> When you had finished ironing me
> I felt like hot silk queueing up to be bathed

> Under a waterfall in Samarkand
> Or a mountain stream in Enniskerry.

It is characteristic of Durcan that he manages to achieve solemnity, tenderness, wit and tongue-in-cheek mock-rhetoric in one short sequence like this. In fact, the poems' effect is gained from an accumulation of such sequences, one of the finest of which is a chaotic, loving description of 'the marine insect life of the family psyche':

> A home of your own – or a sea of your own –
> In which climbing the walls is as natural
> As making love on the stairs;
> In which when the telephone rings
> Husband and wife are metamorphosed into smiling
> accomplices,
> Both declining to answer it;
> Initiating, instead, a yet more subversive kiss
> –A kiss they have perhaps never attempted before –
> And might never have dreamed of attempting
> Were it not for the telephone belling.
> Through the bannisters or along the bannister rails
> The pyjama-clad children solemnly watching
> Their parents at play, jump up and down in support,
> Race back to bed, gesticulating wordlessly:
> The most subversive unit in society is the human family.

Anyone unfamiliar with Durcan's poetry and who reads *The Berlin Wall Café* will want more. It can be found in *The Selected Paul Durcan* edited by Edna Longley or in the excellent anthology *Poets of Munster* edited by Sean Dunne who rightly calls Durcan 'one of the most distinctive voices in recent Irish poetry'.

Hugo Williams' new collection *Writing Home* is another, though very different and far more elegant, celebration of family life – at the centre of which is the poet's relationship with his father. The correspondence is made up of poems which become letters posted from the past by Williams senior – a flamboyant, debonair actor,– and addressed to it by his son who recalls his life at prep school (where he was always wanting 'to do nothing urgently') and an adolescent which seemed a perpetual putting on of style: 'Clothes were a kind of wit. You either/carried them off or you looked ridiculous':

> My jeans I wanted taken in and flared.
> I was very keen on suede.
> 'You should be with someone a full minute
> before you realise they're well-dressed,'
> said my father. I imagined it dawning on people
> in sixty seconds flat

that I was his equal at last.
'Suppose you realise before that?' I asked'
wriggling my toes in my chisel-toed chukka boots.
'Probably queer,' said my father.

Posturing and badinage, underscored by affection and a mutual delight in discreet outrage, characterise the relationship between father and son. The former's letters home, in the sequence 'An Actor's War', are full of fusty Thespian mannerisms – a local pub is remembered as 'the very Elysium of Alcohol' – but speak for themselves and in the context of the whole book are not mocked. As the young Hugo Williams grows in confidence, his father, having returned from the war and failed to pick up his career is wounded by the peace. Out of work at fifty and hardly able to get up in the morning, he becomes a droll and sadly philosophic veteran with 'cigarette burns/like bullet holes in his pyjamas', but in his prime he was the same age as his son is now at the time of recollection and writing. This gives the collection its particular poignancy. *Writing Home* is a portrait of the Actor as Aging Dog, and of the Poet as Young Pup, but even more than that it is about that trick of time which brings them both together as contemporaries on the same stage until the regular programme has to be resumed:

> Now that he has walked out again
> Leaving me no wiser,
> Now that I'm sitting here like an actor
> Waiting to go on,
> I wish I could see again
> That rude, forgiving man from World War II
> And hear him goading me.
> Dawdling in peacetime,
> Not having to fight in my lifetime, left alone
> To write poetry on the dole and be happy,
> I'm given to wondering
> What manner of man I might be.

Postscript

I have been reading *Randall Jarrell's Letters* while putting this piece together (as he would have said). They are full of brilliance, fierce competitiveness, and not a little back-biting. For much of his career, despite his enthusiasm for good new poets, he was obsessively jealous of his, and other poets' ranking. He was a master of the put-down, not least of critics, and given to a childlike one-upmanship boasting – as amusing to observe as it was no doubt exasperating to live with. Like his even more competitive friend John Berryman he spent much of his career teaching in Universities, and as a feted super-achiever he loved being top of the class even while relaxing: 'I've just taken a Rorschach test for Eileen

Berryman – I am about the twentieth poet she's done. It took three hours; apparently I see five or six times as many things as most of the others.' Only in his last months, and after he had come out of a severe depression, did he seem to begin to question the whole break-neck literary ball-game –'as if', comments his widow who has admirably edited these letters into a Life, 'his recent misery had taught him at last that who ranked with whom was truly on the surface of art and that...the surface "doesn't matter compared to our real life and real self"'.

I have had to select the books reviewed in this piece from over forty titles, and many reputations which called for attention have been passed over. One poet, though, I am determined to fit in. He is R.L. Barth whose pamphlet *Forced-Marching to the Styx* is a small collection of outstandingly accomplished poems written out of his experience in the US Marine Corps (1966-9) and as a long-range reconnaissance leader in Vietnam. They are the response of a keen, formal mind to combat and recall the very best of Louis Simpson's and Randall Jarrell's poems of first-hand war experience.

> There are no young men:
> they are hiding, Viet Cong, or dead.
> Only the old folk, children
> and empty-breasted
>
> mothers still remain,
> survivors among all the wreckage.
> Are they trying to retain
> some hold? or to edge
>
> from a commitment,
> patiently waiting out their desire?
> I don't know. Once arrogant,
> bringing aid, the fire
>
> of napalm, and lead,
> I become one of their witnesses
> to history: this seedbed,
> with its crevices
>
> sluicing through earth's crust;
> this seedbed, like a dry pod shaken
> over a dead land, like lust
> without a woman.

12
Plain Truths and Home Cooking
March 1987

Douglas Dunn: *Selected Poems 1964-1983* (Faber & Faber)
Ted Hughes: *Flowers and Insects* (Faber & Faber)
Paul Muldoon: *Selected Poems 1968-1983* (Faber & Faber)
James Simmons: *Poems 1956-1986* (Bloodaxe Books)
Andrew Waterman: *Selected Poems* (Carcanet)
David Sutton: *Flints* (Peterloo Poets)
Anna Adams: *Trees in Sheep Country* (Peterloo Poets)
Frank Redpath: *To the Village* (Sonus Press)
Douglas Houston: *With the Offal Eaters* (Bloodaxe Books)
Lawrence Sail: *Devotions* (Secker & Warburg)
Fleur Adcock: *The Incident Book* (Oxford University Press)
Peter Scupham: *Out Late* (Oxford University Press)
Clive James: *Other Passports – Poems 1958-1985* (Jonathan Cape)
Charles Johnston: *Selected Poems 2, or Writers on the Edge* (Bodley
Head)
R.S. Thomas: *Experimenting with an Amen* (Macmillan)
Jack Clemo: *A Different Drummer* (Tabb House)
Kathleen Jamie and Andrew Greig: *A Flame in your Heart* (Bloodaxe
Books)
John Alexander et al. (eds): *Numbers 1*

SOME YEARS AGO in an interview, Douglas Dunn, whose *Selected Poems* has just appeared, made the following observation about Ted Hughes who has recently published another sumptuous little volume with full-colour illustrations by Leonard Baskin:

> I think Ted Hughes is probably a traditional English nature poet in his heart, but because of contemporary humbug, as well as the humiliations and upheavals of the twentieth century, and the distortions upon the imagination which they've produced – the affront of recent history – he's been deflected away from attention to nature and creatures, which I think is his love, in order to orchestrate feelings within a kind of Lawrentian ideology: it shouldn't really be necessary.

Will the real traditional English nature poet please stand up. There have been so many, attentive to the surface of the seasons, to social change from common and cottage to municipal gardens, and to the still sad music of humanity; not to speak of the moralists of *hortus inclusus* and the celebrants of the force through the green fuse. Ted Hughes, for all the deflection Dunn rightly points out, has always returned his attention to nature. Indeed, in even his most appalling mutations there have been moments of exquisite, exact transcription. It's not so much in his heart that he's a nature poet as in his nervous system, and in *Flowers and Insects* (some Birds and a pair of Spiders) he's as alert and responsively startled as he has ever been. With him, contemplation is quickly transformed into reciprocal animation. The flower of a cyclamen floats free of its neatly earthed, domestic containment in a bowl and becomes 'the lambent, electric shock-waves/Of our simply, quietly gazing at it'. Hughes is the conductor of shock-waves. He's also a micro-biologist with a fine ear. In 'Sketch of a Goddess', burying its face in an iris, in 'the very beard of her ovaries', an overpowered bee 'deafens itself/In a dreadful belly-cry – just out of human hearing'. Watching a pair of spiders through a magnifying glass, he focusses on the female's

>   gentle
> Sinister dance. All legs clinging

> Except for those leading two, which tapped on the web,
> Trembling it, I thought, like a fly, to attract
> The immobile, upside-down male, near the frame,
> Only an inch from her. He moved away,
> Turning ready to flee, I guessed. Maybe
> Fearful of her intentions and appetites:
> Doubting. But her power, focussing,
> Making no error after the millions of years
> Perfecting this art, turned him round
> At a distance of two inches, and hung him
> Upside down, head under, belly towards her.

One reads on, hooked by an evolutionary thriller – 'So, I imagined, here is the famous murder' – or moves out of the *huis clos* to sweeping spaces where a tern is 'swimming in the wind' appropriating all languages to become sheer articulate motion.

> He hangs,
> A blown tatter, a precarious word
> In the mouth of ocean pronouncements.
> His meaning has no margin. He shudders
> To the tips of his tail-tines.
>
> Momentarily, his lit scrap is a shriek.

For all his imaginative energy and affirmation, Hughes's universe is full of shrieks which cannot, as Dunn indicates, be dissociated from those 'distortions upon the imagination' produced by the 'humiliations and upheavals of the twentieth century'. Dunn's own work is more thoroughly civic, though certainly not narrowly parochial. As he acknowledges in that same interview, he has always thrived on melancholy, but this has been far from disabling. Where Hughes, one feels, would view melancholy as an indulgence, for Dunn it is a vital source. Not an English, or even a British, melancholy ('Britain bores me') but a European one which can be heard everywhere in his cadences. He favours the kind of surrealist (and symbolist) method which reinforces social observation and insight, which – as he puts it – 'carries with it a whole world of comment and narrative'. It allows a generous accumulation of scenic dissolves within solidly constructed stanzas. In his early 'Terry Street' poems it carried the effect well beyond that of mere disenchanted documentation:

> They are a part of the silence of places,
> The people who live here, working, falling asleep,
> In a place removed one style in time outwith
> The trend of places. They are like a lost tribe.
> Dogs bark when strangers come, with rent books, or
> free gifts.

The cadence of Mallarmé's 'l'adieu supreme des mouchoirs' can be heard in 'the silence of places'. And Dunn's later work, however closely personal its source, finds the individual voice always committed to community in its widest, aspirational sense. The close of 'An Address on the Destitution of Scotland' shows how effectively he manages a rhetoric which verges on the lofty but does not betray the needs of its subject:

> Share with me, then, the sad glugs in your bottles;
> Throw a stolen spud for me on the side-embers.
> Allow me to pull up a brick, and to sit beside you
> In this nocturne of modernity, to speak of the dead,
> Of the creatures loping from their dens of extinction.
> Who are you waiting for? The stern mountain-preacher
> In his coat of biblical night? I have seen him.
> He sleeps in a kiln, out of the way of dragoons;
> And I met a subversive optimist, at Sanquhar.
> Permit me, then, to join your circle around your fire
> In this midden of warm faces and freezing backs.
> Sing me your songs in the speech of timber and horse.

In Hughes and Dunn we have established masters of *cosmos* and *civitas*. Paul Muldoon is an emergent master of elegant vanishing tricks. His curiously evasive, even sometimes wilfully oblique poems are, at the same time, enticing, sensuous and charged with a kind of compulsive secrecy always just on the verge of revelation. A characteristic Muldoon lyric is as cryptic as it is intimate. It invites the reader's complicity like a wishbone, provoking a nimbus of shared apprehensions and desires but making an enigma of its own designs as if it were bad luck to give them away. The title poem of Muldoon's third collection *Why Brownlee Left* is a clear example of his procedure:

> Why Brownlee left, and where he went,
> Is a mystery even now.
> For if a man should have been content
> It was him; two acres of barley,
> One of potatoes, four bullocks,
> A milker, a slated farmhouse.
> He was last seen going out to plough
> On a March morning, bright and early.
>
> By noon Brownlee was famous;
> They had found all abandoned, with
> The last rig unbroken, his pair of black
> Horses, like man and wife,
> Shifting their weight from foot to
> Foot, and gazing into the future.

That gaze into the future, both intense and listless, is brilliantly contrived to absorb the whole poem into the source of its mystery. The effect is not unlike encountering a grounded Marie Celeste – all the properties are still there, the detailed images of a purpose, but the poet has absconded along with Brownlee from the poem in which they met. The reader is just too late to catch them, and is left to puzzle over the unanswerable question.

Muldoon is a serious writer who plays at being one step ahead. His subjects touch on important issues of history, sectarian politics, identity and faith, but for much of the time he is a poetic secret agent who writes with invisible ink. Even in his more expansive, hallucinatory narratives, 'Immram' and 'The More a Man Has the More a Man Wants', length only compounds the mystery. It simply takes longer to wake from the dream – tight-packed stanzas of libidinous fantasy, surreal juxtapositions and break-neck scene changes – and realise that it *was* a dream. Where responsibilities begin is another matter, and it is hard to avoid the impression that Muldoon sometimes indulges in abuse of the allusive. He writes with the sort of nonchalant authority which expects you to take your own bafflement on trust, although when he does attempt direct transcriptions of personal experience he shapes anecdote into emblem with memorable results:

> Uncle Pat was telling us how the B-Specials
> had stopped him one night somewhere near Ballygawley
> and smashed his bicycle
>
> and made him sing the Sash and curse the Pope of Rome.
> They held a pistol so hard against his forehead
> there was still the mark of an O when he got home.

Muldoon's fellow Irishman, James Simmons, is a very different kind of poet. The troubadour of the Heaney generation, his poems are robust, candid, vulnerable, by turns tender and aggressive. They chronicle his life, his energy – on a steady back burner even when he is at his most contemplative – and his priciples in the face of domestic trouble. 'Responsibility must be particular,/not to every creature under the sun,/not universal love, but cleaving to one.' So he writes in 'On Circe's Island', celebrating 'this stunning stranger' who 'kept me from my own' in the same breath as 'In guilt I remembered my own wife and my son'. His humane, moral but never judgemental verse thrives on the conflict of emotions, guilty recognition and passionate reconciliation – 'I sing of natural forces,/marriages, divorces', of being 'ruefully invigorated,/at home at sea', and when he addresses himself directly to the suffering of his community the awareness that responsibility must be particular results in some remarkable poems which fuse the domestic with a fearful sense that a world elsewhere is on the doorstep:

> That day there flew and fell
> from astonished victims eyebrow, bone and entrail,
> like stars in the sky, like snowflakes, like nuts in May,
> like a meadow of daisies, like butts from an ashtray.
>
> Familiar things, you might brush against or tread
> upon in the daily round, were glistening red
> with slaughter the hero caused, though he had gone.
> By proxy his bomb exploded, his valour shone.

The only compromise Simmons is prepared to understand is the one he acknowledges in a fine poem 'Didn't He Ramble' dedicated to his friend and fellow jazz fan, Michael Longley:

> Jazz is a compromise:
> you take the first tune in your head and play
> until it's saying what you want to say.
> 'I ain't got no diplomas,' said Satchmo,
> 'I look into my heart and blow.'

Simmons himself has got diplomas – he's a university lecturer and improvises inventively on literary themes as in a series of 'King Lear' poems – but it's looking into his own heart and blowing straight out that he does best, and I'm sure he must be aware that Satchmo, for all his lack of academic learning, was paraphrasing the last line of the first sonnet of Philip Sidney's *Astrophel and Stella*.

Andrew Waterman is another university lecturer – from the same campus, in fact (the New University of Ulster in Coleraine), and he shares with Simmons an addiction to that larger campus, the University of Life. He, too, makes a virtue of being at home at sea, of running 'into Life's left-hook/absurdly often'. His earlier work is set in the country of his childhood and youth, and it finds him 'journeying often across the heart of England', celebrating his love of Edward Thomas (often in that poet's cadences) with a strong sense of his own secret sharer, of that 'other' which Thomas has bequeathed to him. Spiritual exile has always been his theme, an ambivalent attitude towards the suburban Eden with its 'water-sprinklers rotating for ever' (a recurring image), his origins, and a succession of bedsits:

> The massive pink door shuddered to let me in.
> And I was led up past landing kitchenettes,
> and round and up to a slope-roofed room, low bed,
> bed-table, tilting wardrobe, cheap bowl fire.
> 'That's it, and there's the meter.' Then,
> 'You're young,' he added' 'where is your home?'
> 'Home?' I replied. 'Home is where I find myself.'

In John Clare's affecting phrase, Waterman finds himself 'homeless at home' wherever home is for him, and he compensates with a fierce, necessary emphasis on friendship, loyalty and betrayal. In later poems which allude to marriage, a court case, custody, and are almost over-whelmingly full of a possessive tenderness for his young son (to whom the book is dedicated), the tone is sometimes grotesquely bitter ('that drivelling judge') but mainly stoical – 'You're what you make, this mess no paradise'. Personal detail moves in and out of generalised statement about the human condition, and the verse – accomplished to a high pitch of virtuosity – is, by turns, poignant and grandiose. The loss of 'family perspectives' tends to get submerged by forceful but attenuated polemic as if the pain (in Simmons's phrase) of 'clinging to one' were seeking refuge in statements about the universal:

> Art seeks to forge atoning sense
> and shapeliness from violence
> and hurt we may be powerless
> in life to help. These lines confess
> sheer impotence, as they complete
> their formal pattern, to defeat
> or solace discord which has ripped
> you from your home and father, stripped
> away known places, play and friends;
> yet while it cannot make amends
> for wrong endured, the poem sustains
> truths life would void; by taking pains
> composes our essential form,
> inviolable through the storm.

Andrew Waterman is an uneven but highly intelligent poet for whom the troubles are, in every sense, on the doorstep, and his *Selected Poems* is a strong volume.

Two attractive new collections from Peterloo Poets are David Sutton's *Flints* and *Trees in Sheep Country* by Anna Adams. Their virtues are those of scrupulous local attentiveness, a close reading of what David Sutton calls the 'domestic unfamiliar text'. In 'Postcard from Pembrokeshire' he contrasts himself with 'My friends,who go so lightly here and there,/...and never care/That none of it is yours:

> I know you'd laugh to see me here perplexed
> Still after two weeks by the rocks and seas
> Of one domestic unfamiliar text,
> Missing my rooted etymologies
> Of Chiltern beech. Yet there's no other way
> For us, the slow ones, who would understand
> The language of the summer clouds that lay
> Their shivering allusions on the land.

We ignore, or lose patience with, the slow ones at our peril. Their poems are unspectacular, modest and traditional in form. They sit four-square on the page, making pleasant conversation, rooted in reassuring common sense, often proverbially wise but lighting up again and again with vivid felicities of observation and phrasing which give the lie to readers who may feel they have heard it all before. These poems are, generically, the well-weathered English stock, feet on the ground and head in the shivering allusions of those summer clouds. The risks they take are minimal, but their deceptive steadiness is so full of the incidental delights of recognition that they often achieve considerably more than the awful daring of those moments of surrender which bring in the diminishing returns of febrile excitement.

David Sutton unapologetically offers 'Small Incident in Library', 'Another Small Incident' etc., but small is far from minimal. In 'Blooding', for example, he describes an incident on a car journey with his children where he comes across a hare

> back legs
> Smashed quite flat: a stuck moth, fluttering,
> And yet not dead, but panicking wild-eyed,
> Arching in the dazzle, pushing up
> On boxer's shoulders, falling, pushing up.
> No one spoke. My children looked and waited.
> Me? What competence had I in death?
> I started off to let the car roll forward,
> All set to do it in the modern way,
> A filthy casual obliteration,
> And could not: took a spanner and knelt down
> Saying words. The great eyes rolled, went quiet.
> I lifted it, the body cold as dew
> Before I even laid it in the bracken.
> No more singing. At the door my wife
> Met us: 'What on earth...' My little one:
> 'Daddy couldn't help it', ran upstairs.

This is quietly moving and unobtrusively skilful. 'My little one', so nearly a sentimentality, avoids being so by gathering strength from its association with the small death which has preceded it. Try placing the emphasis. 'My' or 'little'? That's the genuine, occasional question raised by a real, if otherwise unexceptional, poem.

Anna Adams's particular gift is for empathy with the slow unfolding of organic growth. Favouring tight forms, she relishes the opportunity they offer for manipulation and disclosure. In 'Flowering Berberis and Bees' an intricate variation on the pattern of the villanelle exactly matches her subject:

I am a world, the only world I know,
though humming outer-space-ships visit me
with cryptic messages. They come and go

tickling suggestively. Like yellow snow
my loosened garments fall continuously
from canopy to earth. From space I know

I grope towards blue summer air; I grow
while tenor angels sing of mystery
and probe my roses as they come and go.

If there are other trees that blossom so,
whose sulphur buds unfold successively,
then others know the ecstasy I know.

She can be prosaically sententious when she gets hold of an idea and
works it out through a succession of neat, creative-writing-course metaphors ('A garden is a book whose daily leaves,/turned over by the sun,
relate the year') but when she trusts to her delight in language and the
possibilities of received form she is very good.

More quirkily adventurous but equally firm on the ground are the
poems of Frank Redpath and Douglas Houston. Redpath, whose small
volume *To the Village* deserves more attention than it appears to be
receiving despite an enthusiastic introduction by Douglas Dunn, was born
in Hull where he has spent most of his life, and like the poet who put Hull
on the map he is capable of distilling a lyricism from the compassionate
shrug – 'A moral lesson here? A sign?//Perhaps not –'

But looking up I see the birds:
Grey trills and ornaments along a crest.
They share what he endures: a quite absurd
Hold on the thin edge of the everyday...
And dangerous too, for when they fly how quick
They're hurled – and he; no matter how you look
You'll get a wink, no more, before they're gone...

In 'There' (a nice counterpart, and obvious allusion, to Larkin's 'Here')
Redpath looks closely, with a keen mass-observer's eye, at an unexceptional landscape, carefully accumulating 'small signs to say you're
there':

Evidence
Of other people's lives, they warm
And quicken, stave off death and satisfy.

In 'Seen from the Train' a rain-rinsed vista achieves 'a supernatural
ordinariness', a kind of heightened reality which approaches the
visionary, and there are several moments of this order in Redpath's

enjoyable collection.

For Douglas Houston, a young poet now living in Hull, ordinariness is touched by the surreal rather than the supernatural. It is also infiltrated by a strong individual sense of politics and recent history. One poem in his first collection, *With the Offal Eaters*, carries an epigraph from Auden – 'Another time has other lives to live' – but there is, for Houston as for Auden, no time like the present for locating and focussing global anxieties:

> The glory of the world is passing already
> With white blossoms dropping from the may's laden boughs.
> The heels of the man with shattered kneecaps crush them
> To a moist translucency. Dead prisoners gather
> On the green outside the Methodist Hall to hear
> A moving address on human rights delivered
> By a visiting Belgian milkman, who breaks down
> When whispers inform him of a lost football match.
> People who happened to be listening to radios
> Maintained their politic silence while descending
> To shelters now crowded and firmly closed.

Perhaps Houston's most immediately approachable poems are his least original. He has learnt much about writing of family loyalties and heredity from Tony Harrison who might almost have ghost-written 'Dead Man's Shoes':

> I'm happy in my socks, but, *de rigeur,*
> A man needs shoes to strut his stuff today.
> I'm keeping those calf numbers to ensure,
> If necessary, my feet will look O.K.

but the best work in *With the Offal Eaters* is distinctive, and Houston is without doubt a poet to watch.

The mediaeval illuminator of manuscripts who explores, justifies and acknowledges the precious limitations of his craft in 'Apologia' from Lawrence Sail's new collection, *Devotions*, is, at the same time, a spokesman for this poet's own scrupulous self-awareness:

> I do not pretend, as the truly ruthless do,
> That any pain can be contracted to fit
> The fluency of words or shining paint –
> Or that the world's my cloister. All my art,
> Beneath rich foliage, curling metaphor,
> Commutes between God's world and the trappist heart.

Sail could not be truly ruthless if he tried, nor even pretend to the kind of violence which would seize on experience and bundle it into the confessional. Like the 'God in white gloves', in his poem 'Snooker

Players', who tenderly 'retrieves each fallen planet with love' and replaces it on the baize, he attempts to assert symmetry and balance against all the odds. He knows well enough that just beyond the brightly-lit table 'in the framing/Darkness, doubt dogs the game'. The best poems in *Devotions* are marked by an anxious tenderness for his children, and an acute sense of loss, as in 'Hallowe'en Lantern':

> Crackling waxily, profane,
> Neckless, a drunken dome,
> It stood between curtain and pane
> Facing the frost or the dark rain
> Through which I shivered home.
>
> My mind's a blank. What went on
> Behind that grin, in those banging
> Rooms which belong to no one?
> My children will go, my wife has gone –
> In the darkness I see a face, hanging.

Paradoxically that desolate, declarative sentence, 'My mind's a blank', in so unexpectedly recalling Robert Lowell's 'My mind's not right' from 'Skunk Hour' serves to emphasise the compelling orderliness of Sail's art. Lowell's statement ends a stanza *in extremis* whereas Sail's begins one, moving neatly into the balance of the closing lines. There is no exhileration, nothing ruthless, only a quiet honesty, undemonstrative but affecting. When Sail, as he does on occasion, puts his quick mind through its paces merely for the sake of exercise, the balance does tend to become balancing tricks and produce elegant poems which – in Wallace Stevens's telling phrase – are too much themselves, but there are fewer of these than in his previous volumes, and *Devotions* is an excellent collection by a fine and undervalued poet.

As I was reading Lawrence Sail I found myself recalling a line from Fleur Adcock's 'An Illustration to Dante' in which, countering Ruskin's comment that Rossetti 'didn't know how to do hail', she observes 'Well, he could do tenderness'. Well, so can she, though with a sharp, disenchanted sense of reality underscoring it. Her latest collection, *The Incident Book*, contains some extraordinary chilling moments which could themsleves be Dante-esque illustrations though not by Rossetti:

> Here is a hole full of men shouting
> 'I don't love you. I loved you once
> but I don't now. I went off you,
> or I was frightened, or my wife was pregnant,
> or I found I preferred men instead.'

Her recollections of childhood are witty and poignant, a knee-high view of adult behaviour or, as in the excellent 'The High Tree', that secretive,

omniscient over-view of the shy child on the verge of discovering her
identity:

> It was a refuge. When you sat in its branches
> threatening strangers passed you by.
>
> Nothing could find you. Even friendly people,
> if you invited them to try,
>
> couldn't climb very far. It made them dizzy:
> they'd shiver and shut their eyes and cry,
>
> and you'd have to guide them down again, backwards,
> wishing they hadn't climbed so high.

The Incident Book also contains a set of poems, 'Thatcherland', which
observes a Britain 'going anonymous' with wry accuracy and a valedictory
irony, a marvellous poem about love in middle-age ('Kissing') and, finest
of all, 'The Keepsake', an elegiac, anecdotal meditation in memory of her
friend Pete Laver.

Peter Scupham's has always been a poetry of tutelar deities, and at
the centre of his new book, *Out Late*, there is a substantial set of variations
on 'A Midsummer Night's Dream'. It is ritualistic, ornamental, haunted
by disembodied voices and spectral groupings around the maypole and
the Great Oak. The whole ambitious sequence is a synthesis of Scupham's
affiliations and concerns. Herne the Hunter presides over a box of
delights which is also a Pandora's Box releasing the world's ills in our
midst. It manages to be both antiquarian and contemporary. Sustained
meditations alternate with shorter lyrics, and Scupham's inclusive,
layered imagination shifts continually between an old England of custom
and ceremony and the terrors of a world alienated from nature and
nurture, a world with its 'ribboned maypole blunted into missile' and 'an
acid rain/Eating the heart out of the sluggish lake'. Like Auden, with
whose 'The Sea and the Mirror' his Dream invites comparison, Scupham
understands what it means to be 'lost in a haunted wood', but in a key
poem (dedicated to Geoffrey Grigson) which opens the volume he points
to those 'signs and seals' which speak 'with riddling tongue/Of what we
were, and are' and his own poems amount to talismans of faith and doubt,
carefully wrought, polished and arranged into a collection which we are
the better for sharing with him. Many of his finest poems, such as 'A
House of Geraniums' grow out of meditations upon those 'wraiths who
keep their patience.../Who if we find them voices, only say:/'We were; you
are. Why should you ask for more?':

> The dead are anything that sighs in millions:
> The tossing flower-heads of Queen Anne's Lace,

Moths trawling the dark, those waifs of snow
Flocked against glass, formations of the night

Which grows towards us: ghosts talking of ghosts,
Compounded of old walls, old bones, old stories,
Watching an inch of sun slip to the West,
Playing the revenant to this house and garden

Sleepy with cats down a remembered lane
Where unaccustomed eyes look cleanly through us;
Pity our grey hair, unfamiliar pauses.
Our tongues which trip so lightly over our graves.

When wondering whether he should ask for more or not, Peter Scupham is at his most accomplished and memorable. In a lighter vein he writes excellent parodies. Clive James, whose vein is often lighter, though his concerns weigh in on the heavy side, does not. His real gift is for the lampoon. There's a merciless charm about his copious productivity. *Other Passports* is an overweight juggernaut of a book, great fun to dip into but monotonously smart when read at length. James is a champ for whom every line must pack a punch. His range of interests and learning is formidable, and he demonstrates his mastery of demanding verse forms, often pointing out that he is doing so. Certainly not one of the slow ones, he's quick to hitch his verse wagons to rising stars and the glitterati dazzle on his pages. Armchair readers who want to know where things are at in the metropolitan scene (and in the great Cosmopolitan Elsewhere) will greatly enjoy being entertained by James if his cast of thousands doesn't crowd them out.

Clive James's knack of being at the point where intelligence and energy coincide has made him a prominent supporter of the poetry of Charles Johnston whose *Selected Poems II* contains his outstanding auto-biographical poem 'In Praise of Gusto'. Johnston, a distinguished administrator who died last April, is perhaps best known for his trans-lation of *Eugene Onegin*, and in 'In Praise of Gusto' the Pushkin stanza alternates with the Spenserian. Throughout the volume, which also con-tains dramatic monologues spoken by classical authors who lived on the edge of times of social upheaval, a worldly scholarship is pressed into civil service. Johnston's free verse is as supple, resonant and finely tuned to the speaking voice as his use of complex forms is authoritatively relaxed. His bequest is

The eclectic taste equipped to find
Delight in movements of the mind,
Yet open to the contribution
Of the external world of sense,
The active verb, the present tense.

Of the many other books that have come my way I'd particularly recommend R.S. Thomas's *Experimenting with an Amen* in which he continues with unflagging dedication to push belief to the edge of doubt and then miraculously retrieve it. Also Jack Clemo's rugged, wrestling *A Different Drummer* in which he engages with the strenuous non-conformist inner life of a number of his spiritual heroes; and an engrossing and very affecting enterprise by the young Scottish poets Kathleen Jamie and Andrew Greig. This is *A Flame in your Heart* which is set in 1940 (twenty-two and eleven years, respectively, before either poet was born) and, through a series of poems which explore the courtship, passionate apprehensions and fate of Ken, a Spitfire pilot, and his girl-friend Katie, recreates the uncertain and therefore intense atmosphere of wartime with uncanny accuracy. This is one of Katie's (Kathleen Jamie's) poems:

If you knew that little force
when I press stamps, then unthinking
watch my letter fall into the box...

That gentle touch
I feel beneath my ears
as you raise my face to yours...

I still kiss you, though I know
that soft pressing of the thumb
is all it takes to kill a man.

Finally, a welcome to the new magazine *Numbers* which includes a selection of R.L. Barth's Vietnam poems which I recommended in my last piece. It also contains work by Seamus Heaney, Thom Gunn and a very good lesser-known American poet Timothy Steele. It's excellent value for money and most attractively produced. The Editorial concludes with the reminder 'Above all, good poetry needs good readers and loyal ones'. Indeed it does.

13

The Imperative of Usefulness

July/August 1987

Bertolt Brecht: *Poems 1913-1956* (Methuen)
William Carlos Williams: *The Collected Poems 1909-1939* (Carcanet)
Laura (Riding) Jackson: *The Poems of Laura Riding* (Carcanet)
Anne Stevenson: *Selected Poems 1956-1986* (Oxford University Press)
P.J. Kavanagh: *Presences – New and Selected Poems* (Chatto &
Windus)
Vernon Scannell: *Funeral Games* (Robson Books)
Roy Fuller: *Consolations* (Secker & Warburg)
Alan Brownjohn: *The Old Flea-Pit* (Hutchinson)
John Loveday: *Particular Sunlights* (Headland Publications)
Daniel Weissbort (ed): *Poetry World No.1.*

SOME POETS RISE to the top of the bowl, magical and wholesome as yeast, and Bertolt Brecht, who died just over twenty years ago, is certainly one of them. 'Grub first, then ethics' he once declared, unarguably voicing the one responsible and realistic priority, but in his own work the two are simultaneous, and the ethical richness of his poetry is what makes its nourishment so variously appealing. 'Why should my name be mentioned?' asks the title of a poem. 'Because I praised the useful/Which in my day was considered base' answers the text. Throughout his writing life, Brecht was committed to *Gebrauchslyrik* – 'of all the works of man I like best/Those which have been used' and 'useful works/*require people*':

> Who gives works duration?
> Those who'll be alive then.
> Whom to choose as builders?
> Those still unborn.
>
> Do not ask what they will be like. But
> Determine it.

Reading him again in the long-awaited and revised paperback edition of *Poems 1913-1956*, first published in 1976 and the combined achievement of thirty four translators, including John Willet (one of the volume's editors) and Michael Hamburger, is to recognise that Brecht's vast output is unified by that germinating core of instruction which is still too often mistaken for mere didacticism. 'The truth is concrete' runs his favourite quotation from Hegel, and his own compassionate, stubborn, contentious imagination is firmly located in modest routine and in a heightened sense of the occasional which measures history in terms of what we do to, and for, each other on a daily basis against a darkening backdrop of discredited ideologies.

With an invigorating mixture of humility and conscience-ridden self-denial, Brecht's poetry is all the time questioning the validity of its own utterance. What are these games, these plots, these rhymes that its perpetrator is up to? A consummate, though often unobtrusive, technician he undoubtedly is, but there are several fascinating stages in his career where he quarrels with his own gifts and in doing so only demonstrates them the more forcefully. 'What kind of times are they, when/A talk about trees is almost a crime/Because it implies silence about so many horrors?' The answer is, surely, the kind of times (then as now) that need Brecht's way of talking about trees. 'Concerning Spring', for example, is no crime. Like all his finest lyrical pieces it is light-years from being the gentle notations of a solitary. It's a firm, responsible and necessary celebration of life vividly at odds with its cadences of loss and deprivation, a lyricism which embodies Brecht's instinctive Marxism, too, in that it seems magnificently communal, collective and inclusive:

> Long before
> We swooped on oil, iron and ammonia
> There was each year
> A time of irresistible violent leafing of trees
> We all remember
> Lengthened days
> Brighter sky
> Change of the air
> The certainly arriving Spring.
> We still read in books
> About this celebrated season
> Yet for a long time now
> Nobody has seen above our cities
> The famous flock of birds
> Spring is noticed, if at all
> By people sitting in railway trains.
> The plains show it
> In its old clarity.
> High above, it is true
> There seem to be storms:
> All they touch now is
> Our aerials.

What shines through *Poems 1913-1956* is that ironic point of light at the tip of his big cigar, to which Brecht drew a nicely self-dramatising attention in 'Of Poor BB' in the middle 1920s and which went on glowing as the night closed in with its long knives and the terrible ascendency of the house-painter. Like Auden's ironic points of light in 'September 1939' – a poem I've always felt owes much to Brecht and belongs in the company of both poets' best – it flashes out 'wherever the just/Exchange their messages'. Whether Brecht is urging actors to visit 'that theatre whose setting is the street' because it is useful, serious, funny and, most of all, dignified, or whether he is contemplating his own survival –

> I know of course: it's simply luck
> That I've survived so many friends. But last
> night in a dream
> I heard those friends say of me: 'Survival of
> the fittest'
> And I hated myself

– he weighs his words exactly in a careful balance between the present and those perspectives of 'distant times' – past and future – which gives him a proper sense of his own vulnerability. They give an edge, too, to a poetry which is always on the move because it dare not stay in one place for too long. In the world as it is there are no consoling absolutes outside the scope of human responsibility. Although many of his transcriptions of the natural world are luminously exact he never forgets for one moment that 'beyond the village the elms still bow their fine branches/Gracefully to the man abusing a child'. That adverb displays all the courtesy of a profound indifference.

By the end of his life Brecht was an experienced exile, schooled in *realpolitik*, and a wily internal emigré. He had become a master of the extended ballad, the orchestrated sequence and the allegorical fable, but many of his finest poems are deceptively short – part of their utility factor – and in his last years he makes memorably plain statements, summations which nevertheless in their blend of conscience, fatalism and hope, their celebration of a fragile provisional security, and their self-admonition, address themselves unequivocally to the future: 'Everything changes. You can make/A fresh start with your final breath'. For Brecht, the observation is an imperative, and of these later poems 'A New House' – from *Poems of Reconstruction* – is outstanding:

> Back in my country after fifteen years of exile
> I have moved into a fine house.
> Here I have hung
> My No masks and picture scroll representing the Doubter.
> Every day, as I drive through the ruins, I am reminded
> Of the privileges to which I owe this house. I hope
> It will not make me patient with the holes
> In which so many thousands huddle. Even now
> On top of the cupboard containing my manuscripts
> My suitcase lies.

The last sentence bears witness to Brecht's central importance. He is among the great poets of the century, in one of his own often-used words 'exemplary', and a warning to us all never to entrust our suitcases to the guardians of any system of belief however attractive their promises or flattering their attention to our immediate needs.

Like Bertolt Brecht, William Carlos Williams is a poet committed to the utility factor. As Marianne Moore wrote in a review of his *Adam and Eve in the City* (recently reprinted in her Complete Prose) 'he is honest, prompt to submit his premise, serious to the point of bitterness, compassionate, ruled by affection and the compulsion to usefulness'. She might just as well have been characterising Brecht, and indeed in his study *The Truth of Poetry* Michael Hamburger makes the comparison direct:

> Only one other twentieth-century poet I can think of, William Carlos Williams, succeeded as well as Brecht in integrating his poetic and social selves to the extent of really overcoming the Romantic-Symbolist dichotomies. Both became masters of the seemingly off-hand, seemingly effortless manner that leaves no gaps between the thing said and the way of saying it, between what the poem enacts and the person who enacts it. Of the two, Williams was by far the more sensuous and visual poet, and he presented 'images' rather than moralities; both poets made a new purity out of the very stuff which most of their predecessor poets had condemned in advance as impure, because it was ordinary and workaday.

Carcanet's handsome new edition of Williams' *Collected Poems 1909-1939* is the first in a two-volume edition of the poetry (excluding *Paterson*) in which the editors reverse the poet's decision to put his work in thematic order, thereby restoring the original order of publication and providing the opportunity for a reassessment. What we find is a poet intent on shedding artifice, and as suspicious as Brecht of any theatre which is not the street. Certainly his earliest work is often romantically arch in its diction (quite a bit of fleeing and pangs) but it is never less than firmly crafted with remarkably little puppy fat on the bones. The celebrated phrase 'No ideas/but in things' is the scope of his ambition writ small just as an intimation of 'the universality of things'

> draws me toward the candy
> with melon flowers that open
>
> about the edge of refuse
> proclaiming without accent
> the quality of the farmer's
>
> shoulders and his daughter's
> accidental skin, so sweet
> with clover and the small
>
> yellow cinquefoil in the
> parched places.

It is that proclamation 'without accent' which becomes the hallmark of Williams' work, a poetry in which the candy, the refuse, the farmer's daughter and the wonderful passing detail of her 'accidental skin' are

noted in a precise and equable synthesis which transcribes the variousness of things with no word wasted. The achieved Williams voice is instant,
astonished, full of a finely tuned amazement.His exclamation marks are
emphatic but never shrill, and there's a generous impersonality about his
inclusive method which amounts to a kind of gracious bowing-out from
the scene of his observation. Sometimes, as in 'The Young Housewife',
he seems almost to be parodying the romantic image of the passing
observer, but whereas, for example, Wordsworth appropriates the song
of his Solitary Reaper, bearing it in his heart with solemn emphasis,
Williams applies a gentle pressure to the accelerator and moves on to the
next street corner and the next poem. The song is the momentum of the
street, and the poet's responsibility is to become a part of it, involved but
invisible. And as for the enigmatic smile at the end, it seems the poem's
own contented purr at Williams' restraint, at his letting a small, un-
repeatable moment have its way:

> At ten A.M. the young housewife
> moves about in negligee behind
> the wooden walls of her husband's house.
> I pass solitary in my car.
>
> Then again she comes to the curb
> to call the ice-man, fish-man, and stands
> shy, uncorseted, tucking in
> stray ends of hair, and I compare her
> to a fallen leaf.
>
> The noiseless wheels of my car
> rush with a crackling sound over
> dried leaves as I bow and pass smiling.

Small wonder that in a heavily adjectival extract by Randall Jarrell,
quoted on the cover of this new edition, the greatest weight is given to
'democratic'. Williams' poetry, like Brecht's, offers a working model of
human life rather than a self-congratulatory reflection. As he writes in
Spring and All

> I suppose Shakespeare's familiar aphorism about holding the mirror up
> to nature has done more harm in stabilizing the copyist tendency of the arts
> among us than –
>
> the mistake in it (though we forget that it is not S. speaking but an
> imaginative character of his) is to have believed that the reflection of nature
> is nature. It is not. It is only a sham nature, a 'lie'
>
> Of course S. is the most conspicuous example desirable of the falseness
> of this very thing.
>
> He holds no mirror up to nature but with his imagination rivals nature's

composition with his own.

He himself become 'nature' – continuing 'its' marvels – if you will

And in the earlier 'The Wanderer: A Rococo Study' this central pre-occupation can be seen developing in the exclamation 'How shall I be a mirror to this modernity?' with the emphasis, again, on being and becoming, on achieving what Michael Hamburger calls the 'seemingly effortless manner that leaves no gaps between the thing said and the way of saying it' which can only be done by smashing the frame of literary tradition and carrying off the glass. It is absorbing to follow this risky and courageous adventure through the pages of *Collected Poems 1919-1939*, to watch a poet attempting to 'become nature', failing when he merely notes down what he sees with a randomness which doesn't cohere, then suddenly discovering in his language the 'bite of the actual' which makes it new. After 1939 Williams started the experiments that led to the longer works and finally to *Paterson*. These experiments, though not their final outcome, will be in the next volume. An event to look forward to. It will continue the marvels.

In 1938, one year before Williams began those experiments, Laura Riding gave up writing poetry altogether, renouncing it with a fervent sternness which – in her various subsequent attempts to explain why she did so – has almost amounted to a denunciation. Apparently she believes that poetry has failed her kind of seriousness and can offer no absolute resolution: 'The universal linguistic solution hangs suspended in poetry, and so long as it does, human beings cannot know what kind of beings they are, cannot speak themselves with whole consciousness of their being speaking beings, and what this lays upon them to require of themselves'. It is as if she were claiming that poetry is a deceptive quest that gets you nowhere fast:

> By crude rotation –
> It might be as a water-wheel
> Is stumbled and the blindfolded ox
> Makes forward freshly with each step
> Upon the close habitual path –
> To my lot fell a blindness
> That was but a blindedness,
> And then an inexpressive heart,
> And next a want I did not know of what
> Through blindness and inexpressiveness
> Of heart.
>
> To my lot fell
> By trust, false signs, fresh starts,
> A slow speed and a heavy reason,

A visibility of blindedness – these thoughts –
And then content, the language of the mind
That knows no way to stop.

It is hard to avoid feeling, when comparing the urgency, animation and subtlety of those lines with the inert strictures of the prose comments that poetry has become the scapegoat for Laura Riding's own intellectual overload, that she gave up poetry as the only way of stopping a take-over by the 'language of the mind' (which must, by definition, be self-generating and endlessly exploratory), and that her subsequent obsession with 'truth-telling' has been the restlessness of a brilliant mind chasing its own tail. Instead of the bite of the actual we get the snap of frustration, a magisterial snap, but one which cannot disguise the source of its discontent in the failure of artistic nerve. Riding's polemical voice is wilfully unattractive, with a kind of MENSA exclusivity. Admirably committed to mind-expansion, believing as she did for a time in the 'implications of a general human potentiality secreted in the poetic demonstration', she nevertheless gives the impression of holding a lofty contempt for mere mortals every time she adds a further layer of explanation to her copious introductions and appendices.

However, this proud emphasis upon failure, upon complex and often unfathomable reasons for dismissing the 'false weight of authority attached to the term "ordinary", in contexts of reference to human behaviour' while it leads one to suspect that she would give little credence to the humane achievements of Brecht and Williams should not go on reflecting on her own poetry. It's high time this fine body of work leapt free of its author's denigration and the paraphernalia of her rhetoric. The best way to approach this new paperback edition of her poems would be to seal off all the surrounding apologia and analysis, and come to it without prejudice or fear of its legendary 'difficulty'. It will charge every reader's imagination with the responsibility of thinking big:

To the microscopy of thinking small
(To have room enough to think at all)
I said, 'Cramped mirror, faithful constriction,
Break, be large as I.'

Then I heard little leaves in my ears rustling
And a little wind like a leaf blowing
My mind into a corner of my mind,
Where wind over empty ground went blowing
And a large dwarf picked and picked up nothing.

Everything comes of nothing and nothing of everything. The more Laura Riding races over the switch-back of her own paradoxes the more engrossing her poetry becomes. She negotiates that 'crossed estate/Where reason's loud with nonsense/And nonsense soft with truth'. It's the condition of her reality and the landmark of her *own* truth. She claims that the American reviewer Schuyler B. Jackson (who later became her husband) let the 'cat of trouble-ahead out of the bag' when he wrote of her that 'language that would seem clear in Shakespeare or Mother Goose may seem obscure in Laura Riding'. In the short term, maybe, but that term has lasted long enough. All serious readers of poetry expect the cat to jump over the moon and are disappointed if it doesn't. The last thing they want is for it to sit on the wall complaining that there never was a moon after all. What Laura Riding's poetry requires is the innocence of a fresh start. Its absolute authenticity will do the rest.

The central section of Anne Stevenson's *Selected Poems 1956-1986* takes up over a third of the book's length. It's an historical narrative in verse letters (and a variety of forms) in which between 1829 and 1972 several generations of an American family write to each other – admonishing, encouraging, advising and reproaching. They win and lose, leave home, marry, divorce, cross borders between the North and South (geographically and temperamentally) negotiate between the Puritan morality with its work-ethic ('Work is next to Godliness; a man should keep books when dealing with the Deity'), the delights of frivolity ('Frivolity is an armor of lace/against the mind's inner vengeance and poisons') and the encroaching dissolution of *Civitas Mundi:*

> 'New England is dissolving like a green chemical.
> Old England bleeds out to meet it in mid-ocean.
> Nowhere is safe.'

This enterprise, *Correspondences*, is an epistolary saga, an oblique and poignant narrative which develops a cumulative force of mood and attitude. It is also, of course, interesting in that the many branches of the Chandler Family, whose genealogy amounts to an intricate fiction, are clearly the stock of Anne Stevenson's imagination. In the first letter of Part One, Adam Chandler, reverend father of all that follows, rebukes his daughter for preferring 'the precarious apartments of the world/to the safer premises of the spirit' and in the last letter of all the poet Kay Boyd – born in 1932, one year before Anne Stevenson herself, – writes back from England to *her* father in America, describing herself as living 'a long way from Eden. The tug back/is allegiance to innocence which is not there'.

In her subsequent collections, considering her own life, her uneasy but determined commitment to putting down roots in England, Anne Stevenson thrives on a creative tension between 'now' and 'then', between the historical past – her New England origins – and a present of 'contemporary voice and dislocation'. Flux and change are stemmed by family love, loyalty to friends and a celebration of seasonal recurrence but an anxious sense of vacancy is never far from the surface. In 'Transparencies' the writer of *Correspondences* sends a letter to her own sons in which a more modern, alienated, self-doubting sententiousness wavers between rejection and continuity – a contempory Eve pained but fascinated by the consequences of her exile:

> This is a letter I'd never write if I could
> send you counsel. Cicero, Polonius – thistles
> preaching their beards to their blown seed. Oh,
> it's your particular selves I need to hold
> to the light as you cross the impossible lens of now
> and now. Solid enough to believe...until
>   the river ripples under your melting faces
>   mouthing at me from its thin windows.

The title of P.J. Kavanagh's New and Selected Poems, *Presences*, comes from one of the small selection of new poems entitled 'Late Acknowledgement':

> We never know whom we shall miss.
> Some deaths leave a gap that heals over
> But others leave presences.

Like Geoffrey Grigson whose gift for precise natural observation was inseparable from his fine sense of mortality, Kavanagh finds his poems are full of ghosts, and several of the most moving of them – such as 'One' and the deeply affecting 'Beyond Decoration' – recall his father, and his first wife who died at a tragically early age. These ghosts are benign, if often desolating, presences constantly alerting Kavanagh to a keen apprehension of loss and transience in the midst of the natural world:

> Why else do they seem to turn to us today?
> For now they know we do not know we relish
> The end of love, evaporation of children,
> While we enjoy them, love our own death even;
>
> That melancholy is our atmosphere. Like autumns
> We watch our own departing...We must like it.

Someone once commented that autumn is the curse of English poetry, but Kavanagh avoids it more often than not. Melancholy is certainly his atmosphere but, as with his admired Edward Thomas for whom 'there must be doubt in heaven to accommodate him', Kavanagh takes to it with vigour, writing at his best with a plain, declarative lyricism which is often very moving indeed.

In 'Satire 1' he writes to his friend Patrick Creagh that 'a poet's a burdensome, touchy thing to be' and there are times when he collapses under the burden into prolixity and a rather rambling sententiousness, but there are poems in *Presences* which go straight to the heart and, in that telling phrase of his, are beyond decoration. Outstanding among these is 'Sometimes', threading its way through a delicate syntax, full of quiet deliberating pauses and coming out exactly right:

> There was one who was perfect, who had
> faults doubtless, but they were for God
> to see, not for us who loved her, though whatever
> I think of her is usually mixed with my
> own falling short. But sometimes I see her
> as she was, nothing to do with me:
> as sometimes a cloud leaves the sun alone
> and every leaf on a tree is a plate for light,
> the tree become solely itself, and stays itself
> though another cloud crosses and it goes dull again,
> its secret kept; puzzled at by the eyes
> of one who wants it always to stay gilded,
> isolated, amazing, resentful of its patience,
> obscuringly angered by what he sometimes sees.

Vernon Scannell is another poet whose autumnal meditations avoid the curse, but then he's always been a contender. Risking the accusation that some of his more fanciful sentiments may sound 'like anthropomorphic gush' (as they occasionally do) he rounds disarmingly on his readers with a firm 'and yet' which closes in on the next line hooking them immediately and carrying on without pause for further doubt.

His new collection, *Funeral Games*, though often dark in tone, is a hugely enjoyable volume, the pleasure lying not so much in any startling originality as in its candid appeal to common experience. Of 'Hands' he writes

> I like to watch them rest on tables, knees,
> Lifting a pint of beer or with deft ease
> Rolling a fag which later burns between
> Dark oaken knuckles which have never been
> Surely as soft and sensitive to pain
> As this pen-pusher's hand I look at now;
> But most of all I like to witness how
> They lift small, tired grandchildren and hold
> Them curled and safe, how gently they enfold
> Their always welcome, always cherished guests,
> Become protecting, gnarled and living nests.

To anyone who claims that this kind of strict, though never constricting, metrical conversation looks easy the answer must be 'You try it'. Scannell is the kind of poet who hits the nail on the head and is never afraid of using phrases like 'hits the nail on the head' though he'd never dream of placing inverted commas round them. Time and again he achieves remarkably exact passages of description. The words themselves may be commonplace but their combinations are often quietly startling – as in those 'dark oaken knuckles' or a camera which is 'black-cowled' as it gives its blessing to an image while at the same time freezing it to death.

A deservedly popular poet, Vernon Scannell exemplifies Robert Frost's dictum that a poem begins in delight and ends in wisdom. In its modest way, too, his work is committed to that idea of usefulness which concerned Brecht. He will go on being read and remembered.

By chance, the title poem of Vernon Scannell's *Funeral Games*, where a widow looks around her husband's favourite room after his death, contains an inventory which provides a convenient link with Roy Fuller's new collection:

> The recorded Brandenburgs, the piano-lid
> Still raised and on the music-rest the Liszt
> Consolation Number Three, the pages cold,
> And, underneath the window, on his desk
> Pencils and speechless sheets of lined A4
> With one apart on which a few words walk...

With very little shift of emphasis, this could be Fuller posthumously casting his ironic eye on his own work-place. Although there is no direct reference to them in the book itself, the opening bars of Liszt's Consolation Number One appear as the design on its cover so that we read the announcement: *Consolations* – Andante con Moto – Roy Fuller. This is Fuller's pace and character exactly. Published to coincide with his seventy-fifth birthday, there is a resourceful liveliness about these meditations on age, accident, apparently random events and the intimations of an inscrutable design. Fuller has grown old with a debonair stoicism, developing a self-deprecating and quizzical persona in his poems which relishes the mock-dismissal or send-up of its own deliberations as 'further triads of essential bosh' even as it raises important questions about human existence. His bosh is certainly of the essence.

As in the poem of that title, his 'Garden Queries' are insistent speculations, and a bird's song (or a composer's attempt to transcribe it) is exemplary. The digitally precise timing with which the poem is set in motion is not, as Fuller would playfully suggest, old age's fussy preoccupation with minutiae. It is part of his imaginative precision in charting the natural processes of recurrence by which, as he approaches the time when he will no longer be able to 'command an action replay of the Spring/And see the detail inattention missed', he has become increasingly absorbed:

9.25: the throstle's resourceful song
Goes on. To whom or what, is the question raised.

Later, the garden's silent in the night,
A crescent moon aloft. And equally

One speculates as to inherent wrong
In the cosmos. When that initial atom blazed

How could the mystery of reflected light
Have been foreseen, after dusk's melody?

If, as he claims, 'lingering unease in moments of unhappiness' is a feature of old age, Fuller's consolation must surely lie in the fine gift he possesses to succeed in what 'James said of the notebook habit: "To catch/and keep something of life..."', and his modest claim to 'try my best with poetry to match/Everyday's marvellous and varied prose' should not lead to an undervaluing of several ambitious forays outside the everyday. One of the most successful of these is the reminiscent monologue of a Shakespearean actor, 'The Marcellus Version', although even here we are referred with humour and a crusty resilience to the perennial question:

'To be or not to be?' Eh? There's the point.
'To die, to sleep, is *that* all?' There it goes.
You get the answer simply by surviving.
There's nothing after death, not even dreams.
But life's worth living. Yes, despite the fact
That wives die far too early or too late;
And rotten luck; and botched ambition.

Alan Brownjohn is adept at producing witty fables of middle-aged anxiety. Twenty years Roy Fuller's junior, he shares that gift for treating personal subject matter with a wry, deceptive detachment, and can distil a considerable lyricism from a mix of memory, desire and social obser-vation. He is at his least convincing when he joins the the tribe of incipient buffers, itemising the symptoms with a familiar, rather predictable pan-ache:

I limp, and ask myself
How much longer has this machine? It prolongs
Its life with meticulous arrangements, hating to leave
A chair not parallel with a table, or find
The Co-op coffee granules on the wrong shelf;
But it grows slower with its diligence.

What gives Brownjohn's work its real strength and character is the manner in which he projects his unease onto the world around him while remaining scrupulously aware of doing so. 'Walking the streets I see too easily/A confluence of the worst in us, beyond/Arranging into calm or tenderness'. Realising that he sees it 'too easily', that he has a weakness for the soft-focus of melancholy effects, he compensates by giving his anxieties the weight of firm detail. Several of the poems in *The Old Flea-Pit* are cinematic dream-fantasies in which he finds himself on a slip road of his imagination. Even an apparently straightforward January walk assumes the rather chilling properties of a location (or dislocation) shot.

> In the salt-marshes, under a near black
> Sky of storm or twilight, the whole day
> Dark on the creeks where the wind drives wavelets back
> Against the filling tide, I have lost my way
>
> On a path leading nowhere, my only guide
> The light half-way up a television mast
> Five miles across the waste; and if I tried,
> I could imagine hearing, under this vast
>
> Raw silence of reeds and waters, the deep drone
> Of generators, gathering up the power
> To send its message out; and, stopped alone
> By this channel's edge, revisit a lost hour
>
> At a restaurant table, in a vanished place
> (An organ chiming in the hushed cave below)
> When three sat smiling in an alcove space
> And saw their futures, thirty years ago...

It is as if Brownjohn had been given an unscripted walk-on part in a movie by a director who seems to be setting him some kind of initiative test to see whether he will be able to find a route towards the meaning of his own life – which is, of course, what so many of Brownjohn's scenarios are about. The director is his alter-ego, his secret sharer, and Brownjohn the bit-part actor is perpetually auditioning in the hope of landing the main role and achieving an over-view of the whole script. For him the 'Cure' (one of his titles) would be to become 'free of his own mists', and in another dream-fantasy he considers how, having one day gone off leaving 'the rest of you behind with your confusion', he might

> one unexpected day, sail back
> With another persona, yes, like someone
> Else altogether, and nothing like myself,
> As an unknown *deus ex machina*, making
> Everyone stop and listen and behave
> Striking clarity into your souls at last, at last!
> – And then pull off my mask and sing it out:
> *It was me! It was me! This is what I had to do!*

It is that snap into clear focus, that sudden clarity, which the drift of Brownjohn's poetry hankers after, but Brownjohn's own talent remains one for exploring the doubts rather than finding the answers.

With John Loveday's attractively produced *Particular Sunlights* there's a return to a firm sense of location which is confident but seldom taken for granted. Loveday's is an affectionate, gently reverential poetry full of ancestral voices, and the poems themselves are carefully crafted objects – many of them small, neatly turned, and with the scent of the woodshed still on them. Not all of them succeed in going beyond the mere accuracy of their particulars, but the best of them are little miniatures of revelation. 'Noah's Flood', for example, could be the vision of Stanley Spencer's Cookham transferred to the Norfolk of Loveday's childhood:

> 'It rained for forty days and nights'...and so
> Out there beyond the high window
> It did, in our imaginations, grey-
> Brown water rising till the village lay
> Submerged in Noah's Flood. The ark was made
> In our own yard; long planks of poplar laid
> End-on made do for gopher wood; the beasts
> Stayed safely vague and credible; south-east,
> Near Diss, lay Ararat; on Ashton's roof
> Of red, washed tiles, I saw the dove.

And a welcome to *Poetry World No.1 – Modern Poetry in Translation* by another name and under a new imprint. This first issue contains the entire text of Vasko Popa's volume *The Cut* and, among several other contributions, this appropriately named poem 'Encounter' by the West German poet Elisabeth Borchers. It returns us to William Carlos Williams and the imperative of usefulness:

> Sometimes it keeps getting colder
> and it's high time to learn what counts.
> As with W.C. Williams,
> doctor to the poor in New Jersey
> for his entire life.
>
> When I ran into him the last time
> he said: An end to dreams.
> I wrote it down. A phrase that appears
> useful to me.

14
Accentuating the Positive
March 1989

David Constantine (ed): *The Poetry Book Society Anthology 1988-1989*
(Hutchinson)
John Heath-Stubbs: *Collected Poems 1943-1987* (Carcanet)
George Barker: *Collected Poems* (Faber & Faber)
E.J. Scovell: *Collected Poems* (Carcanet)
Patricia Beer: *Collected Poems* (Carcanet)
Jack Clemo: *Selected Poems* (Bloodaxe Books)
Thomas Blackburn: *The Adjacent Kingdom: Collected Last Poems*
(Peter Owen)
Martin Bell: *Complete Poems* (Bloodaxe Books)
George Szirtes: *Metro* (Oxford University Press)
Gerda Mayer: *A Heartache of Grass* (Peterloo Poets)
Peter Scupham: *The Air Show* (Oxford University Press)
Donald Davie: *To Scorch or Freeze* (Carcanet)
Michael Donaghy: *Shibboleth* (Oxford University Press)
Christopher Wiseman: *Postcards Home* (Sono Nis Press)
Bernard O'Donoghue: *Poaching Rights* (Gallery Books)
Harry Chambers (ed): *Peterloo Preview 1* (Peterloo Poets)
Marge Piercy: *Available Light* (Pandora)

IN HIS WISE and heartening introduction to *The Poetry Book Society Anthology 1988-1989*, David Constantine writes: 'Contemporary verse, whether it will last or not, has peculiar importance in that it shows what we face today, it shows what might be done, it discovers our truth: the harsh facts we would rather not see and the authentic life we *might* be capable of. In nihilistic, mercenary and cynical times poetry is a ground and means of opposition. It can persuade you of two things simultaneously: that there is something worth fighting for, and that the fight has not yet been lost.'

This needs saying, and Constantine says it well. In a climate of cleverness, instant communication and the feverish collage of marketing imagery, poetry sells nothing but offers a unique chance to stop and listen. In Seamus Heaney's often-quoted phrase, it can 'set the darkness echoing' and catch the hearer miraculously off-guard. 'You know the real thing because it surprises you. That surprise is very significant: in it lies proof of the infinite shifting variety of life, and of poetry's agility.'

Two poets who have, throughout their long careers, witnessed to this infinite shifting variety and never cut their poems according to the cloth of fashion are John Heath-Stubbs and George Barker. Both are fighters, in Constantine's sense of the term, and have survived into old age with their relish for the authentic life undimmed. Their combined *Collected Poems* total just under 1450 pages, accentuate the positive with an untrammelled generosity and are never dull. These are huge, talkative books, abounding with lyricism, learning, an unabashed emphasis on the spiritual and a determination never to confuse seriousness with solemnity. Heath-Stubbs, though he inclines to epigram, can be elegantly garrulous, and Barker, whose leanings are towards extended dogmatic rhapsody, often rushes full pelt into unstoppable passages of banal overstatement, but what is so envigorating about both these poets is their sheer faith in the poetic calling. They are, though temperamentally very different, a pair of subversive cubs who have grown into properly awkward, unclassifiable literary lions. Incapable of parsimony, both celebrate what Barker, in his poem 'To David Gascoyne' calls 'the human perennial' and seek to

counter, through force of imagination, what Heath-Stubbs in his address
to the same influential poet characterises as 'the voices, the voices –
accusing, denouncing,/Mouthing obscenities, nattering and chattering'.
And in the poem immediately next-door to this, written for Barker himself
on his 70th birthday, Heath-Stubbs adds the fuel of approval to his friend's
fire:

> Continue,
> George, to instruct and delight
> Exasperate, excruciate. In the centre of each poem,
> Among the smoking cinders, lies
> A new-hatched Dionysian deity, imprudently
> Wobbling his thyrsus.

Of the two, Barker is, by reputation, the more celebratedly imprudent –
his new Collected, unlike its predecessor, includes *The True Confession*
in which some of his best, most candid writing is to be found – but in
Heath-Stubbs' introduction to his book although he observes 'as for the
purpose of poetry, I can only fall back on the familiar Horatian tag that
it is "to instruct by pleasing"' he nevertheless side-steps the sententious
with a knowing wink: 'I aim to tease you sometimes as well as to please
you.' He can be a wicked parodist, does a host of birds, bees and insects
in different voices (my own favourite among these is 'Robert Herrick's
Pig' wrily and earthily observing its master as he 'squeals his little songs
to Julia,/And other possibly existent ladies,/And I join with him in the
accompaniment *Hunk hunk hunk, snortle snortle snortle,/Gruntle gruntle
gruntle, wee wee wee wee!*'), and his humour is always firmly rooted, playful
but seldom whimsical. He can wobble a modest thyrsus himself, and he
relishes the Martial as well as the Horatian art. Much of his most elegant
writing has a saturnine air and a sardonic edge, setting up a kind of
antiphony between the lyke-wake dirge and the courtly love lyric:

> When my heart was young I wasted my body
> *In every sense of the word Love*
>
> Now my body is older I waste my heart
> *In every sense of the word Love*
>
> My mind and my spirit reproach me both
> *In every sense of the word Love*
>
> There will come a wind and disperse all four
> *In every sense of the word Love*
>
> They will meet again on the Judgement Day
> *In every sense of the word Love*
>
> For Heaven can burn, and Hell can burn
> *In every sense of the word Love*

Judgement Judgement Judgement Judgement
In every sense of the word Love...

It is this kind of echoing tension which sounds throughout John Heath-Stubbs' best work, and in 'David', one of his 'Triumph Songs for the Nine Worthies', he seems to define it exactly:

> Smooth stones in the brook;
> Ten strings on the harp.
>
> 'Death!' whines the sling;
> The harp utters 'Praise!'

The sling and the harp, death and praise, mortality and eroticism, are the intimate opposites of his poetry, and they are nowhere more evident than in his remarkable long poem *Artorius*. Here his love for 'platonic England' (Geoffrey Hill's phrase, but borrowed tellingly as the epigraph for one of his own shorter poems), his keen sense of the overlap and interplay between Christian and pagan cultures, between the classical and contemporary worlds, come together in a fine display of erudition and formal skills – a sustained and lofty alliterative verse, prose discourse, masque and anti-masque, pageantry and song. The result is a dense, layered, often theatrical meditation on myth and its continuing relevance to our lives. The whole enterprise is heroically unfashionable but far from being wilfully archaic, and – as befits the Arthurian theme, abandoned by Milton and bequeathed by Tennyson – with the elegiac note struck throughout. For Heath-Stubbs, though, elegy is never defeatist, and the poem ends just about as far from the Tennysonian dying fall as you can get:

> She ceased; and Silkie and his two brothers
> Shook themselves out of their trance, and saw
> The strangers standing by.
> Then Saehund gave a soft and sudden 'Bao!'
> They slid into the sea, following the raft
> Far out from shore. They bobbed and plunged,
> Joyfully, in the rolling waves.
> The unfallen creatures danced in the salt element:
> The source and origin of all life.
>
> Hang up Euterpe, on the coral bough your harp:
> Take down, Calliope your trumpet.

One of the *Collected Poems*'s most delightful sequences is 'Bird's Plenary Session', but in fact the whole book is a plenary session, a colloquy of wit and wisdom, and John Heath-Stubbs has become the wisest old bird of them all.

Nothing in George Barker's work achieves, or seeks to, the quaint magnifence of *Artorius*, but the reach of his poetry is, in its different direction, equally spectacular. In early sequences such as 'Calamiterror', 'A Vision of England '38' and 'Holy Poems' he comes on stage like a prophet loudly inspired – punning, alliterating, shouting out that 'the chaos of experience is kaleidoscope'. This is not Platonic England but 'the tremendous panoply of England' falling vertical. 'The historical curtain exuding blood on my pillow'. His response to historical events, as they came to a head in 1939, is sensational, and often as deafening as the rhetorical climate that occasioned them – a feverish imagination, seeming to activate the scenario from which it recoils. In this Barker offers a fascinating contrast to the more measured intensity of Auden and Mac-Neice's foreboding:

> In the red theatre of the flesh I stage
> The anatomical tragedy of this sad age
> Whose sweat of tears cannot put out rage.
>
> Now the guns rock my vision as I look
> With blood-prognosticating eyes on Europe
> Whose weeping map invades all my books.

In some ways, this kind of writing, of which there is a great deal, is not unlike the worst excesses of the so-called Apocalypse movement to which it became attached, but what distinguishes Barker is the authentic vagabond visionary perspective he achieves, where Villon meets Blake, the street leads to the confessional, and the rhetoric alights suddenly on a modest particular and illuminates it:

> I see the flamingo involved with the hanging fruits,
> The hand of horror the claw of bananas and
> Mr Salisbury the proprietor greengrocer,
> The magnificently actual unit the human.

George Barker's later work, though still often remorselessly *con brio* and continuing to apostrophise with a vengeance, manages more of that humane fusion of the oracular with the domestic which gave such a rumbustious luminosity to his famous sonnet 'To My Mother'. The *Collected Poems* (apart from two appendices) concludes with the familiar incantatory dogma of 'Anno Domini', but the closing pages are also graced by the mellow inclusiveness of the 'Villa Stellar' poems in which Eros seems surprised by an unaccustomed, almost valedictory gentleness, and Venus is in the ascendant:

> The Contessa sat by the window fingering the black notes of the piano.
> I saw the sunset begin to fight its way over the Mediterranean
> in a noiseless allegory of the futility of speech
> and indeed of everything save the cloudy mutations we think we believe in:

those cloudy mutations in which all aspirations and all dreams
and all human determinations, as the sun falls,
fade into the supercession of night and stars. Are they, these cloudy
                                                    presences
the hereafter of yesterday's equally futile illusions,
the hallucinations of which there is no original
excepting that first dream of an ejection from a garden
where we once walked without knowledge?
The Contessa rose and led me out into the arbour
where we sat without speech, looking at the sky.

It is typical of Barker that silence should be conveyed so explicitly and
with so many words, but the emphasis is firmly on the authentic life and
the search for meaning. The poet may protest too much. He is loud even
in his privacy. But his total commitment to the poetic life is rare enough
to discourage carping.

Several other Collected and Selected poems have appeared recently,
two of the best coming, like Heath-Stubbs', from Carcanet. E.J. Scovell
began publishing in the 1940s, seemed to stop with *The River Steamer* in
1956, then reappeared in 1982 when Secker and Warburg published *The
Space Between*. Now her *Collected Poems* provides an opportunity to
measure the intensity of her quiet commitment to the inner life. At first
glance, her world is one of familiar, even cosy, appearances – gardens,
flowers, domestic interiors, framed perspectives, family occasions – but
her intelligence, and the grace of her accuracy, fuse what might seem
random perceptions into a unity, a singleness of theme which is nothing
less than a sustained, restlessly wondering meditation on the mysteries of
creation:

> The grass heads, filled with air-like fountains pause
> Over their drenched green – blade and moss,
> And those least flowers that take the grass
> For cover and for sky, stars in its space –
>
> Till water, air and hanging meadow seem
> Of one continuous substance, each
> So fixed in flowing, and the touch
> Seems deft and light of time creating them.

'Fixed in flowing' catches the nature of her gift exactly. Reminiscent of
Edward Thomas's wish to be held 'fixed and free/In a rhyme', hers is a
poetry of surfaces animated by the pressure of immanence. Attracted to
'where deepest silence lies' or 'the look of utterance on the silent flower',
she transcribes minute particulars with an enchanted but entirely unsentimental directness, and although the range of her subject matter may
appear limited when compared with that of Heath-Stubbs or Barker, her

scrupulous attentiveness ensures that every poem is a new beginning, a fresh encounter however brief:

> One day at noon I crossed
> A sandy yard planted with citrus trees
> Behind a small hotel. I walked slowly in the sun
> With feet in the hot sand which the leaf-cutting ants
> Crossed too, under their little sails of green, filing
> Intent; and I thought, this
> I will keep, I will register with time: I am here;
> And always, shall have been here – that is the wonder –
> Never, now, not have been here; for now I am here,
> Crossing the sandy yard
> Between the citrus trees, behind the small hotel.

And behind poetry of this quality lies Rilke's question: 'Are we, perhaps, *here* just for saying: House,/Bridge, Fountain, Gate, Jug, Fruit tree, Window?...but for *saying*, remember,/oh, for such saying as never the things themselves/hoped so intensely to be'. E.J. Scovell's poems certainly, in her own words, 'register with time', and so indeed should this very welcome collection of them.

Writing 'In Memory of Stevie Smith', Patricia Beer observes that 'She struck compassion/In strange places'. The verb is aptly ambiguous, containing both the sense of discovery and the note of admonition. Patricia Beer's work is, of course, very different from Stevie Smith's but both poets share a wily delight in irony, a keen appreciation of the droll and the dotty which can often be found at the heart of serious matters:

> Dear Husband, Please come to me.
> Yesterday I fell on these stern rocks
> And lie in hospital. I was wrong to walk
> Here alone. Please come, for both our sakes.
>
> As I fell I noticed the seagulls above me.
> Legs dangling, wings pumping, they yelled
> Out of white breast feathers and spotted beaks.
> Then their cliff drew them back...

There is more than an echo of 'Not Waving But Drowning' in this, and the short, childlike sentences of the first stanza with their apologetic note of self-chastisement and fear of rebuke are at the same time moving and odd. The body of Patricia Beer's work is firm – if precariously sober-toned – in its celebration of the 'continuity of love', of history, faith and literature, but as she writes in a delightful new poem 'Looking Sideways' 'The corner of the eye lets in lunacy/More accurately than the whole body' and much of her best, most memorable poetry becomes so precisely because of what she catches in the corner of her eye and allows to shape her field of vision. This is especially true when – as she often does – she retraces the course of her own life from a strict, secure world, which she recalls only to reject with baffled affection, to a less secure but more assuringly unresolved present. In 'Called Home', for example, the phrase 'squinnying down' in the penultimate line is Patricia Beer's unmistakable watermark, the tender, bizarre twist in the poem's tail:

> 'Called Home' the Plymouth Brethren used to say
> When someone died. Warm, bright corridors
> Led to eternal domesticity
> And from outside we heard the sound of tears
> Being wiped away by God. Shall we gather
> At the river? In the sweet by-and-by?
> Yes, I sang then. Beyond the bright blue sky
> Dead families would always be together.
>
> Loving an atheist is my hope currently.
> Believers cannot help. I must have some
> Ally who will keep non-company
> With me in a non-life, a fellow tombstone
> Stuck senseless in cold grass, squinnying down
> At father, uncle, grandfather, called home.

And the ghost of Thomas Hardy is there too. Patricia Beer knows how to transcribe the frisson of life's little ironies.

Jack Clemo is the author of two engrossing spiritual autobiographies, *Confession of a Rebel* and *The Marriage of a Rebel,* as well as a novel, *Wilding Graft,* which was admired by T.F. Powys. Writing of Powys in *The Marriage of a Rebel*, Clemo stresses a fundamental affinity: 'His work had impressed me for many years despite my rejection of his pessimism and obsession with death. He too had chosen the unworldly borderline, the terrible wrestle with God'. Clemo ends his poem 'A Kindred Battlefield', dedicated to Powys, with this stanza:

> Chalk heart and clay heart share
> A wilful strategy:
> The strife you learned to bear
> Breaks westward over me.

That wilful strategy, acted out in the stark, scabbed landscape of the Cornish clay-pits, is the theme of Clemo's strenuous poetry of grapple and hard-won grace. The earlier poems, shot through with a self-wounding, exclusively tortured spirit of Calvinism intensified by the awareness of his own encroaching blindness and deafness, are an extraordinary achievement. Dismissive of the civilised church or chapel goer – 'so civilised...so dextrous in control/Of the tricky signals' – and seeing himself as 'outside, a truant soul,/Deep in the Word, stung by the dirt/Of primal clues', Clemo nevertheless struggles for the kind of reconciliation voiced in this closing stanza of 'Beyond Trethosa Chapel' which provides a good example of his charged, evangelical language:

> Mediate, then, beloved; let tension cease,
> Dune-grit and pews be reconciled:
> Let not the peak be cut away,
> Nor the fold reviled.
> Harsh clang of the prophetic tip
> May yet be blent, through you,
> With hymn of fellowship
> My childhood knew.
> Bless with your dreams my broken clay
> As you take the broken bread;
> Fuse the corporate flame with our lonely ray;
> Show me that Bethel wine is red.

This 'beloved' is clearly the elusive object of what Clemo has called his 'mystical-erotic search'. This has found eventual fulfilment in his marriage to a wife whom he addresses thus in 'Wedding Eve':

> You chose pure heavenly grace
> To mirror the image of your man:
> No veiled carnality could pass
> The test of that altar-glass;
> But it showed you a face, my face,
> Scarred, yet singing against earth's ban.
>
> To plant the Cross in the nerves
> Intensifies the wedlock sun;
> Faith's ravaged fibre now revives
> Where the blood thrives,
> And I feel in your flushed curves,
> In your kiss, the world-renouncing nun...

The intensity of this does not lie easy on the imagination, and Clemo's poetry is often chillingly austere and not a little claustrophobic in its charting of the authentic life. There's a remorseless emphasis on the 'striving flesh', the 'storm-flash of grace', tunnelling through darkness, wrestling with the angel, not only in the personal poems but in the many that recreate the lives of his heroes – Lawrence, Melville, Browning, Karl Barth – , but if, as William Empson once said, the purpose of literature is to give us access to worlds of experience removed from our own then Jack Clemo's *Selected Poems* must be considered a rare and unusually revealing book. It is certainly as compulsive as it is discomfiting, and it contains writing of undeniable splendour.

'A relentless and probing critic of his own psyche' might be one way of describing Clemo but it is, in fact, Roy Fuller on Thomas Blackburn.

Blackburn died in 1977, and his *Collected Last Poems* have been gathered and edited by Jean MacVean who also contributes an informative introduction. Once read, this introduction, which leads towards the extraordinary and moving circumstances of Blackburn's death, makes it easier to come to terms with the unpromising announcement of many of his clinical case-book titles: 'Alcoholism', 'Schizophrenia', 'Maturation', 'Insomnia', 'Ageing' etc. These are, in fact – though the spiritual quest is entirely different from Clemo's and could, for short-hand convenience be described as Jungian – brave poems. They are often wordily abstract, circling the metaphors they are unable to grasp, but particularly when recognising aspects of selfhood in the suffering of others a reminder of the true, if uneven, poet Thomas Blackburn was:

> I remember on my last day in the asylum
> On my way to the shop to buy cigarettes
> Being accosted by one in madness continuum
> And progressed in that shuffle they have and little leaps.
>
> He gripped me by the throat and announced –
> I remember still that grip and my spasm of fear –
> 'You're dead, you're dead, you're dead',
> And then he let go of me and began to caper,
>
> Singing, 'I'm the only man in the world left alive',
> Down the corridor he vanished singing,
> In the extremis of that solitude lunatics have.
>
> I bought my cigarettes and packed for leaving.

More than a reminder of Martin Bell is provided by the reissue, with a long introduction by Peter Porter, of his *Collected Poems* along with a selection of what he wrote between 1967 and his death in 1978. Bell was an influential founder member of The Group during the 1950s but seemed to vanish as Porter, Peter Redgrove, Alan Brownjohn and others came to prominence. Despite his virtuosity, which drew high praise from Anthony Burgess, the admiration of his friends, the ambitious younger poets, an appearance in the Penguin Modern Poets series, and a copious knowledge and love of European literature, he seems to have remained far less read than spoken of. Although his *Complete Poems* could have done without the rather bitter squibbery that his increasing disenchantment lapsed into, everyone should read the first part of the book in which Bell's sardonic relish for the tropes of anger is a match for Amis and Osborne at their early best. As Peter Porter observes 'his style is a yoking of salient detail to rhetorical projection' and his poems of celebration (of which 'To Celebrate Eddie Cantor' is a fine example) demonstrate much of the surrealist-inspired energy he called on to counter the urban drabness, timidity and cautious bourgeois respectability which he felt to be surrounding him:

> Voice soaring in gleeful lubricity,
> Scandalous coloratura at full tilt!
> Excited wide eyes rolling
> And hands that have to clap that joy's too much.
> Energy, wanton small bright ball
> Leaping on top of the fountain –
> Living water, extravagant
> Flooding and cleansing the movie-house.
>
> No endless exits down the sad perspectives,
> The avenues of infinite regrets,
> For you, Sir, No Siree!
> Palmy Days, ample a blue sky
> And the gross bull lulled to an euphoric calm,
> Contented cows, O Don Sebastian –
> The lineaments of gratified desire
> Making whoopee with the whooping red-skins.

Bell's encouragement of George Szirtes can now be seen not only in the context of a friendship – they met when Bell was Gregory Fellow at Leeds University and Szirtes was a student at the Art College – but, given his European outlook, a prescient liaison. If, while he has increasingly searched out and consolidated his Hungarian identity, Szirtes can be said – in Peter Porter's words – to have 'taken England into Europe', one of the ways he has done so is by marrying his natural gift for surreal leaps of the imagination with a determined study of the English pentameter:

> The writing on the wall says *Carpe Dym*
> attached to the name of a national hero, or
> it could well be the local football team.
> Upstairs are voices I have heard before
> that hook and draw you up as on a line,
>
> to something cramped, imprisoned and defined
> by yards and corridors. I run my hand
> along the wall and feel it sweat and grind
> its teeth. A brilliant light is in command,
> a fist of light within an iron frame.

In his earlier work, Szirtes seemed to settle for the shorter lyric and essentially pictorial sequence, but he has been working towards the kind of extended meditation which has now found its form in the title poem of his new collection. 'Metro' is a solemn phantasmagoria, a Dante-esque journey through the underground set in fascist-controlled Hungary of 1944–45. Against a background music of what should never have happened but did, images of everyday living are glimpsed everywhere under threat. 'Metro' is at once domestic and chillingly universal. This double image is what gives it its power. Led through the nightmare of his family and nation's recent history, Szirtes asks the most difficult question of all concerning the implications of his own apparent freedom:

> Disorientation, loss: the doors that close
> Just when you think that you have gained your entrance.
> A glimpse of hallway, hat-rack, mirror, more doors.
> Beyond the doors and on the left perhaps
> A window giving on to a neat yard
> With trees and flowers. Straight ahead of you
> A lift-cage dressed in iron broderie,
> A smell of coffee brewing, an envelope
> Slit like a wound, the darker recesses
> Of sitting rooms, momentarily opened.
> What troubles me is the uncertainty:
> Is this really a valuable darkness,
> Or am I part of the darkness that's locked out?

Gerda Mayer is a Czechoslovakian who came to England in 1939 when she was twelve. What she brings to her art is the ability to recreate that blend of the knowing and the insouciant, a kind of wise-child irony which subverts what appears to present itself with all the friendly ease of anecdote. She is particularly good at building her beguiling shock-tactics into little songs like 'Anon' which might almost be sung in one of George Szirtes' darker recesses:

> I was resting my feet between two pogroms
> And cooling them in a stream,
> When through the tender leaves above
> I saw an angel gleam.
>
> My guardian angel: I knew him at once.
> He floated about the tree.
> *Now carry me off and carry me high.*
> And he said *presently.*
>
> And presently means by-and-by,
> And by-and-by, anon.
> He settled his halo and flapped his wings;
> He kissed me and was gone.

Peter Scupham's wartime childhood is the subject of his outstanding new collection *The Air Show*. Throughout it runs the image of his 'Journeying Boy' who is, literally, travelling between Derby, Cambridgeshire and Lincolnshire, changing homes and holidaying with his grandparents, but who also becomes the lost self for which the poet seeks:

Under my sandals
The shining parallels race on,
Haul our lost luggage into nowhere
Over cinders, torrents of oily stone;
Our stuffed compartments, weary cubicles,
Whistled dolorously downwind
Under the gantries of the blinded Midlands.

. The first two lines, there, are vivid but unexceptional nostalgia for a secure seat in the carriage, but then suddenly with that 'lost luggage' and its blank destination you can hear the points change, and the journeying becomes the mysterious, haunted quest for identity which controls the enterprise. Scupham has never written better. He catches so well the child's apprehension of adult anxiety. War Games are played on the nursery floor with intense concentration while the Air Show overhead turns from display into a puzzling cross-fire. Deliberate whimsy sets trap after trap, and some of Scupham's most memorable effects are rather as if the child he was is handing back to his adult self a crowded pop-up book to remind each other that there is still a war on:

They pushed their gravy trains into my tunnel
And stuffed me up with garden slugs and snails.
My salad days were crisp and limp as lettuce,
Then all the clockwork toppled off the rails,
The little foxes jumped from all the foxholes
And ran about the world with blazing tails.

Of the many books that have come my way over the past year since I last wrote a piece for *Encounter* there is space to mention only a few more, but if anyone uses this kind of omnibus as a guide to what he or she should go out and buy then each of them comes with the seal of strong approval.

Donald Davie's seriously witty investigation of what it means to be 'god-fearing' – a God who is 'steadily weighing/your airy, your weightiest, saying' – makes a fascinating counter-balance to Jack Clemo about whom he has, elsewhere, written with great insight. Davie is an expert on the Dissenting tradition. He once described C.H. Sisson as 'the devout Christian constantly battling his own instructed scepticism'. *To Scorch or Freeze* could be seen as presenting a devout sceptic battling, and attending to, Christian instruction.

Michael Donaghy's first collection, *Shibboleth*, is a debut marked by fine and full tuning – the kind of attentiveness that notices how 'the dive was there before the hawk was' and knows how to register it in a verse which is both sensuous and crisply intelligent:

Forget the here-and-now. We have no time
but this device of wantoness and wit.

Make me this present then: your hand in mine,
and we'll live out our lives in it.

Christopher Wiseman, British born but living in Canada since 1969, deserves to be far better known outside his adopted country. The poems in *Postcards Home* appear to be written from 'such an ordinary address' and to inherit the 'calm unshaken/Handwriting' of the forebears a number of them pay homage to. They are mainly quiet and conversational, although they occasionally attempt a satirical vein which Wiseman doesn't quite have the nerve or conviction to force home. His postcards are, in fact, at their sharpest when they are most loving, and Wiseman's strengths are his conscientiously troubled sense of responsibility and an unsentimental gentleness:

Sirens. Gas masks. Bombers based nearby. A searchlight battery.
And I in my uncle's study watching him work, waiting for my life.
Such things have shaped me, catch me unaware, tease my dreaming.
Now it's peacetime and I'm at war with myself, and I'm undone
when I catch the smell of apples, of empty rooms, of forked soil.
O uncle, my life, your old age. Sit at peace in your pipesmoke.

Bernard O'Donoghue stood out as one of the best poets in Faber's *Poetry Introduction 6*, and *Poaching Rights* is his welcome first collection. He has a sharp sense of the humour and incongruities of behaviour in small communities (there's something of the flavour of Synge's *Playboy* and that language 'as fully flavoured as a nut or apple', but there's nothing archaic about his approach). O'Donoghue can be an up-to-the minute ironist too, and several of the poems achieve broad perspectives while remaining wittily exact in assembling the pieces of the jigsaw. 'Pompeiana' is a good example:

Scratching away for shards of singed, green tile,
They'll be trying to assemble Sunday mornings
From our pre-atomic age. Infinitely
Careful, they'll fit them all together
To display medals and competition shields,
Serenaded by their much-loved pumproom trio,
And sell postcards of unoccupied bikinis.
Will they be able also to decode
The stern prohibition on petting and horseplay,
Or to account for that funny, male strutting
At large through the changing-rooms? To rebuild
That miserable, suggestive, chlorinated ache
From girls trailing toes in the blue water?

The newly established *Peterloo Preview* series looks set to rival the Faber and Chatto Introductions. The first volume assembles six diverse talents, each of them worth watching in the future, and one of them, Brian Waltham, more than ready for a book of his own. Waltham's sardonic, disenchanted sense of absurdity, of opportunities missed, of being in the right place at the wrong middle-aged time, is reminiscent of the later Louis MacNeice. The tone is one of edgy regret, a nervous, reflexive humour which refuses to become mellow. Even his 'Maison de Vacance' is not quite the good place one feels it wants to be:

> Doors with a grudge, a book open where it was left,
> Last year's woodsmoke, another fall of plaster,
> A damp patch, shutters that will not budge;
> House, you're in a sulk like a neglected girl.
>
> Come, we'll light a fire, such a fire,
> And you shall show me your winter trophies;
> Fly husks in shabby webs, a shrivelled mouse,
> Moths and wasps in their window graveyard.

This is Peterloo's 100th volume, and it is typical of Harry Chambers' commitment to new talent that the press's century should be scored by a new team. Waltham is the senior member. The others are Donna Dickenson, good on childhood and quirky recollection, Stephen Duncan who writes about love and the birth of his son without causing that rather too recognisable response ' 'tis new to thee!', Tony Roberts, a dogged explorer of myth and history, the mercurial Raymond Tallis whose 'In Memoriam Roland Barthes' is the volume's bravura performance, and Maureen Wilkinson who won the 1987 Peterloo Open Poetry Competition with 'Bringing the Night Cow Down' and now proves that she has a body of work of equal quality. This is a volume that gives real pleasure. It could serve, not least for the reluctant reader, as a most approachable introduction to the middle ground of contemporary poetry.

And, last, for a book that talks a dozen to the dime, full of engaging personality and taking its material from whatever comes to hand. Marge Piercy's *Available Light* is readily available and shed around on topics as diverse as housework, apartheid, menstruating in a traffic jam, and the effects of radiation. She has no time for emotional restraint, and clearly identifies with 'the driven' of her poem 'The Fecund complain they are not honoured':

> The driven get ideas in the bathtub
> and sit down still dripping and spoil
> the chair. The driven get a great idea
> at the worst moment, panting and heaving
> and blow the orgasm or lose their erection
> as the case may be. They burn the beans,
> disconnect the phone, are rude to callers,
> and yet in the middle of the down-filled

> night, the muse walks back and forth
> across their belly in boots with cleats
> cursing and kicking and singing the praises
> of the unborn poems and the untold stories
> till they swarm like fish babies nipping
> the flanks of sleep. When the driven die
> their real inner stone reads: you did
> a little piece of it, a little piece.

Marge Piercy not only burns the beans, she spills them. She also most certainly eliminates the negative, and is not to be found messing with Mister In-Between.

To return to David Constantine, 'Poetry combats stasis, combats the hardening of our postures and perceptions, by being itself agile. I know places where at first sight it is not easy to distinguish between the quick and the dead. Among poems it is, and the quick poem is a powerful illuminator of quickness and deadness in the lives we lead'. Quickness in the word's other sense – a febrile urgency – has little to do with it. Poetry is not naturally attracted to the fast lane. A true poem can never be a quick read, either. Still less does it seek to oblige. Although in the speedy world of journalism it may be short enough to serve, conveniently, as a column-filling mark of 'quality', it enlarges the meagre space which surrounds it and insists upon its unique authenticity. For poets, this is the condition of their service and the continuing renewal of opportunity. As W.H. Auden declares:

> After all, it's rather a privilege
> amid the affluent traffic
> to serve this unpopular art which cannot be turned into
> background noise for study
> or hung as a status trophy by rising executives,
> cannot be 'done' like Venice
> or abridged like Tolstoy, but stubbornly still insists upon
> being read or ignored...

Auden wrote these lines twenty-five years ago, addressing them to the companionable shade of Louis MacNeice. More than ever they need to be heard now.

Index

The number beside each book corrresponds to the chapter number in which it is discussed.